BY DESIGN

**SCIENCE AND THE
SEARCH FOR GOD**

LARRY WITHAM

ENCOUNTER BOOKS
SAN FRANCISCO

Copyright © 2003 by Larry Witham

All rights reserved. No part of this publication may be reproduced, stored in a retrieval system, or transmitted, in any form or by any means, electronic, mechanical, photo-copying, recording, or otherwise, without the prior written permission of Encounter Books, 665 Third Street, Suite 330, San Francisco, California 94107-1951.

Published by Encounter Books, an activity of Encounter for Culture and Education, Inc., a nonprofit tax exempt corporation.

Encounter Books website address: www.encounterbooks.com

Manufactured in the United States and printed on acid-free paper.

The paper used in this publication meets the minimum requirements of ANSI/NISO Z39.48-1992 (R 1997) *(Permanence of Paper)*

FIRST EDITION

Library of Congress Cataloging-in-Publication Data
Witham, Larry, 1952–
  By design : science and the search for God / Larry Witham.
  p. cm.
  Includes bibliographical references and index.
  ISBN 1-89355-64-3 (alk. paper)
  1. Religion and science. I. Title.
BL240.3.W58 2003
215—dc21

                                   2003040778

10 9 8 7 6 5 4 3 2 1

CONTENTS

PREFACE

For the past twenty years, new curiosity has arisen about an age-old question: Does nature point to something beyond itself—toward a God, perhaps, or a transcendent order? Since the demise of natural theology in the 1800s, there have been strong taboos against using science—the measuring of physical matter—as a gauge of God or a higher reality. But in our time we have seen that stigma slowly fall away, allowing a renewed interest in what used to be called "reading the Book of Nature," a metaphor suggesting that there is either an Author or, at the least, a text imbued with meaning.

One survey of well-educated Americans, conducted by *Skeptic* editor Michael Shermer and MIT professor Frank Sulloway, found that the strongest reason for believing in God was seeing "good design, natural beauty, perfection, [or] complexity" in the world. The journal *Science* wondered recently about a "thaw in the ice between science and faith," and *Scientific American* reported that four in ten ranking scientists can investigate nature *and* believe in a personal God. Though the legacy of late-nineteenth-century science is antagonistic toward the concept of a deity, God-talk has nevertheless come back into favor at the beginning of the twenty-first century.

What is the modern-day believer to make of this turn of events? Well, the issue at stake rarely entails claims of proof or disproof of God, except when the most ardent skeptics and evangelistic ministries engage in battle. A truer picture of the situation is this: slowly, almost imperceptibly, science may be giving believers more ways to argue that God's existence is a *better explanation* of the cosmos than atheistic materialism. Even that qualified assertion, needless to say, is quite sufficient for raucous controversy and a lively story.

In this book, I summarize the new mood in a series of sketches, venturing descriptions of the events, ideas, people, institutions and controversies that are part of this ongoing debate between science and belief. Another goal is to give the reader a condensed overview of those areas of contemporary science that impinge on the ultimate questions: the origin of the cosmos, of life on Earth, and of humanity especially. Evolution theory, genetics and neuroscience are of course central to the biological issues.

The new interest in a possible rapprochement between God and scientific rationality is manifested in two recent developments. The first can be traced to the dialogue between the Catholic Church and the science establishment. With beginnings in mid-twentieth-century discussions, it became prominent on the world stage with Pope John Paul II's celebration of Einstein's birthday in 1979, and with the establishment of the John Templeton Foundation, which in the 1990s poured millions of dollars into such projects as research on "evidence of universal purpose in the cosmos."

The second movement goes under the portmanteau name "intelligent design." A very distant cousin of modern creationism, it has become flag-bearer in the debate about natural theology and the limits of science: under its banner are gathered a motley war party of credentialed scientists and thinkers who ardently wish to loosen the grip of what they view as dogmatic naturalism. What marks this coalition is its ability to put aside the Bible as an issue, revisiting instead the design arguments and the evidence from physics and biology that, according to the Shermer/Sulloway survey, are still quite persuasive as reasons for belief.

According to public opinion surveys in the United States, belief in God or a universal spirit is the rule, not the exception, so this book is not offered as an antidote to religious doubt. And the American people's strong tendency toward metaphysical belief arises from a vast array of motives and experiences; persuasion by the evidence of science can be one reason for belief, but perhaps a relatively minor one.

Yet this is a scientific age, and believers willing to acknowledge the power of science will want to reconcile their convictions with the latest findings. For atheistic materialists, the "scientific naturalism" promulgated by Thomas Huxley still holds sway—a stance that either denies God's existence or relegates the question itself to irrelevancy. At the opposite pole are the biblical creationists: hoping to harmonize nature and science with a literal reading of Genesis, they are willing, in cases of conflict, for revelation to trump factual discoveries.

In the following pages, the champions of the materialist school will appear frequently; after all, they voice the orthodoxy of establishment science. The Bible creationists make only cameo appearances as part of the historical background. My interest is situated in the middle ground between the atheists and the fundamentalists: this is where the dialogue emerging from the science-and-religion and the intelligent design movements truly takes place.

Among the occupants of this territory are the "Spinozans," named after the formidable Dutch Jewish philosopher Baruch Spinoza, the hero of Einstein, who himself acknowledged a "cosmic religious feeling." For these thinkers, God is mysteriously *one* with the laws of nature. This pantheistic view of deity has been labeled by proponents the "God of the philosophers," and by more traditional theists "no God at all." But that is part of the debate. Entering the science-and-religion dialogue with zeal, Spinozans reject what they regard as the humdrum reductionism of the materialists. Instead, they prefer to talk about "emergent properties"—qualitative changes that manifest in unforeseeable phenomena. And they are not afraid of using words like *purpose, meaning* and *design.*

Another party inhabiting the middle ground are the classic monotheists, who differ on how a personal God may actually operate in nature. One faction—comprising modernist Christians and theistic evolutionists—prefer to see God in the Big Bang origin of the universe and in its perfection of fine-tuning; but they don't see God as intervening directly and miraculously in nature. Alongside them—and frequently rivals in the fiercest arguments about God and science—are the design advocates themselves.

These people accept that God may actively intervene in nature, in addition to working through natural processes. They search for "marks of intelligence" in the universe. And, as in the boisterous days of Victorian natural theology, they argue that a sufficiently complex signature must point to a Signer. Design arguments today are usually made with an accompanying attack on Darwinism, doubling the emotional level of an already intense debate.

The modern search for God has another, age-old component: the classic question of evil. Many have used the existence of moral and natural evil—torture and genocide, or catastrophes such as plagues and earthquakes—as arguments against God's existence. In similar fashion, God has been persuasively defended by comparing such realities with the overwhelming goodness that arguably is necessary, not only for unforced acts of individual generosity, but for the existence of the cosmos in the first place. This great enigma lurks in the wings, and I have no intention of elaborating on it here.

A century ago, the American psychologist William James, in his Gifford Lectures on Natural Religion, stressed that evil is an inescapable fact of human life, and that people who tend toward a morbid or melancholy view of life have a more realistic response than people who are inattentively sunny and optimistic. His point was that temperament often determines one's belief system.

As a conclusion for this book, James is apropos. He has received much attention of late for the centennial of his famous 1902 lectures, *The Varieties of Religious Experience*. While his views remain controversial, some of his enduring insights will provide touchstones for the contemporary fanfare over science and faith. But we begin with another one-hundredth anniversary, the Darwin Centennial of 1959, a time when science was feeling far more certain of its victory over God than it is today.

RETHINKING SCIENCE

1

DARWIN TRIUMPHANT

The East African midday calm was shattered by Mary Leakey's scream, "I've got him!" She had just brought the Land Rover to a rattling halt, sending a swirl of dust through the base camp. Her cry shook her husband, Louis, the white-haired fossil hunter, from a feverish nap: "I've got him! I've got him!" This was in July 1959.

Since 1935, when Mary left England to follow Louis to Africa, they had been repeatedly scouring the Olduvai Gorge in Tanzania. This earthen gash, which reveals two-million-year-old hardened sediments, as yet had yielded only animal fossils, stone axes and snakes. But now the "long quest had ended," said Louis, a Cambridge-educated scientist and adventurer. "After all our hoping and hardship and sacrifice, at last we had reached our goal—we had discovered the world's oldest known human."

That morning, Mary had gone alone to the gorge with their two Dalmatians, wearing her broad-brimmed straw hat and crawling among the lowest rocks of the three-hundred-foot walls. The noon heat usually signaled quitting time, and Mary had her epiphany just before that when she came face to face with a bulky cranium, jaw and molars. When Louis went to the dig with her, he too felt exultation. "The teeth were projecting from the rock face, smooth and shining and quite obviously human," he later reminisced. "At last we had found him." They called him *Zinjanthropus,* for "East Africa Man."

The discovery could not have come at a better time. In four months, Louis Leakey and "Zinj" would journey to America for the greatest science celebration ever held, the Darwin Centennial. Convened during Thanksgiving week at the University of Chicago, the event drew thousands after its opening on November 24, the date in 1859 when Charles Darwin received the first copy of *On the Origin of Species* off the presses. In the book, Darwin had said only that "Much light will be thrown on the origin of man and his history," but a few years later, in 1871, he boldly pointed to Africa, home of the gorillas and chimpanzees, as the likely place where man was born.

There had been debate in England over whether tropical Africa with its "lowly natives" could produce the noble human, and the discovery of humanlike fossils in Asia had directed attention there. But Darwin's prediction appealed to the young Louis Leakey, a child of British missionaries in Kenya, who since 1926 had striven to prove Darwin right. Now, at the age of fifty-six, he would make his first trip to the United States, a vacation from the scorching Olduvai heat in snow-swept Chicago. And then, with Mary, he would go on to international fame. "After Zinj, the days of shoestring budgets and quiet times exploring Olduvai together were finished," his biographer Virginia Morell wrote.

Though a backwater compared with London or New York, Chicago became the focal point of the Darwinian centenary by managing to attract bigger names than other cities. Two years in advance, organizer Sol Tax, a University of Chicago anthropologist, had set his sights on Sir Julian Huxley, the "spokesman for the twentieth-century evolutionary edifice" and grandson of Thomas H. Huxley, who as Darwin's "bulldog" had promoted scientific naturalism. Whoever secured the presence of Sir Julian Huxley had *the* Darwin Centennial. And other big names in science were no small draw: there was Sir Charles Galton Darwin, grandson of the great naturalist; Harlow Shapley, the most famous living American astronomer; and Leakey himself.

Chicago got them all, and for five days in 1959 the university, with its secular Gothic ambiance, became the cynosure for international scholars and for the public. There were exhibits and lectures and a showing of the evolutionary film *The Ladder of Life*. Sir Charles kept audiences spellbound with talks such as "Darwin the Traveler." Visitors gawked at an exhibit and illustrated lecture by Louis Leakey on *Zinjanthropus,* humanity's ancient ancestor, and every state in the U.S. sent a biology teacher on a federal scholarship. Most evenings, the university's cavernous, Baroque Mandel Hall was packed for performances of an original showboat-style Darwinian musical, *Time Will Tell.* The media was enthralled.

On Thanksgiving afternoon, a bell tower carillon echoed across the snow-dusted campus, the peals breaking out as a long procession of robed scholars reached Rockefeller Chapel. Huxley took the pulpit. Age seventy-two, he was tall and bulky in his robe, his oiled hair straight back, his glasses heavy. He eloquently declared the late 1950s to be "the period when the process of evolution, in the person of inquiring man, began to be truly conscious of itself." In what became known as his "secular sermon," he said that man no longer needed to "take refuge from his loneliness in the arms of a divinized father-figure" such as God. It was time to recognize that "all aspects of reality are subject to evolution, from atoms and stars to fish and flowers, from fish and flowers to human society and values." The context as much as the content made for arch newspaper headlines, and Huxley, recalling the subsequent mild scandal in his memoirs, agreed that it was not the most appropriate speech to have given in a church.

Yet Huxley's account, an epic tale of cosmic evolution culminating in humanity, did nothing more than state how science viewed reality at mid-century. He referred to religion as a mere stage in the ascent of *Homo sapiens,* which took us from subsistence to civilization, through organized religion to the level of "secular activities," or what Sir Julian called "the threshold of the evolutionary grade." Here, human thinking is "naturalistic," for "it has rejected the supernatural idea of creation for that of material progress."

Progress had now brought the atomic age, an era of physics and mushroom clouds and unending scientific triumphalism. Just three weeks after Zinj was found, the United States boosted its first satellite into orbit. Science had succeeded spectacularly by breaking matter down into its smallest bits, and the confident spirit of reductionism spilled rapidly into chemistry, biology and even the human sciences. Indeed, it was applied reductionism in the 1950s that brought about two of the greatest discoveries about life itself. In late 1952 at the University of Chicago, a graduate student named Stanley Miller produced amino acids, the building blocks of life, in an experiment simulating the primitive earth. The next year in England, young James Watson, an American, joined Francis Crick in deciphering the double helix structure of DNA, the code of life.

During the Second World War, computers had been built to crack enemy codes and the power of radio detection had been amplified. These developments increased science's ability to probe bodies in outer space and to speculate on the computational powers of the brain itself. Already in 1956, the first meeting of computer aficionados had gathered to dream about a humanlike mind in a machine—what became the quest for Artificial Intelligence (A.I.).

The mystery of the stars had also been solved in the 1950s. They were found to be great nuclear furnaces that cooked hydrogen into oxygen, carbon and iron, the elements of biological life. While this practical astronomy was advancing, the speculative cosmologists also came on the scene, talking about the beginning and ending of time itself. Their theorizing might annoy the bench astronomers, but the public was riveted by their debates on the expanding universe, and whether its apparent motion started with a cosmic Big Bang or was merely the churning of a continuous steady state that had been around for eternity. What this explosion in knowledge meant for humanity's self-image was obvious, according to the astronomer Harlow Shapley. "We are no longer at the center of the universe," he said. "Science has freed us from that illusion."

Professor Sol Tax, the Darwin Centennial's organizer, was an energetic man who liked bow ties and sported a crew cut and pencil mustache. To capture some of the sweep of contemporary science, he had organized the centennial around five major panel discussions, and despite the hoopla and the celebrities, he said later that "the panels *were* the celebration." They convened in Mandel Hall, where klieg lights glared for documentary footage and a thousand ticket holders jammed in daily for the three-hour discussions. Each forum lined up about ten leading experts, older men barely distinguishable from each other in their gray suits and tweed coats, but often differing in their views. The program was intended to give Americans "a larger view in which human society and culture are seen again as part of the natural order and subject to the same laws of evolution as the rest of nature."

Professor Tax's hope that "history would take a new turn" as a result of the centennial proved somewhat exaggerated. When the centennial week was over, its memory lingered on for another year as the proceedings were published in a three-volume tome, and the event's documents and memorabilia relegated to boxes for archival storage. But as an intellectual and symbolic event, it dovetailed with a political and financial acceleration of American science. In the late 1950s, Congress began pouring billions of dollars into the U.S. space program and science education. This included publication of biology textbooks and teacher training, an agenda that emphasized Darwinian evolution. The new president, John F. Kennedy, would tell the National Academy of Sciences that the age of basic, or theoretical, research had begun, and that the taxpayer would understand and be supportive.

The other turning point was cultural. Both the centennial and its promising new celebrity, Louis Leakey—whose first wife had commented on his "showbiz manner"—represented science's bid to do what religion had done before, which was to compel belief while defining the human. The centennial's last afternoon in Mandel Hall was given over to questions of evolution, science and religion, with Sol Tax stating his wish for the future: "I would hope that in the next hundred years our religious leaders may come to quote the Gospel as saying, 'Render unto science that which belongs to science.'" Much of the news coverage of the centennial was in fact about the philosophical debate, giving top play to Huxley's "secular sermon" and the final forum on religion—a topic that sold newspapers and one the American people, who are accepting of science and faith in roughly equal measure, could identify with.

Yet if the Darwin Centennial had conciliatory words for modernist or secularized religion, it handed no olive branch to America's Bible believers. As Huxley told Midwestern television audiences, "Darwinism removed the whole idea of God as the creator of organisms from the sphere of rational discussion. Darwin pointed out that no supernatural designer was needed." In tandem with this view, the 1950s were closing with the first intimations of the moral revolution that would erupt in the sixties. In the year of the centennial, *Look* magazine dispatched twelve veteran reporters to survey the nation's moral attitudes, which editor William Attwood characterized in the words of a young Pennsylvania woman: "Who am I to say what's right and wrong?" He elaborated: "Whatever you do is all right if it's legal or if you disapprove of the law. It's all right if it doesn't hurt anybody."

IT TOOK TWO YEARS AFTER THE DARWIN fête for the creationists to fire back. Their weapon was "creation science," spawned by the book entitled

The Genesis Flood. Written by the Bible-believing engineering professor Henry Morris and the Old Testament theologian John Whitcomb, the book aimed to prove a literal Genesis by arguing from geological evidence for a recent global flood. This, they said, was "scientific creationism"—science in the service of God's revealed Word. Its narrative could not have been more different from the Darwin Centennial's: humanity had miraculously appeared on a young earth a few thousand years ago; the natural world was cursed at the Fall; and then in the days of Noah came the great global Flood. For creation science, also called "Flood geology," the Deluge was everything, for it had shaped the earth and left behind the fossil record.

Creation science was not the only religious response to naturalism at a time when believers struggled to reconcile their faith with modern science. But as the most fundamentalist and the most activist, it threw a sharp light on the wide gulf separating the religious outlook and the seemingly triumphant naturalistic worldview represented by the centennial and epitomized by the lives of Shapley, Leakey and Huxley.

Sir Julian was more publicist than scientist. He wrote popular books, hosted the British quiz show *The Brains Trust,* and headed the London Zoo until fired by the board of governors. The first director of the United Nations Educational, Scientific, and Cultural Organization, he was viewed by many as "the man who put the *S* in UNESCO," and he tirelessly advocated the preservation of the Galapagos Islands as a memorial to Darwin and Darwinian evolution. In fact, his 1942 work, *Evolution: The Modern Synthesis,* gave the next generation of evolutionary biologists their umbrella theme of a synthesis between genetics and zoology. For all his atheism, however, Huxley wrote a foreword for the 1959 English translation of *The Phenomenon of Man,* an epic meditation on the spiritual evolution of humankind by the French Jesuit paleontologist Pierre Teilhard de Chardin.

Both Huxley and Harlow Shapley were active statesmen for science. They had both participated in the drafting of the UNESCO charter in London in 1946. Shapley, as the science representative in the U.S. delegation, was credited with persuading Congress to back the charter, and it is still debated who actually ensured that science became an integral part of it. If Huxley had truly put the *S* in UNESCO, "Shapley almost single-handedly prevented the deletion of the *S,*" according to one later writer.

What divided Huxley and Shapley most in the centennial year, however, was a matter of cosmic emphasis: was Earth or outer space the proper context for science? When Professor Tax had planned the centennial, some biologists had urged him, unsuccessfully, to exclude the topic of extraterrestrials. They found theories about aliens an embarrassment to natural science, viewing the evolution of the human mind as an event so improbable that it seemed preposterous it could have occurred elsewhere.

With his Earth-centered emphasis, Huxley was not shy in saying humans were the apex of nature. Later on, at his 1964 dedication of the Darwin Research Station in the Galapagos Islands, he declared that "man is the latest and highest type produced by the evolutionary process, and that his destiny is to guide his future course on this planet." An earthbound optimist, he had little interest in extraterrestrial life. "It is very nice to think they are there," he said to Shapley during the centennial. "But what have they to do with us? They do not help us out of our present mess."

As an astronomer, however, Shapley had invested much thought on alien life, and was for his generation a herald of the Copernican Principle—the conviction that humans have no centrality in the universe. A rural Missourian, Shapley was born in 1885. He had been a news reporter for "a miserable little daily" when, for lack of a journalism school in the Midwest, he decided to take up astronomy. With a gift for using telescopes, Shapley went to Princeton and became an expert on bipolar stars. At Mount Wilson, near Los Angeles, he used the 100-inch telescope, then the largest in the world. And in 1918, Shapley determined that our Milky Way galaxy was ten times larger than previously believed. What was more, he found that the solar system was peripheral to the Milky Way, whose center was situated toward the constellation Sagittarius. After these discoveries, he moved to the Harvard Observatory for the rest of his career.

Shapley had been reared by a "hardshell Baptist" mother, but working as a crime reporter for a daily newspaper may have soured his piety. Early in the 1930s he derided scientists around him for "becoming soft and religiously traditional." But with the rise of fascism followed by the Second World War and its Cold War aftermath, Shapley became newly impressed by believers, particularly modernist and liberal Protestants on the East Coast who were allies of the movement against nuclear arms. An internationalist who worked with Soviet scientists, Shapley was probed by the House Committee on Un-American Activities in the mid-1940s and then, in an act of solidarity by the scientific community, was elected president of the American Association for the Advancement of Science. His latter-day pessimism, often evident at the Darwin Centennial, seems to have hinged on his political experiences.

By the 1950s, Shapley felt that modernist religious leaders could be the allies of his global vision. In 1954, he helped found the Institute on Religion in an Age of Science (IRAS), and was the president of this annual forum in its opening years. The movement was strongly led by New England Unitarians and humanists, followed by liberal Protestant groups, and at its core was the pursuit of a rational, almost scientific, religion. "It gets away from superstition and miracles," said Shapley during the centennial. "Science can strengthen religion, and not upset it."

Perhaps his most far-reaching contribution to religion, he believed, was the cosmic dethroning of Earth. "After I saw that mankind was peripheral, it occurred to me that this had philosophical implications," Shapley wrote in his memoirs. "Later I found it one of the most important thoughts I have ever had.... If man had been found in the center, it would look sort of natural. We could say, 'Naturally we are in the center because we are God's children.' But here was an indication that we were perhaps incidental." He called this a "shocker" for ordinary people, including the clergy. "The ideas reached the preachers and theologians and worried them a bit," he said. "I had conversations with them, and they invited me to come and talk in their churches." During his time with the IRAS, he saw scientists speak with theologians and called it a worthwhile "confrontation of religion and science," though he thought that only the scientists came off well. "Theology is in a bad way," he concluded.

Three days before the Darwin Centennial opened, these two great spokesmen for science, Huxley and Shapley, were featured on the major Midwestern television talk show *At Random,* which aired in prime time on the CBS affiliate. They were a contrast of scientific egos, each with a prognosis for a world facing nuclear war, overpopulation and countless other problems.

Shapley was by far the most pessimistic, offering the opinion that humans are "one of the worst things" to have befallen planet Earth. Boosting the Copernican Principle, he emphasized the small part played by humans in a gigantic cosmos: "I think we fool ourselves in thinking that we are important in the universe. . . . We are a little vain or anthropocentric if we consider ourselves the center of life and the highest being in the universe." Like many astronomers, he believed that the "probability is exceedingly high" that there is intelligent life somewhere in the cosmos, although perhaps not amid the one hundred billion stars of the Milky Way. Why should *Homo,* Shapley asked on television, rule out a race higher then itself? Some of those distant stars may have planets with living beings holding aspirations similar to ours, and "to deny them this high privilege of having philosophers talking about the universe is not fair."

Huxley, a terrestrial optimist, was puzzled by these exhortations. "Unfair to stars?" he asked. As an atheist, however, Huxley understood one part of Shapley's attack on anthropocentric hubris, the part that arose from religion. "There was a time when we might say we swore by a one-planet god, or deity," Huxley said. "That's over!" For Shapley the pessimist, the stars remained an important solace. "One of the best things to be said for this planet is that it is a wonderful place on which to set up laboratories and mount telescopes to study the rest of the universe," he told television viewers. For Huxley this was too much. He retorted sarcastically, "Make the world safe for astronomy!"

Louis Leakey's role at the centennial was dramatic but momentary, for afterward he set out on a lecture tour of the United States. Rather than comment on where science put humans in the cosmic or global context, the fossil hunter from Africa sought man's place in the evolutionary past. This meant defining the origins of the genus *Homo.*

For two centuries before Darwin, the great naturalists of Europe were creationists who categorized living things into kinds designed by the Creator. After Darwin, the taxonomic categories were placed on a tree of life ascending from the very simplest organisms—what Darwin called "one or a few" original ancestors. On a high branch comes the class of mammals, which includes the order of primates and finally the genus *Homo.* From these beginnings, *Homo* branched into species such as *Homo erectus* and *Homo sapiens* and then into further subspecies—*Homo sapiens sapiens,* for example, was truly modern man.

In the search for *Homo,* the debate raged over Asian or African origins. Though Asia had prevailed through the first part of the twentieth century, by the 1940s the palm had gone to Africa. Because hominid skulls were the primary evidence in this debate, their features tell the story. In Asia's favor, advocates claimed that the first humans were possessors of a big brain and an ape-like face. Indeed, the famous Piltdown Man, uncovered in 1912 in Sussex, England, had just such a combination. Always suspected to be a fake, the Piltdown fraud was conclusively exposed in 1953: it was an antique human skull with an orangutan jaw. The new consensus, that the first humans had small brains and more modern features, was looking good for Africa—and for Louis Leakey.

Still, the tendency in the field was to view human emergence as a straight-line march in three stages from hunched ape to erect modern man. Leakey disagreed, calling this fashionable view simplistic. "As a result, attempts are made to fit all available fossil hominid material into one or another of these three supposed stages."

At the centennial panel on "Man as Organism," he chided the straight-line march schema and suggested that the human line had divergent branches and crisscrosses, much like other animal evolution: "I doubt very much whether man went through a stage with short legs and very long arms, such as we find with the great apes today." It is more likely that man arose directly from a quadrupedal primate such as *Australopithecus,* an ape that Leakey believed had also walked erect.

The evolution of the human brain was another matter. This was called "the mental Rubicon," or the point at which the brain became large enough to mark humanity. The standard set by anthropologists as the crossover point was 700 cubic centimeters, but Leakey was having none of it. His Zinj skull, "the oldest known human," came in at 600 cubic centimeters, and not for the last time in his career, Leakey wanted to lower the bar. At the centennial, he railed against big-brain bias. "Mere size of brain is not so important as people like to believe," he averred. To illustrate his point, he cited a study in Britain in which he had participated, which found that the brain sizes of scientists were smaller than those of pugilists, or boxers. "Looking at those sitting around this table," Leakey joked with the panel, "I can see a tremendous variety of absolute brain sizes. And I stress that quality rather than brain size is important." From his seat at the end of the long table of experts, the biologist Marston Bates smiled and offered, "It may take more intelligence to be a pugilist!"

Whatever the threshold of brain size, Mary and Louis Leakey had abandoned any idea of God as the arbiter. Though Louis was reared by missionaries, and Mary in her mother's Catholic faith—it had been a priest in France who introduced Mary to archaeology—science and personal predilections had erased those influences. Louis met her in the 1930s, not many years after Mary Nicole had been expelled from a British parochial school. He was thirty and she, a brunette archaeologist with blue eyes, was twenty. She smoked, had a sharp wit and piloted gliders. Leakey left his first wife for her, and they met up in Africa.

Leakey was and remained a lady's man his whole life, likened to an "alpha male" of an ape troop by a sympathetic biographer, while Mary unswervingly devoted herself to fossils. Years later, in 1984, she traveled to the American Museum of Natural History in New York City for the greatest exhibit of hominid fossils ever held. Her most memorable remark was about the risk of gathering them all in one place, where a religious "fundamentalist could come in with a bomb and destroy the whole legacy."

Together, Louis and Mary inaugurated the field of paleoanthropology and produced its most famous dynasty. Their son Richard, in the 1970s, took on the first great rival of the Leakey family, the American fossil hunter Donald Johanson. "I was still in high school when I read about Zinj in *National Geographic,*" Johanson recalled. In the coming years, he was awestruck as scientists—redating the Olduvai Gorge sediments—pushed back the age of *Homo* from hundreds of thousands to 1.8 million years. At one stroke Leakey and his associates had tripled the known age of humans.

After many more discoveries, even Zinj had been downgraded. With new fossil finds, the next candidate for the oldest human was *Homo habilis,* or "handy man." It took Leakey three years to persuade his primary collaborator in Africa, Phillip Tobias, to declare the new find more than an ape, but the trade-off was to classify Zinj as an ape once more. Biographer Virginia Morell has said that Leakey was unique in paleoanthropology for his propensity to revamp theories and standards without compunction. And in this case, she wrote, by "assigning Olduvai's oldest stone tools to *Homo habilis,* Louis effectively stripped *Zinjanthropus* of his human standing." To confer this status on *Homo habilis,* Louis had opted, in his own words, for a much more complex definition, which included more than just cranial measurements or tool-making abilities. In defining man, he said jokingly in 1963, "we decided we must exclude the chimpanzees from the United Nations."

Before Louis died in 1972, his son Richard shared with him his own spectacular find, a *Homo habilis* skull numbered 1470, which, he said, "did for me what Zinj did for Louis; it made me famous, put me on the international stage." The Johanson challenge was not long in coming. He arrived in Africa in 1973 and promptly discovered the 40 percent intact hominid skeleton known as "Lucy." Dating her to three million years ago, he declared Lucy the true branch-off point for human beginnings and proclaimed, "We have in a matter of merely two days extended our knowledge of the genus *Homo* by nearly 1.5 million years.... All previous theories of the origins of the lineage which leads to modern man must now be totally revised."

Biblical creationism had been galvanized by the publicity associated with the Darwin Centennial, and so it was to confound this alarming development that in 1981 Walter Cronkite invited Richard Leakey and Johanson to his television program *Universe* to expound the true story of human origins. That was a pretext—the real agenda was to pit two of the competing giants in the field against each other. By then, Leakey and Johanson represented two rival schemes of human origins. For Johanson, it was a Y-shaped scheme, with Lucy the crucial point three million years ago at which one branch split off from another branch of ape cousins. Leakey rejected such a simple formula; his scheme resembled a complex bush of many splits extending further back in time.

On the Cronkite show, Johanson went on the offensive while Leakey seemed mired in the uncertainties of the science. "I've seen fossils in favor, out of favor, back in favor, out of favor," Leakey said. Johanson pulled out a chart with his Y-shaped family tree and challenged Leakey to draw his alternative next to it. "I think in probability that I would do that," Leakey said as he drew an X on the Lucy tree.

"And what would you draw in its place?" Johanson asked.

"A question mark," Richard said, sketching it in with a laugh.

The early fossil hunters had believed that more finds would bring more historical clarity on the origins of the genus *Homo*. But by the last quarter of the twentieth century, the opposite was true. "Nobody really places a great deal of faith in *any* human tree," Johanson wrote in his 1989 book *Lucy's Child*. Richard Leakey acknowledged his father's tendency to alter criteria to make his fossils *Homo,* and said the *Homo habilis* category was "a grab bag mix of fossils; almost anything around two million years that doesn't fit the robust [ape] definition has been tossed into it."

By the new century, paleoanthropologists were divided over two models of human origins, one "tidy" and the other "untidy." The first envisioned a direct march to *Homo sapiens,* while the second saw hominid origins as a crazy quilt. Both approaches were rocked in the year 2002 when, after twenty-five years of digging, the French paleoanthropologist Michel Brunet found a small-brained skull with a human-like face in the Djurab desert of Chad, in central Africa. Dated to seven million years ago, it was the oldest hominid yet found. "It's a lot of emotion to have in my hand the beginning of the human lineage," Brunet said. With a touch of personal affection, he called his find "Toumai," reminiscent of how Leakey had personified "Zinj" as the beloved first human.

The Toumai skull showed that human origins went beyond East Africa (the Leakey hunting ground), and that molecular dating schemes could be inaccurate. Some likened the discovery's significance to the 1920s skull that shifted the search for early humans from Asia to Africa. For the tidy model, locating Toumai at the root of the hominid tree would displace the ape-faced fossils that had been linked to *Homo sapiens,* while for the untidy model, he just made science harder. "Anybody who thinks this isn't going to get more complex isn't learning from history," said Bernard Wood, a paleoanthropologist of the untidy school. The excitement notwithstanding, he said "it will be impossible to prove" whether Toumai is the immortal ancestor. Indeed, a few months after the find a group of paleoanthropologists (writing in *Nature*) attacked Brunet's interpretation, calling it a gorilla or an ape.

THE YOUTHFUL SCIENCE OF PALEOANTHROPOLOGY had dug its way into the great debate about science itself. Since the Enlightenment, the scientific enterprise had been viewed as a steady accumulation of sound knowledge. Unlike the hoi polloi, scientists were rational. The science of human origins began with that self-image and it was perfectly captured again at the Darwin Centennial, a celebration that located science at the peak of the evolutionary climb.

This stately and triumphal view, however, was soon to be challenged. During the 1970s, the decade when Louis Leakey, Huxley and Shapley passed into history, two other readings of science emerged. One reading described it as an utterly human institution that, while successful in its task, was accompanied at every step by prejudices, misconceptions, irrational hopes and stifling orthodoxies—all the things deemed wrong with religion. To an extent acknowledging this critique, scientists became more willing to concede they were possessors of a "faith," but they insisted that it was a faith in nature itself, or simply "naturalism."

A second assessment appeared as science began to occupy the highlands once trodden exclusively by philosophers and theologians. This is the domain of the very large, the very small and the very complex. It includes the distant past, the distant future and what is unseen by the human eye or instruments. Science, according to this opinion, might have reached its limits. While for some scientists this pessimism is anathema, and while optimists are correct in saying "the end of science" has been erroneously declared before, gone are the self-certain days of Louis Leakey, who told his audience how "reasonable" it was to "accept the genus *Zinjanthropus* as being in the direct evolutionary line leading to *Homo*."

After the discovery of Zinj, *National Geographic* editor Mary Smith in 1962 visited the Olduvai digs. Leakey urged her to put the "evolution of early man" front and center in her magazine. "You can't have those Bible people hold back the knowledge we're learning," she recalled him saying. "It must be brought to the public. Promise me, Mary, that you'll look into this." She had said, "Yes, sir, I certainly will."

Decades later, the "Bible people" were quite a diverse array, not just the creation scientists whose growth was spurred by the Darwin Centennial. Now, they ranged from modernist theists to Bible believers who looked for divine design in the universe. Aware of and encouraged by the secular debate about the all-too-human reality of science and its ultimate limits, a good number had entered the field, arguing that the scientific facts might make a case for God. What aspects of nature, they asked, reveal the mind of the Creator?

2

SCIENCE IN THE DOCK

At the Darwin Centennial, the power and knowledge of science were seen most dramatically in the panel on "The Evolution of Life." It was a showcase for the modern synthesis, the greatest achievement yet of evolutionary biology and a reigning orthodoxy in modern science.

Eleven of its captains sat on the stage at Mandel Hall during the session. None were more emblematic of the triumph of the movement than two white-haired gentlemen: Sewall Wright, a geneticist, and Ernst Mayr, a bird expert and naturalist. If Wright was "perhaps the single most influential evolutionary theorist of this century" and the the leading exponent of the modern synthesis, a sympathetic biographer later said, Mayr was its chief organizer. In 1946, Mayr founded the Society for the Study of Evolution, the first collective effort of its kind and flagship of the modern synthesis.

When Julian Huxley had written his book of that title, he was giving a name to the theory. The modern synthesis, arrived at between 1937 and 1947, proposed that all organic evolution arose through the agency of natural selection, which eliminates the unfit by acting on variations caused by genetic changes, or mutations. It was a two-part mechanism with the power to create everything in the natural world and, as Huxley had told centennial audiences, "removed the whole idea of God as the creator of organisms" from discussion: "Darwin pointed out that no supernatural designer was needed." And it was true, for Darwin had dramatically replaced one explanation with another. "The old argument of design in nature, which formerly seemed to me so conclusive, fails, now that the law of natural selection has been discovered," Darwin had written. Creation had become a fictive way of talking about nature, a refuge for obfuscation. "It is so easy to hide our ignorance under such expressions as the 'plan of creation,' 'unity of design,' etc., and to think that we give an explanation when we only restate a fact."

The stakes were high for the modern synthesis, for it had to explain everything, not just restate a fact of natural diversity. So high were the stakes that it could not fail to produce personal and professional rivalries. Sewall Wright was sixty-one when he traveled to the centennial, having retired to Wisconsin from the University of Chicago. It must have been bittersweet, for he had long felt misrepresented and unappreciated for his contribution as one of the few geneticists among those who forged neo-Darwinian theory. As the field of evolutionary biology climbed in professional stature, a disagreement arose: which factor was most important in the modern synthesis—the gene and the geneticist, or the organism and the naturalist?

Darwin, it is said, had made the generations of biologists after him evolutionists, but not necessarily selectionists. Until the synthesis, many scientists doubted the power of natural selection to produce new species. With the first formulation of scientific laws of heredity in 1900 and later of mutations and the mixing of genes, it was believed that the driving power of evolutionary change lay there. While there was some inclination, particularly in Germany, to look for abrupt, gigantic mutations that produced novelty, Darwin's belief in the gradual accumulation of small changes had prevailed, especially in England.

In that country, the mathematics of heredity and the hypergradualism of Darwin were combined in a new field called "population genetics." The English theorist Ronald Fisher, who would end up as Sewall Wright's great rival, proposed a "fundamental theory" in which gene mutations spread widely through a population. After that smooth and statistical dispersion, natural selection would determine the entire population to be fit or unfit; it would die out or evolve to some new and viable level.

In disagreement, Wright believed that the genetic changes spread in small, isolated populations and natural selection worked upon these. This was the idea that opened the way to the modern synthesis. And it had come as something of an epiphany to Wright himself. The son of a Midwest college professor, he completed his advanced study at Harvard fully persuaded of Darwin's gradualism and natural selection. But then he began to notice the small or local group effect in cattle breeding and in experiments with guinea pigs while he was working at the U.S. Department of Agriculture outside Washington.

Back in the 1930s, Wright's published work struck the Darwinian naturalists like a bolt from the blue. Lacking field studies, they had been stumped on how speciation, or the rise of new species, actually took place: did selection work on an individual, a small group, or an entire population? What provided sufficient variation—a gradual buildup or a major mutation? Naturalists such as Ernst Mayr, who handled massive bird collections, had mounds of information on the shapes, habitats and varieties of creatures, and on the fossil record. But now Wright gave them a genetic basis for a description of the process: genetic variation, then isolation and selection.

Wright argued that a subgroup could evolve at rates, and with a versatility, unlikely for a large group. The subgroup could subsequently influence the rest, dragging them up an "adaptive peak" to create a new species. The breeding of higher-grade shorthorn cattle, Wright said, put flesh on the theory. "There were always many herds at any given time, but only a few were generally perceived as distinctly superior," he wrote in the *Journal of Animal Science*. "These herds successively made over the whole breed by being principal sources of sires."

This was not very different from Darwin's observation in Victorian England that pigeon breeders, using their power of "human selection," could crossbreed birds and come out with new variations. Wright assigned this power to nature in a small isolated group he called a *deme,* which by its limited size could accomplish the heavy lifting of evolution. What was not Darwinian, however, and therefore a source of growing controversy, was Wright's suggestion that gene mixing was the main engine of evolution. This downplaying of natural selection as the chief mechanism for evolution put him on a collision course with orthodox Darwinians such as Mayr, who was selectionist to the core.

Wright's work greatly influenced the godfather of the modern synthesis, Theodosius Dobzhansky. A Russian émigré, Dobzhansky was both a geneticist who worked in the "fly room" at Columbia University and a field naturalist who watched wild populations of fruit flies and beetles. He "fell in love" with Wright's theory, which he incorporated in a set of lectures, published in 1937, that launched the synthesis. The lectures had a domino effect. Dobzhansky encouraged Mayr, the ornithologist, and others in botany and mammal paleontology to apply the variation, isolation and selection schema, and more books tumbled forth.

Thanks to Wright, said his partisans, the modern synthesis was born and gave coherence to a field in disarray. Before the synthesis, geneticists, taxonomists and paleontologists went their own way. They "appeared to be getting farther apart in their conclusions," reported the journal *Evolution,* founded by Mayr in 1947 to promote the modern synthesis. By the time of the Darwin Centennial, a mighty research program was in place, and the synthesis had become orthodoxy in textbooks and university biology departments, having been established, some would say, by a very small, exclusive group. Indeed, when the Society for the Study of Evolution was founded, Mayr was its first secretary and Wright and Dobzhansky its first council members.

But the great "explanation" promised by Darwin had not yet succeeded, and below the surface amicability of the centennial panel lay theoretical tensions. The panel opened, however, with an emphasis on agreements. After much speciation, the panelists agreed, evolution produced dominant types. Successful organisms had achieved adaptive fitness—they were fit to survive and reproduce. Fitness often came when an organism sprouted a new feature, and the feature was often a compromise between genes and the environment. Some features were pre-adaptations, not useful at first, but in the long run allowing an evolutionary breakthrough. As Ernst Mayr said in his German accent, "The fishes that gave rise to terrestrial vertebrates had fins that were already like legs."

As a young man, Mayr had trudged through the jungles of New Guinea to collect birds. Their differences showed up from one mountain to another, hinting at the role of geographic isolation in forming different species. An aura of adventure surrounded Mayr, who was once reported killed by a hostile tribe and who survived waterfalls and malaria during his collecting years. From experience, he passionately argued that geographic isolation—not just Wright's genetic isolation—was an essential factor.

This all-important topic received much attention from the panel, with Dobzhansky arguing that both kinds of isolating mechanisms were operable, one geographic and the other reproductive—giving credence, in effect, to both Mayr and Wright. But in general, participants disagreed on how many isolating mechanisms existed, so chairman Sir Julian Huxley summarized: "I think everyone agrees that some degree of isolation is a prerequisite for the changes that may later lead to speciation."

The disagreement between Wright and Mayr, however, chilled their professional relationship down through the years. And when Mayr organized a major retrospective on the modern synthesis in 1974, Wright was not invited. A typical statement by Wright seemed to focus everything on genetic mixing: "Evolution as a process of cumulative change depends on a proper balance of the conditions which at each level of organization—gene, chromosome, cell, individual, local race—make for genetic homogeneity or genetic heterogeneity of the species." Indeed, it was this kind of emphasis that prompted Wright's critics to say he didn't need natural selection—the very backbone of Darwinism—at all.

The battle between the geneticist and the naturalist was quietly waged on the 1959 panel, with the occasional side remark that population genetics had tried to make evolutionary biology "almost a branch of genetics." Mayr stressed the adaptive breakthroughs of an organism. "Occasionally a species will make a major 'discovery'—for instance, the first fish that got out onto the land 'discovered' the land niche and gave rise to the terrestrial vertebrates," he said. Similarly, a reptile "discovered" the air niche and gave rise to the birds. With trademark passion, he argued that in all such cases, natural selection worked on an organism's body, not on its genes. "Selection operates on the phenotype, the final product of the interaction of all the different genes."

But when it came to larger evolutionary controversies, the two men were allies. They both agreed on Darwinian gradualism, the key to Darwin's explanation. Wright's theory of genetic mixing required just such an infinitesimal building up, "step by step, by thousands of little steps, to results that are utterly unthinkable as occurring at a single step." A big genetic mutation could not bring about that unthinkable change because it was highly unlikely that a novel mutation would be favorable and survive. Mayr could not have agreed more. He had grown up with German biology, where evolutionists favored big jumps and mutations. Ever after, he fought such ideas. He told the audience that such a jump was "like believing in a miracle."

Explaining how evolution worked had become more complicated than science had anticipated. So with the advent of computers, scientists turned hopefully to the powerful new tools at their disposal. The mathematics that Wright had used to elucidate nature took a leap of its own into the world of computation, bringing new explanatory models of how evolution worked; the lament could now be heard that evolution had become a branch of computer science. Mayr, the old-fashioned Darwinian, would call some of these techniques "gimmicks," though in truth naturalists who had not also majored in mathematics were soon at a disadvantage. The most popular of the computer-driven approaches were game theory and complexity theory.

During the Korean War, the U.S. government had recruited International Business Machines to build what was called the Defense Calculator, which was IBM's first fully electronic digital computer. Two of the scientists on the project were John H. Holland and Arthur Samuel. It was Samuel who began to think about how machines learned to play games and what this might say about the laws of nature. Holland popularized the new outlook that trafficked in chaos theory and promoted a new buzzword in biology: emergence.

In 1959, Samuel created the Checkersplayer program on one of the largest existing computers. The program created a learning machine by first setting an optimum goal, measuring trial and error success against the goal, and pruning away errors with every new game; it gradually became strong enough to beat Samuel hands down. As Holland would write later, "Board games are a simple example of the emergence of great complexity from simple rules or laws." Holland had a name for this new science, and put it in the title of his classic 1989 book, *Emergence: From Chaos to Order.*

Earlier in the century, before the modern synthesis, some biologists talked of "emergent evolution," and even Huxley in his seminal book spoke of "emergent properties." The word had always had a feel of "vitalism"— the idea, heretical by the late fifties, that mystical, mental or organic forces worked from within organisms to guide their evolution. Now that vitalism was dead, slain by the reductionism of physics, genetics and natural selection, the utter complexity of biology could still be acknowledged in the novel and essentially materialistic approaches of emergence and chaos theory.

And they could only be understood on a computer. "It is at first surprising that a wide range of concrete objects and processes can be represented by numbers and the manipulation of numbers," Holland explained. He would join a cadre of researchers at the newfangled Santa Fe Institute, where biology was turned into mathematical models. Traditional naturalists looked askance at the project, and others called it faddish. But Holland said that emergence and chaos were pure Darwinian natural selection, the force of trial and error, so that in a system, "more comes out than we put in"—a perfect definition of creation by evolution.

Yet to explain evolution, computer science in 1959 still had a "creation problem," for it was intelligent humans who created the machines and programs to start with. In comparable fashion, Victorian pigeon breeders had picked which birds to crossbreed. By analogy, then, the computer programmer and the breeder were both creators of something after their own thoughts. Darwin had used the pigeon breeder as an example of intelligent selection, but he of course rejected an Intelligent Breeder behind nature. Evolutionists, on the other hand, claimed that computers proved that godless creation was possible. Design theorists disagreed; just as humans must program computers, a Cosmic Programmer must design nature.

The computational power of computers also revealed how improbable it was for a random mix of particles to produce a functionally designed organism. This was the debate in 1966 at the Wistar Institute of Anatomy and Biology in Philadelphia, where a group of mathematicians skeptical about Darwinism met with some of its leading biological defenders. Mayr was among the fifty-two people who attended, and Wright defended himself in a paper afterward.

The leading skeptics were Murray Eden of MIT and Marcel P. Schützenberger, a French doctor and mathematician who would teach at MIT and Harvard and be elected to the French Academy of Sciences. They both thought it was mathematically impossible for Darwin's tiny variations to add up to a new organism. "Nowadays computers are operating within a range which is not entirely incommensurate with that dealt with in actual evolutionary theories," Schützenberger told the Wistar gathering. In the age of computer power, Darwinians could not use assumed "astronomical numbers of small variations" as a magic wand. And they still could not explain the major gap in their theory: how does the random shuffling of a one-dimensional string of genetic codes create a highly coordinated multidimensional organism? "We believe this gap to be of such a nature that it cannot be bridged within the current conception of biology."

Under pressure, Darwinians at the Wistar Symposium accused the agnostic Schützenberger of believing in special creation.

"No!" he protested.

By the 1990s, the intelligent design movement would herald Schutzenberger as a gutsy pioneer in modern anti-Darwinism.

Given the newness of computers, however, their impact on Darwinian theory was a sideshow to the principal upheaval that came to evolutionary biology in the 1970s. It was no less than a declaration of war on the modern synthesis. Though the Darwin Centennial had ended amicably enough, the "Evolution of Life" panel had already revealed cracks in the consensus. For example, Mayr would speak of how few examples of speciation really existed: "Most of our knowledge of speciation is based on a few species of birds, butterflies and moths."

The best examples of evolution were the same kinds of "microevolution"—evolution below the species level—that would still be emphasized in textbooks after the year 2000. One of these, cited enthusiastically by Huxley, was the case of the peppered moth *(Biston betularia)* in England. A 1953 experiment supposedly showed that the population of moths changed from light to dark—they evolved—as tree trunks darkened from industrial pollution and hungry birds ate the now more visible lighter-colored moths. The other examples cited by Wright were the "evolutionary" processes by which insects develop resistance to pesticides and by which bacteria produce immunity to antibiotic penicillin. These examples were about extermination and disease, Wright admitted, and thus "beautiful only from the evolutionary standpoint."*

---

*By 2002, the claims about the peppered moth were being attacked as a "myth" and a "fraud" in science articles and in a book, Judith Hooper's *Of Moths and Men,* which ably exposes the bad science behind this Darwinian icon. Hooper writes, "To be uncritical of science is to make it into dogma." Likewise, pesticide resistance is now questioned as a relevant example for evolution of new species.

The other conundrum of the centennial panel was the frequency of extinctions, particularly since Darwinian theory envisioned a gradual transformation of one species to the next, with one methodically replacing another. The fossil record was beginning to show, however, not only that most species died out but that they did so by what seemed to be mass extinctions and major upheavals in the history of life. As Mayr had put it, "The whole pathway of evolution is strewn left and right with bodies of extinct types."

The fossil record showed one other anomaly, Mayr said with candor: some organisms had stayed the same for 120 million to 140 million years. Then they showed an abrupt change that "suddenly broke out during a new evolutionary outburst." He called it a "loosening up of tightly knit systems," and asked how it might have happened.

In 1959, the modern synthesis was an edifice of triumphant certainty. Behind the edifice, however, was modesty and doubt—and Dobzhansky offered some of it: "There is a great temptation, especially when one reaches a certain age, which I have reached, as have most of my colleagues on this panel, to speak about things as really known and to represent them as cut and dried." Huxley agreed, saying, "I think if Charles Darwin had been alive for this panel, he would have been bewildered by the many new problems, new terms, and new ideas that have come up." A century hence, he added, science would be "equally excited and equally bewildered," and biology would remain "a wonderful field full of problems."

It took far less than a century, however, for others in science to bemoan the heavy hand of the modern synthesis. Again, it seemed that all the features of the evolutionary explanation were up for grabs. Was evolution a smooth, adaptive process, or was it a pluralistic, messy, clumsy and cataclysmic force? This latter view was preferred by paleontologist Stephen Jay Gould, and it was he and colleague Niles Eldredge who, in 1972, set out to unsettle the modern synthesis by characterizing it as hidebound and rigidly orthodox.

Gould had studied at Columbia University, hard by the American Museum of Natural History, where he was exposed to the thinking of Dobzhansky and Mayr. But the fossil record caused him to think along new lines. As Mayr had before him, Gould noticed the pattern in which long periods of stasis were suddenly interrupted by evidence of rapid change. On the vast scale of evolutionary time, it looked to Gould and Eldredge like a jump, and so they called it that, publishing the new theory in 1972 in their paper, "Punctuated Equilibrium: An Alternative to Phyletic Gradualism." The punctuations, or jumps over thousands of years, appeared in populations that had moved off to the side of a larger group. In this, the two theorists drew on the isolation principle of the modern synthesis.

Like Mayr, Sewall Wright also fiercely opposed these brash young punctuationists. As his biographer William Provine noted, "Wright disagreed strongly with Gould's suggestion that something like Goldschmidt's hopeful monster theory was required for explaining the observed geological record."

Richard Goldschmidt, a geneticist at the University of California at Berkeley, had argued in the 1940s that evolutionary change that produced new species was so dramatic it required massive genetic mutations, or hopeful monsters. If Mayr visualized a fish's fin as the first sign of a reptile's leg, Goldschmidt theorized that a full-blown reptile might appear in a fish's egg. Goldschmidt for his pains became the butt of the Darwinian gradualists' scorn. However, such a view, also called "saltationism," was not unprecedented. The British geneticist J. B. S. Haldane argued for major mutations for the same reason that Thomas Huxley, Darwin's ally, had: there was limited geological time in which all of Earth's organic diversity had to appear. America's early geneticists, such as William Bateson and T. H. Morgan, also believed that a species was fixed until a major mutation transformed it into something else.

A talented polemicist, Stephen Jay Gould rehabilitated Goldschmidt. He also argued for pluralism in evolutionary theory: evolution as a fact, but with any and all explanatory strategies welcome. He also rehabilitated Wright, whose genetic theory had been sidelined by what his biographer calls the "extreme selectionist attitude" of the fifties. Finally, in 1980, Gould delivered what he hoped was a stunning blow to the tottering modern synthesis. He declared it "effectively dead" and asked, "Is a New and General Theory of Evolution Emerging?"

In his polemic, however, Gould was a young Turk, not a seasoned veteran. That kind of sophisticated dissent came instead from across the Atlantic in the work of Pierre P. Grassé, France's leading naturalist. In 1972, he wrapped up a long career with a work that set out to "destroy the myth of evolution as a simple, understood, and explained phenomenon." The French, whose evolutionary theories predated Darwin in the likes of George Buffon (d. 1788) and Jean Baptiste Lamarck (d. 1829), had never entirely warmed to the English way of thinking about it—individual organisms gradually progressing in a competitive free market of evolution. Grassé's *Evolution of Life* argued that Darwin and his interpreters had proved so ineffective in explaining the origin of species that "it is possible that in this domain biology, impotent, yields the floor to metaphysics."

Dobzhansky was commissioned to beat back Grassé's "frontal attack on all kinds of 'Darwinism.'" The Frenchman knew his zoology, Dobzhansky said: "One can disagree with Grassé but not ignore him." (He had been president of the Académie des Sciences and editor of the twenty-eight-volume *Traité de Zoologie*.) Dobzhansky surmised, however, that Grassé had succumbed to undue pessimism, and had further erred by reverting to "oriented evolution." This last was a kind of directed evolution, a force—usually anathematized as "vitalism"—that was wholly opposed to the spirit of the modern synthesis. While Grassé insisted that the synthesis amounted to evolution by chance pure and simple, Dobzhansky rejoined that he was guilty of using fuzzy notions of chance.

When the National Association of Biology Teachers met in San Francisco in 1972, the debate over Darwin's explanation and the creationist response dominated the sessions. To bolster the biology teachers' confidence, Dobzhansky delivered the oft-quoted judgement, "Nothing in biology makes sense except in the light of evolution."

Dobzhansky was no atheist in the academic mold. He had never lost his inherited faith in traditional Russian Orthodoxy and was also a follower of the Catholic philosopher Pierre Teilhard de Chardin. Drawing on this background, he told the gathered biology teachers that the modern synthesis was on God's side:

> I am a creationist *and* an evolutionist.... Disagreements and clashes of opinion are rife among biologists, as they should be in a living, growing science.... Anti-evolutionists mistake, or pretend to mistake, these disagreements as indications of the dubiousness of the entire doctrine of evolution.

Their favorite sport, he added, was stringing together disagreeing and negative quotations, always out of context.

DESPITE THE BROUHAHA AND CLASHES of opinion, at the time of the Darwin Centennial science could at least claim that it was on the right track; its methods and outlook were sound, apparently unassailable. But by the 1980s, those claims were being called into question as a result of a robust debate over the authority of science, which proved to be a major windfall for those anxious to defend God against ever-encroaching materialism and reductionism. Beginning quietly in the 1950s, the debate peaked around 1973, the time of the next major science celebration: the 500th anniversary of Nicolaus Copernicus's birth, held in Washington, D.C., and sponsored by the National Academy of Sciences and the Smithsonian.

This was a time when, for reflective scientists, theoretical disagreements among themselves, or worries about creationism, seemed almost trivial compared with a looming problem: the strange phenomenon of a widespread and documentable disenchantment with science and technology in the advanced nations, especially among young people. The year of the Polish astronomer was thus eagerly awaited by the faithful—the return of an ancient comet proclaiming the accomplishments of the West. As the sociologist Wilton S. Dillon explained, scientific congregations also need their feast days.

Anniversary celebrants forecast a future of endless new gateways. "We can believe that the discoveries of the future will outnumber those of the past," enthused physicist John Wheeler with his customary eloquence. "But will they be greater? Nothing so much encourages the answer 'yes' as the mysteries encountered wherever we turn."

There was a defensive undercurrent, however. "We know that the cycles of antiscientific agitation have come and gone away before," said science historian Gerald Holton. He recalled for the august Washington audience the hostility of the masses in the time of the great German astronomer Johannes Kepler, when peasants ransacked his town. And in England in the 1830s, someone wrote a book entitled *The Decline of Science.* After the "bankruptcy of science" was declared in 1900, Holton went on, came the discovery of

X-rays and the revolution of quantum mechanics. Beware of the "alleged disenchantment," he concluded. Other Copernican-year speakers tied the antiscience mood to the social crises of the day, including the economy, environmental problems and political cynicism.

The Copernican year revealed the vulnerability of science both as a tool of knowledge and as a social force. The increasingly public debate would also be a crossroads for those struggling over the questions of God and science. Was science so fallible and destructive that it must be met by a counterculture of antinomian creativity or by a "faith alone" religious fideism? Alternatively, could science be redefined so that it was friendlier toward theological belief?

In the aftermath of the Copernican year debate, this option was tried. Attempts to redefine science so that it allowed concepts of design or mind proved the most promising. This was a time also when traditional materialist ideas about science came to be increasingly questioned. Some of the people doing the questioning were Michael Polanyi, Arthur Koestler, Thomas Kuhn and Theodore Roszack.

The influence of Polanyi, a scientist turned philosopher, peaked in the 1950s in England. Born to a Jewish family in prewar Hungary, Polanyi had been a medical doctor and research chemist. He converted to Christianity in 1912 after reading Dostoevski's *The Brothers Karamazov*. Soon after that he fled politically volatile Budapest for Berlin, where he worked with German scientists. By 1933, the German political atmosphere had darkened as well, so Polanyi left for England. He became head of a research laboratory at the University of Manchester and, not surprisingly, began to speak and write against the Nazis and against Soviet oppression of scientists. Though he waxed romantic about "the republic of science," a world brotherhood that spoke the same language, he warned against even democratic governments taking control of laboratories and technology.

By the time Polanyi retired from his laboratory, he had published two hundred papers, made significant advances in chemistry and taught the likes of Melvin Calvin, the American Nobel laureate. Yet around 1937, Calvin recalled, "It often became difficult for me to talk with him because he was thinking in terms of economics and philosophy, and I couldn't understand his language." This difficulty marked Polanyi's crossover from science to philosophy, which he studied at Oxford University. Though baptized as a Catholic, Polanyi joined the Anglican Church. He moved in a learned circle of Christian thinkers that included T. S. Eliot, and in 1961 addressed the World Student Christian Association on "The Science Revolution." Polanyi also studied with the modernist theologian Paul Tillich; as Tillich fought religious fundamentalism, so Polanyi fought scientific fundamentalism. It was a man of religion—the Scottish theologian and cleric Thomas Torrence—and not a man of science who became executor of Polanyi's papers when he died.

Whatever the ambiguities of Polanyi's personal view of God or "divine reality," his idea of tacit knowledge—or personal and intuitive knowledge—changed the entire debate in science. He summarized his ideas in the 1953 Gifford Lectures on natural theology. They were published five years later as *Personal Knowledge: Towards a Post-Critical Philosophy.* With this opus, Polanyi seemed to have emerged as the knight who had slain the materialist dragon of scientific positivism, with its Enlightenment myth of science as purely objective. He argued that personal, subjective insight motivated the best scientists. While Polanyi opened a space in the scientific mind for mystical insights, he never plainly stated that God made an appearance in that space. For many, however, the assertion that the opening existed was Polanyi's great appeal. He never declared himself on whether God or the afterlife existed, but he did argue that the mind was programmed for transcendent experience, a mode of knowledge just as important as the mode of science.

For one group of Christians in science, Polanyi would be remembered for his 1967 article in *Chemical and Engineering News* titled "Life Transcending Physics and Chemistry." Drawing on his expertise in chemistry, Polanyi explained how the chemical bonds that were fundamental to the structure of biological life were mechanical and repetitive. Unlike a computer program, repetitive complex chemicals do not produce something new. They lack "information content." Polanyi wrote: "The pattern of atoms forming a crystal is another instance of complex order without appreciable information content." Citing the unique information content of a DNA molecule, he asked, "can the control of morphogenesis by DNA be likened to the designing and shaping of a machine by the engineer?"

The idea of information content that transcends chemical bonds and the picture of an engineer shaping the organism would be picked up by the group that formed the intelligent design movement about a decade after Polanyi's death in 1976. Conceptually, Polanyi provided grounds for the attempt to detect "irreducible higher principles [that] are *additional* to the laws of physics and chemistry."

Not surprisingly, Francis Crick, who had co-discovered the DNA double helix, believed that life was "nothing but" the chemical bonds, and thus dismissed Polanyi as a "vitalist." But the Polanyi legacy spread through the works of Arthur Koestler, who thanked him for encouragement in his first history of science, *The Sleepwalkers,* a story that begins with Pythagoras and runs through the age of Isaac Newton. The novelty of the book hinges on Koestler's obtaining the first English translation of the diaries of Johannes Kepler, the formulator of the laws of planetary motion. As he dramatically showed with Kepler, scientists down through history have walked more of a zigzag path than a straight one. They could be beguiled by fanciful ideas and often propagated obsolete notions while overlooking plain empirical truths. These sleepwalkers nevertheless made the discoveries of science, and were honest enough to think of themselves as "natural philosophers."

Now in the age of credentialed scientists, Koestler hoped to "counteract the legend that Science is a purely rational pursuit, that the Scientist is a more 'level-headed' and 'dispassionate' type than others (and should therefore be given a leading role in world affairs), or that he is able to provide for himself and his contemporaries a rational substitute for ethical insights derived from other sources." While Koestler did not attack Darwinism in *The Sleepwalkers,* he was heading in that direction. A decade later, in 1969, he brought biologists who doubted Darwinian orthodoxy to picturesque Alpbach, Austria, for a discussion called "Beyond Reductionism," which followed up on the Wistar Symposium.

What Koestler marveled at most in *The Sleepwalkers* was the persistence of old-fashioned "materialist philosophy." Here in the age of quantum physics, when "matter itself has evaporated," brute materialism had still "retained its dogmatic power over [the] mind" of the average scientist. Worse still, science had banned "purpose" from nature, even a purpose unrelated to an "anthropomorphic deity." Koestler concluded his book, which came out a year before the 1959 Darwin Centennial, with the observation: "The basic novelty of our age is the combination of this sudden, unique increase in physical power with an equally unprecedented spiritual ebb-tide."

A few years later, the Harvard historian and physics instructor Thomas S. Kuhn stirred the pot some more in a monograph for the *Encyclopedia of Unified Science,* which turned into the blockbuster book *The Structure of Scientific Revolutions,* published in 1962. Unlike Polanyi or Koestler, whom he did not mention, Kuhn described how institutional science worked. Establishment science, which he called "normal science," operated on the most successful and agreeable theory of a given era. But as anomalies in the theory appeared in increasing numbers, the establishment became defensive, like an insecure orthodoxy—or like the Nixon White House before the Watergate hearings. Scientists in a rival camp, typically outsiders, were eager to move to something new. But that either took time—until the passing of the old guard—or it took upheaval. When the "palace coup" was successful, Kuhn said, it marked "a paradigm shift" in a field of science.

The book was galvanizing. Many scientists, historians and people in the humanities doubtless read more into the book than Kuhn intended. (He spent the next three decades explaining himself.) But the implications of his work were clear: Far from being magisterial in its objectivity, science was conditioned by history, society and the prejudices of scientists.

Kuhn's work catalyzed the nascent discipline of the history of science. This new historical approach to science could fit well into the decorum of a setting such as Harvard. It could also be a rabble-rousing intellectual activism on the political left, as in the case of an equally popular work by Theodore Roszak, *The Making of the Counter Culture.* Roszak was a leftist history teacher at a college in Hayward, California, a stone's throw from Berkeley, and he saw the youth rebellion of the sixties as a clash with "technocracy," which had become "a grand cultural imperative, a veritable mystique" embraced even by the general public.

The mystique was rooted in Western science and it produced a "society in which those who govern justify themselves by appeal to technical experts who, in turn, justify themselves by appeal to scientific forms of knowledge. And beyond the authority of science, there is no appeal." Roszak prescribed an antidote: subjectivity, art, sensual expression—in a word, the antinomianism of the sixties. Soon enough, the political left identified science with the arms race and the Vietnam War. And because of this, science advocates tried to humanize their worldview.

This was a challenge not only to the technocrats, but to the Darwinians as well. To their rescue came the scientific humanist Jacob Bronowski, a mathematician and Polish Jew who had emigrated to England. He delivered his science in his unprecedented television series, *The Ascent of Man,* which aired in 1973, the Copernican year.

Bronowski pioneered a new approach to science and the public. He called it "a personal view." And in his final product—evolutionist, reductionist, humane and arty—scientists were seen to be quite as interesting as giants of art and literature. The show inspired astronomer Carl Sagan's *Cosmos* series, which punned on a Christian doxology by claiming, "The cosmos is all that is, or ever was, or ever will be." When astrophysicist Stephen Hawking decided to write *A Short History of Time,* he too took a cue from Bronowski's work. "I was very impressed," Hawking said of *The Ascent of Man,* although he added, "such a sexist title would not be allowed today." Hawking's book cleverly ended with a hope that science would "know the mind of God," but without such a God having to exist.

Unlike Bronowski, Sagan or Hawking, the 1973 Copernican celebration in Washington was not so caught up in the cause of refuting God's existence. Instead, it celebrated the humaneness and wonder of science with an April medley of banquets, academic sessions, musical compositions and ornate prose by astrophysicist Fred Hoyle, the onetime Cambridge don and science fiction novelist. The year featured Copernicus postage stamps. Congress, mindful of the Polish-American vote, issued a Copernican resolution. A satellite bearing the astronomer's name circled the earth. With all this fanfare, it was hard to avoid assessing what had happened to Western science between Copernicus and the present.

One theory argued that perhaps science itself had lost confidence, letting the flame that lit the scientific revolution—the belief that people could apprehend reality—flicker out. "We must be prepared to raise afresh the question, how far that original self-confidence is still alive for us today," cautioned the historian Stephen Toulman. The Copernican endowment may have "at last begun to crumble away, leaving us, apparently, at the end of the intellectual era that he inaugurated."

Philip Handler, president of the National Academy of Sciences, offered a different twist: ordinary people had a loss of nerve in the face of science. Human society itself, he proposed, was being challenged to its philosophical core by the objective findings of science. It was the stinging implications of both the Copernican and the Darwinian revolutions, he said, that brought a backlash that was deeply psychological, a welter of "dual emotions." There was delight in knowledge; but there was also "the lonely pain which such understanding brings as each of us confronts our fleeting, earthly passage, our puny places in the flow of history and the vast reaches of the cosmos."

Later that year, the celebration of Nicolaus Copernicus continued in his homeland of Poland. Set in cities such as Torun and Cracow, under communist rule in a tense era of the Cold War, the assemblies did not feature criticisms of government, society or low funding for science, as in the West. But even behind Poland's Iron Curtain they could talk about the situation of human beings in the cosmos. The talks included a new breed of astronomers who, as they strove to understand the truth of affairs, were surprisingly like Copernicus in spirit. They were known as cosmologists.

INTIMATIONS OF DESIGN

3

THE COSMIC CENTER

Torun's heritage as the city of Copernicus's birth had made it the hub of Polish astronomy, and throughout the Copernican year, visitors streamed across the Torun Observatory's parklike grounds to see the three small domed buildings with their antiquated telescopes.

Yet despite these artifacts of astronomy, the Copernican revolution was mostly about mathematics. Early science had struggled with the deceit of the senses, and often, as in the case of figures like Pythagoras and Plato, turned to mathematics as a perfect realm that did not lie. When it was published in 1543, Copernicus's book *De Revolutionibus* was filled with mathematical ideas. It had no more than thirty astronomical observations, all made by others.

People today hail Copernicus for cracking the "problem of the cosmic center"—proving that the cosmos did not revolve around man and his earthly home. Copernicus's contemporaries, however, cared only about his ability to calculate compound circles, says historian Owen Gingerich, and "ignored the heliocentric idea." Fellow historian Ernan McMullin adds, "Copernicus was a powerful mathematician rather than an observational astronomer."

In our time, a tension between sensory observation and abstract mathematics is at the heart of the God-and-science debate. For some centuries now, physical science has increasingly consigned humanity to a backwater of the cosmos. Modern mathematics, however, has seemingly put biological life back at the cosmic center, and as always, the human address in the universe is inextricably linked to how—or whether—people believe in God.

Until Copernicus made his mathematical case for a Sun-centered universe, astronomers and theologians had relied for their understanding of the universe on Aristotle's nine books of physics, which were descriptive, not mathematical. When the heliocentric controversy had its denouement in Galileo's clash with the Inquisition, the issue was still primarily about ousting Aristotle and his notion of a fixed Earth at the center of an eternal universe. Inevitably, science and common sense concluded that Earth did indeed move, but were unable to truly verify Earth's motion for 175 years after *De Revolutionibus,* when the aberration of starlight was discovered.*

The story of Copernicus illustrates how knowledge from the physical senses, such as sight and touch, can rival what is known by mathematical abstraction. Science still has that challenge as it discovers a universe vastly larger than Copernicus could have dreamed of, and an atomic world he might have found unbelievable. Just as the atomic world seems governed by quantum uncertainties, the large-scale universe is beholden to Einsteinian relativity with its strange effects.

These were the kinds of points that the British astrophysicist Fred Hoyle and the German physicist Werner Heisenberg toyed with in the Copernican year. Hoyle wrote a little book about Copernicus, but he clearly wanted also to celebrate the brilliance of Ptolemy. True, Ptolemy had believed the Earth was at the center of the world system (as Aristotle had believed), yet in terms of the calendar of sky movements, he had done quite well. Copernicus, with his belief in the Sun-centered system, could only improve somewhat on the ancient Alexandrian.

With the arrival of Einstein's theory of relativity, an entirely new system was in play. The observer and the speed of light became constants, while space and time became relative. Acting as provocateur, Hoyle said that now the senses had become deceptive once again. By one measure of science, the Sun was definitely at the center of the solar system. But by another strange measure, the human observer was back where Ptolemy had put him—at the center of things.

As Hoyle was playing with the idea of the cosmic center at astronomical scales, Heisenberg went to the subatomic realm to make a Copernican-year case that mathematics will be the only true measure for future science.

---

*The aberration of starlight is the small periodic displacement in the apparent position of a star caused by the motion of the Earth around the Sun.

In the simple world of the senses, scientists had once hoped that atoms might behave just like tiny solar systems, with electrons neatly orbiting a nucleus as the planets orbit the sun. On the contrary, Heisenberg's "uncertainty principle" explained, electrons jumped around, as if by magic. Given such physical uncertainty, Heisenberg closed his controversial career by arguing that mathematics was the only true resort for science:

> Mathematical forms … if I can express it in a theological manner, [are] the forms according to which God created the world…. Or you may also leave out the word God and say the forms according to which the world has been made. These forms are always present in matter, and in the human mind, and they are responsible for both.

Heisenberg was a Platonist, declaring that God or an ideal mathematical order preceded the world, and in this he was an heir to Copernicus. Not only had Copernicus concluded by mathematics that the Sun must be at the center of the celestial movements, he also believed that God had designed it that way. The Sun in fact was "enthroned" in its divine glory, according to Copernicus, a pre-Renaissance Catholic mystic and alchemist; it was the physical center for "the movements of the world machine, created for our sake by the best and most systematic Artisan of all."

A few centuries later, however, science's rejection of a universe existing "for our sake" would be called "the Copernican Principle," since he had begun the displacement of humanity from the physical center. The Copernican Principle would become a central and powerful belief of science as further discoveries of human non-centrality mounted. After the American astronomer Harlow Shapley showed in 1918 that the solar system was not at the center of the Milky Way galaxy, he became the evangelist for the philosophical implications of the human displacement. "The solar system is off center and consequently man is too," Shapley said. "Man is not such a big chicken. He is incidental."

The astounding facts kept pouring in. Beyond the Milky Way there were other "island universes," great spiral galaxies just as beautiful as the Milky Way. Because the galaxies are made out of the same chemical elements as the planet Earth, "Copernican modesty has been pushed a stage further," said Astronomer Royal Martin Rees. "Even particle chauvinism has to go."

With similar chagrin over human arrogance, the search for extraterrestrial intelligence began in 1959. The guiding principle of this search could well have been borrowed from Giordiano Bruno, the remarkable Renaissance monk and heretic who believed that other worlds might contain "creatures similar or even superior to those upon our human earth." Finally, as the contemporary hypothesis that the universe may be mostly "dark matter" takes humans down yet another notch, the theory of multiple universes represents "the ultimate Copernican idea," says cosmologist James Gunn: "Not only are *we* of no conceivable consequence, but even our *universe* is of no conceivable consequence."

For religious reasons, this trend in thinking would have troubled even Nicolaus Copernicus. And thus it was ironic that many in science used the Copernican Principle to chasten the hubris and arrogance of religion, as portrayed, for example, in medieval Christian paintings of man and woman in the middle of the cosmos. This ridiculing of anthropocentric religion has worked, but historians have also noted its excesses. Writers from Aristotle to Dante, for example, had never exalted the Earth. In fact, they viewed it as made of a lower substance, far coarser than the supernal heavenly substance (not to mention Hell at the Earth's core). The medieval mind clearly viewed humanity as theologically central, but physically lowly. Even today, physical centrality is not essential to conservative Bible belief, says Bible scholar Robert Newman, who has a doctorate in astrophysics from Cornell University:

> If we are the only intelligent beings native to this universe, then in some sense we are central. But that doesn't mean we're what the universe is all about necessarily. The Bible says we are central, but it also is silent on the topic. We are dwarfed when it says, "What is man that you are mindful of him." But on the other hand, God loves us enough to send his son. That still doesn't tell us that the universe is all about mankind.

Under the influence of astronomers such as Shapley, and the preference in science to see the cosmos as everywhere homogeneous, the Copernican Principle was eventually extrapolated into the Principle of Mediocrity. While mediocre could mean average, in the sense that nothing is special in a homogeneous universe, it has also come to have a moralistic ring when used by scientists: thou shalt not make theological claims of human centrality.

THE COPERNICAN YEAR, WHICH MARKED a half-millennium since Copernicus was born, was filled with celebrations, scholarly conferences and dreams of the future. But a quiet revolt was instigated at Symposium No. 63, which was convened by the International Astronomical Union in Cracow under the title "Confrontations of Cosmological Theories with Observational Data."

Symposium No. 63 produced perhaps the only talk in the entire global Copernican celebration that seemed to have any staying power. Given by the Cambridge astrophysicist Brandon Carter, it was designed to rock the scientific boat. The youthful Carter spoke on "Large Number Coincidences and the Anthropic Principle in Cosmology." He was obviously eager to debunk a bit of tired conventional wisdom in the field of cosmology, namely the Copernican Principle. Ever since, the modest alternative concept of the "anthropic principle" has kept astronomical tongues, and even those of laypeople, wagging.

Carter asked why the unique observational role of humans could not again be taken seriously by science. He remonstrated against an "exaggerated subservience to the 'Copernican principle.'" And he called the scientific version of the Principle of Mediocrity "a most questionable dogma." But his punch line about the human location in the scheme of things was what galvanized his audience. "What we can expect to observe must be restricted by the conditions necessary for our presence as observers," Carter said. Thus, "although our situation is not necessarily *central,* it is inevitably privileged."

In his paper, Carter noted how coincidental it was that certain numerical ratios governed the mass of stars and the expansion rate of the universe. He commented on how certain fundamental parameters of physics allowed biological life to exist. The presence of observers—according to the anthropic principle—would predict that these coincidences and parameters are necessary for their existence in the first place, which would explain why the numbers are what they are.

By giving humans a privileged status in the universe, Carter opened the doors for a future of scientific, philosophic and theological debate. The simplicity of the anthropic principle has also made it abstruse, says philosopher John Leslie, a chronicler of the debate. The confusion arises for this reason: the anthropic principle is a tautology, saying the same thing in two ways. For example, says Leslie, what Carter called the "weak" and "strong" applications of the anthropic principle could translate this way: "Observers must be at times and places compatible with observership, and they must be in a universe compatible with observership." Yet even as a tautology, the anthropic principle would begin to shake the Copernican dogma.

"Brandon Carter saw this as an interesting way of explaining the fine-tuning of the universe," Leslie says. "But he got fed up with how people misinterpreted him." Carter wrote a few more papers on the "observational principle" over the years, but never grandstanded the anthropic principle again. He didn't have to. There were plenty of others to do that.

Those with a theological bent were impressed by the connection between biological life, which meant observers, and the cosmic constants of physics. In this view, the vast impersonal universe is actually imbued with a biocentric meaning and purpose, just now being hinted at by science. As a scientist, Carter would deny that his idea was freighted with any implication of meaning or purpose. But once the idea was out, it snowballed into a kind of natural theology. The foundation was both biblical and scientific: King Solomon once wrote that God had "ordered all things by measure and number and weight," and Galileo said God's book of nature was "written in the language of mathematics." The fine-tuning was not proof of God, but more good evidence of the same, says the physicist and theologian John Polkinghorne: "The existence of the Creator would explain why the world is so profoundly intelligible, and I can't see any other explanation that works half as well."

In the new cosmology, the uttermost beginning or ultimate end of the cosmos were garden-variety topics. Carter had entered the field at Cambridge University just as it and Princeton were becoming the two hubs for the new cosmology. Their common aim was how to apply Einsteinian theory about gravity and curved space-time (general relativity) to structural questions about the universe.

At Cambridge, Dennis Sciama led the way. A radio technician in World War II, Sciama had a taste for the philosophy of Ludwig Witgenstein and for nonconformity. He threw in his lot with the "steady state theory," which held that the universe was eternal and had no beginning—the chief rival to the ultimately victorious Big Bang theory. Sciama's students became some of the brightest stars in the cosmology establishment, from Martin Rees, the Astronomer Royal, to Stephen Hawking, George Ellis and, of course, Carter. When members of the Sciama "family tree" held a tribute to him in the summer of 1991 in Trieste, Italy, when he was sixty-five, they looked back upon what they called the "renaissance of general relativity and cosmology." Sciama's students got much of it going. Before anyone had heard of the wheelchair-bound Hawking, he and Ellis, a South African mathematician, had in 1973 written a slim volume that became a classic in the field: *The Large-Scale Structure of Space-Time.*

At Princeton University, meanwhile, the physicist John Archibald Wheeler had the reputation necessary to take an exotic subject like large-scale space-time and make it a respectable field of study. Scientists had for the most part steered clear of it. Wheeler, a quantum physics expert, wanted to tackle what relativity meant for the expanding universe. According to Einstein's theory, relativity expresses itself over the vast reaches of the universe in the dynamics of curved space-time. The curvature is gravity, which leans toward a collapse, a pulling together of all the mass in the universe. To counterbalance this Big Crunch, energetic matter pushes back. This balance of forces on a cosmic scale intrigued Wheeler.

"By coming into the field, Wheeler single-handedly brought respectability to it," says Charles Misner, a cosmologist who studied under both Wheeler and Sciama. "Sciama brought a much wider astrophysical viewpoint to the subject. He was very good at finding the right questions, bringing good young people together."

Wheeler is known for his flashing insights into physics and a knack for putting them into memorable sayings. For example, this on general relativity: "Matter bends space, and space gives matter its marching orders." He relishes what Misner calls "the deep questions" that have traditionally bedeviled science. "He wanted to be more philosophical than was fashionable in American scientific circles," says Misner. "He wasn't afraid to push those edges of science." Wheeler may have acquired the inclination from working with Neils Bohr at his institute in Denmark, a center of philosophical muscle-flexing and home of the "Copenhagen School" of quantum physics. It was there that physics became the spooky world of Heisenberg's "uncertainty principle," a world in which particles behave probabilistically and where the observer alters the outcome of events in the very act of observation. Wheeler has a saying for this, too: "No physics without an observer." In time, Wheeler would take the observer idea to cosmic levels, ending up as a big supporter of the anthropic principle and, unlike Carter, its quasi-theologian. As for Carter, he had no theological preoccupations; he was grappling with another of the great debates that intrigued his generation of cosmologists. As usual, most of those debates began with Einstein.

In 1917, Einstein had published his "cosmological considerations," which, set in mathematical equations, was the first quantitative model of the entire universe. He knew well the instability of curved space-time, and yet the universe he observed was one in equilibrium. Indeed, with something similar to religious belief, Einstein posited an eternal, placid, evenly spread and mathematically beautiful universe. To explain its stability (despite the collapsing force of space-time gravity), he inserted into his equations a number that stood for the "cosmological constant," a force that counterbalanced gravity. The beauty of math is its ability to solve a cosmic problem on a pad of notepaper.

At first, Einstein resisted the early theories of an expanding universe, but he finally came around. The most persuasive interpretation of that expansion was the Big Bang universe, and its rivalry with a steady state view lasted through the early 1960s. For his popular BBC talks on *The Nature of the Universe,* Fred Hoyle coined the phrase "big bang" somewhat derisively as the alternative to his steady state universe. "Explosions do not usually lead to well-ordered situations," he argued amusingly on another occasion, and said that without a steady universe there could be no "assumption that the laws of physics are constant." He and his allies, Thomas Gold and Hermann Bondi, proposed that the apparent expansion of the universe resulted from the "continuous creation" of new hydrogen atoms in space—what one wag called a "steady bang" rather than a big one.

The 1973 meeting in Cracow was a historic turning point in this debate, according to the British astronomer Michael Rowan-Robinson. It was "the moment at which the Big Bang model of the universe became *the* model accepted by most cosmologists," he wrote in his book *Ripples in the Cosmos.* At Symposium No. 63, "almost every paper seemed to show" that the Big Bang made sense.

But the allure of Brandon Carter's paper was not his support of the Big Bang. It was his assertion that the mathematical "coincidences" in the expanding universe were worthy of attention. By trying to explain the observable universe through mathematical equations, Carter was building on a tradition—mystical at its ancient beginnings—that in modern times was exemplified by Einstein and expanded on by Sir Arthur Eddington, England's leading astronomer up through the 1930s.

Both a mathematician and an adventurer, Eddington made a trek in 1919 to Principe Island, West Africa, to photograph a solar eclipse, confirming Einstein's idea that light bends with gravitationally curved space (the Sun's mass here doing the work). A Quaker with faith in an "unseen world" of transcendent reality, Eddington believed that the basic numerical values that organize the universe are eternal and can be arrived at by pure logic. What he found was that nature, from the scale of atoms to the size of the universe, seems organized around a few ratios with very large numbers— such as 10^{39} or $10^{78.}$ Eddington's numbers have checked out accurately enough against observation, and these are what Carter has called the "large number coincidences" in his Copernican-year paper.

Eddington had begun the quest for a mathematical consonance between the largest and smallest parts of the universe, a quest the Cambridge mathematician Paul Dirac would take up next, calling it the search for a "comprehensive theory of cosmology and atomicity." Dirac, a Nobel laureate in physics, had noted how Eddington's numbers from the 1930s had "excited much interest." But he rejected eternal constants, saying the ratios "are so enormous as to make one think that some entirely different type of explanation is needed for them." He theorized that some constants of nature, such as the force of gravity or number of cosmic particles, change over time, so the ratio "increases as the world grows older"—hence the very large numbers.

Obviously, this rarified debate was of no consequence to the man on the street, but denizens of the ivory tower thought it worth fighting over. The Princeton physicist Robert H. Dicke, both a theorist and a hands-on technician, rejected Dirac's speculations regarding the changing constants and in 1961 arrived at a very practical explanation for the large numbers. He began by reminding us that physicists are people, people are biological, and biology is based on carbon atoms. So humans couldn't evolve until carbon was around, and according to the nuclear physics of how stars burn and throw off elements like carbon, humans could appear only at a stage of the universe's history corresponding to the present. The possible numerical values that humans could observe in the evolving universe, therefore, would have to be "limited by the biological requirements to be met during the epoch of man." By referring to the "epoch of man," Dicke foreshadowed what Carter would call the "anthropic principle."

This allusion to human significance was bound to cause controversy, and a controversialist such as Hoyle pointed out with glee that biological life may mean that "a commonsense interpretation of the facts suggests that a superintellect has monkeyed with physics, as well as chemistry and biology." And for theology, of course, the idea that the universe was fine-tuned for biological life was a welcome message after scientists' constant harping on the theme of humanity's unimportance; Shapley, for instance, had liked to sermonize that humans were unlikely to be "God's children" because they were "on the perimeter of this operation." But now some scientists felt quite free to harmonize a religious outlook with the fine-tuned universe.

One of them is George Ellis, a South African Quaker who arrived at Cambridge in 1961 as Sciama's first student. He says that the anthropic notion simply emerged unbidden in the course of everyone's technical work on general relativity. There was no theological intention at all, but new directions were taken anyway. "The new thing that came through was the concerted effort after Brandon Carter, and Wheeler and Dicke tried to relate the fundamental physics to the existence of life. That was a new round of thinking, although its roots are very old. But nevertheless, it sharpened it and brought it forth."

Ellis is a Christian who is entirely open to the idea that God monkeys with physics. Still and all, "the number of theists involved in the anthropic debate was very small. Those on the scientific side of the debate would not have brought that forward. It's a slippery debate."

Like Eddington, Ellis speaks of faith and religion at sessions of Friends, or Quakers, but in his talks on modern cosmology he avoids the quicksand of scientific proofs of God: "I carefully separate when I'm talking science talk from when I'm talking about things beyond science."

Though the religious implications of the anthropic principle have caused a sharp, even antagonistic, division among scientists, Ellis thinks it has scientific merit. "Clearly it is gaining credibility," he said of the principle in 2001, after an Oxford seminar on the topic. Even Nobelist Steven Weinberg, a staunch atheist, is stumped by the origin of the cosmic constants, Ellis remarks, "so he's willing to work with the anthropic logic."

Though a believer himself, Ellis warns against hanging faith on a scientific finding. "In the end science can't answer those questions. Anyone who thinks they can has been misled." But he argues that the anthropic principle may be part of an individual's faith and theology. Indeed, during a 1991 conference on science and theology at Castel Gandolfo, the papal summer residence and home of the Vatican Observatory, he presented perhaps the first paper on a "Christian Anthropic Principle." Here he did not reason from design to God, but the other way round. "From this viewpoint, the fine-tuning is no longer regarded as evidence for a Designer, but rather is seen as a consequence of the complexity of aim of a Designer whose existence we are assuming."

Basing his argument on the standard Big Bang cosmology, he said that the universe may have originated in a creation event, and that this possibility, and the fact of the perfectly balanced physics of life, are not in contradiction with belief in a Creator; a universe that is designed and that produces a moral sensibility in human beings is reasonable. And there was a novel addendum to his theology: If Christ died to reconcile the universe to God, then he came not only for life on earth but for life wherever it may be— since as every cosmologist must concede, there may be life elsewhere, and other universes may abound.

EVER SINCE NEWTON OUTLINED A SELF-RUNNING, clockwork universe, and the French cosmologist Pierre Simon de Laplace responded to Napoleon's query about God in his model of the universe by saying, "Sire, I have no need of that hypothesis," physics had not been kind to the concept of deity. The new physics, however, opened a door for God's return, according to the Jesuit thinker W. Norris Clarke:

Natural theology is, from one point of view, on better terms with contemporary science than it has been in a long time. The notion that mind has a place in nature, that nature points to mind as its completion, is much more acceptable, even plausible, to many scientists today, especially theoretical physicists and cosmologists.

Although Brandon Carter's 1973 paper spoke of significant coincidences, it did not mention "fine-tuning." The notion that the forces of nature had just the right balance led easily to wonderment at what this might signify. As Wheeler would cast the issue: "Imagine a universe in which one or another of the fundamental dimensionless constants of physics is altered by a few percent one way or the other. Man could never come into being in such a universe."

After Carter's short list in 1973, the catalog of fine-tuned constants expanded in the work of others. In a 1979 article in *Nature,* B. J. Carr and Martin Rees ranged across the scale of nature—from protons and atoms, to habitable planets, asteroids, stars, galaxies and up to the all-inclusive universe—showing how "just a few physical constants" were at play throughout. The two authors moved on to other fundamental constants, but concluded that while life is "remarkably sensitive" to all these numerical values, the fact of the human observer was still "unsatisfactory" as a scientific explanation. Three years later, the British physicist Paul Davies built upon their article in a book titled *The Accidental Universe,* which detailed the "surprisingly fortuitous accidents," the numerical coincidences and proverbial "magic numbers" that were now befuddling science. As a Spinozan, Davies does not believe in a personal God. But he went on to write about a "rational universe" revealing "the mind of God," and for his enthusiastic pantheism and popularization of the anthropic principle he received the Templeton Prize for Progress in Religion in 1995.

The anthropic idea gained even wider exposure in 1986, when John Barrow, the British mathematician and science writer, and American physicist Frank Tipler came out with *The Anthropic Cosmological Principle.* They were all for undermining "Copernican dogma." And they challenged Carl Sagan's argument that disproof of the existence of extraterrestrial life would be the first time in history for anthropocentrism to be rehabilitated. They believed that a fine-tuned universe might restore a human-centered outlook even more effectively. Life everywhere was founded on an astonishingly delicate balance:

> The sizes of bodies like stars, planets and even people are neither random nor the result of any progressive selection process, but simply manifestations of the different strengths of the various forces of Nature. They are examples of possible equilibrium states between competing forces of attraction and repulsion.

The balance is most often illustrated by the four primal forces in nature: the strong nuclear force, which holds nuclei together; the weak force, which governs the decay rate of atoms; electromagnetism, which energizes chemistry, electrical currents and light; and gravity. If their exquisite balance were lost, one among countless possible consequences might have been that the cosmic hydrogen would have burned up before stars could form. Electromagnetism balanced against gravity enabled long-burning stars and chemical bonds, the basis of chemistry and biology; the strong nuclear force has to be precisely what it is in order for the ninety-two elements of the periodic table to be generated in the stars; perfectly calibrated particle masses permit all the kinds of stable atoms; and having a proton far heavier than an electron (though their charges are equal) ensured that the universe was not souplike.

For most physicists, each constant in nature—from the speed of light to the force of gravity and the mass of an electron—is taken as a brute fact that is "provided by Nature, cannot be calculated, and is not in any way related to other numbers," as Dicke puts it. But physicist Paul Davies thinks the constants point to a deeper order of nature, which raises new philosophical questions about design:

> What we're seeing is a sort of resurrection of natural theology, but not applied to biological and physical systems, but to the universe as a whole. To use a loaded term, it is looking for "design" in the underlying laws of the universe, not in the specific structures.

Religious believers are going further still with the implications of fine-tuning for the God of the Bible. The astrophysicist Hugh Ross, an evangelical Christian, built the Reasons to Believe ministry based on the argument of how twenty-seven "just so" constants hold the universe together, and how thirty-five features of the galaxy, solar system and Earth make human life viable. And he draws a conclusion about God's character from the data: "The simplicity, balance, order, elegance, and beauty seen throughout the whole of the creation demonstrate that God is loving rather than capricious." Drawing on the "wisdom" of God in the Hebrew scriptures, former MIT physicist Gerald L. Schroeder has reached an equally theological conclusion after surveying physics and biology, calling this evidence-seeking a "science of God."

Such theologizing would be expected to draw blunt reactions from many scientists, especially when even the secular anthropic principle has grated on materialist nerves. The hard-nosed physicist Heinz R. Pagels calls the anthropic craze "much ado about nothing." Declaring it a spineless quest for a "cozy" universe, he says atheists probably felt it was the closest they could get to God. Stephen Jay Gould summoned the ghost of Houdini, the famous magician who relished debunking supernatural fakes, to take on the anthropic principle. An absurdity (like God) was wishful thinking, said Gould, and he counseled: "Always be suspicious of conclusions that reinforce uncritical hope and follow comforting traditions of Western thought" (though design pervades Eastern traditions as well).

Long before the current debates, there was a humorous assault on the anthropic outlook as exemplified in the great German philosopher Gottfried Leibniz's view that humans find themselves in "the best of all possible worlds." His tormentor was Voltaire, whose novel *Candide* makes fun of Pangloss, a Leibniz-like teacher who advises the witless Candide that life's misfortunes, absurdities and sufferings are all for the good. It was a world, joked Voltaire, in which noses fortunately exist for the abundance of spectacles; a world in which Europe's rivers flow unerringly through its cities and under its bridges.

Darwin, too, used up a good amount of ink criticizing the scientific presumptions of natural theologians that the world seemed designed. "I cannot persuade myself that a beneficent and omnipotent God would have designedly [willed] that a cat should play with mice," he famously said, or that parasites should consume a poor worm.

Yet if the idea of design in nature has been a magnet for sarcasm, the problem of a harmonized, fine-tuned physical universe, the "world machine," was not always so easy to attack. In the eighteenth and nineteenth centuries, England's believing naturalists such as Robert Boyle and John Ray pointed to finely balanced constants in air, water, fire and wind to justify their faith, and the theologian William Paley sermonized on the law of gravity. He noted that the spinning Earth did not wobble or collide with other planets. Nor did it fly into, or away from, the Sun. The high mark of such natural theology, promulgated by eight British scientists in the Bridgewater Treatises, included this escape clause from piecemeal attacks: "The argument of design is necessarily cumulative; that is to say, is made up of many similar arguments."

Because the anthropic debate has centered on the rise of biological observers, questions about the fine-tuning of chemistry have also been revived. This had been the theme of the Harvard professor Lawrence Henderson's classic work, *The Fitness of the Environment,* which came out in 1913. With such elements as water, carbon and the rest "fully determined from the earliest conceivable epoch and perfectly changeless in time," he wrote, "the biologist may now rightly regard the Universe in its very essence as biocentric."

His presciently anthropic way of thinking also included a "teleological" view of nature, which saw a purpose behind the constants. For these kinds of quasi-religious arguments, the red-bearded Henderson was called "the pink Jesus" by the hardheaded men of science at Harvard who, since Darwin, had dedicated themselves to expunging design and purpose from nature.

Naturally, theologians would build on Henderson's novel arguments. Most prominent was Britain's H. R. Tennent, called an "empirical theologian" because of his attempt to use modern physics to point to divine order in the universe. He relied on works such as *Fitness* to argue for a "wider teleology" that stayed away from biological detail. And his 1930 work, *Philosophical Theology,* coined the term "anthropic categories."

To explain the stunning fact of human existence, and the fact of a reasoning brain that comprehends a mathematically rational universe, Tennent argued that "anthropocentrism, in some sense, is involved in cosmic teleology." This big-picture order, he said, "no longer plants its God in the gaps between the explanatory achievements of natural science, which are apt to get scientifically closed up." A new "comprehensive design argument" was possible, he said, made up of innumerable causes in nature that by "united and reciprocal action" produced and maintained the general order of Nature.

Similarly, in the 1950s Royal Society fellow Edmund Whittaker wrote on the numerical quest taken up by Eddington and the implications of finding any physical constants at all. During that time, the new "process philosophy" of the mathematician Alfred North Whitehead was gaining ground, as was its pantheistic notion that God was inside nature and emerging creatively as nature evolved. In contrast, Whittaker argued that a more traditional Creator, a Platonic and absolute deity beyond nature, was disclosed by the constants. As a Catholic, Whittaker was overtly theistic, but the argument was the same as Heisenberg's: "Mathematical law is a concept of the mind, and from the existence of mathematical law we infer that our minds have access to something akin to themselves [such as an original Mind] that is behind the universe."

The astrophysicist Freeman Dyson comes to a similar conclusion, though he is not a theist: "I claim only that the architecture of the universe is consistent with the hypothesis that mind plays an essential role in its functioning." Dyson, like Davies, would also get a Templeton Prize for Progress in Religion.

AS SPECULATION ON THE POSSIBILITY of mind or God behind physics and biological life grows bolder, the materialists have essentially come up with two responses. The first has been, "So what?" Or as the arch-atheist Bertrand Russell said in an earlier era, "The universe is just there, and that's all." The second strategy has been to explain away the apparent significance of the fine-tuning by saying that there must be an infinite number of universes, so that by the cosmic law of chance alone, something like the human habitat was likely to have come into existence.

At the Copernican year event in Cracow, Brandon Carter had concluded his paper on the anthropic principle by pointing out that the multiple universe option was gaining more attention from physicists than ever before. "That there may exist many universes, of which only one can be known to us, may at first seem philosophically undesirable," Carter said. But it was based on a new approach to quantum physics, he added, and it was catching on.

Belief in "many worlds" or an infinite number of realms unseen by the human eye has ancient roots. Naturally, Bible belief and Western science had both focused human thinking on the one universe that may be observed. After Einstein, however, when cosmologists began to ask how the expanding universe originated, one option was to say that the Big Bang erupted from a "quantum fluctuation" in another realm of the cosmos.

Paul Davies thinks putting faith in infinite universes is a wild gamble: "This 'cosmic lottery' theory comes with its own problems." He suggests that it is an escape from the anthropic implications of the one universe we do see. But when religious believers resort to this argument, Steven Weinberg, the Nobel laureate and a convinced atheist, is firm in his rebuttal: the theory grew strictly out of quantum physics, which "doesn't prove it's true, but I think it defends it from the argument that this is just a last ditch struggle of materialistic or naturalistic scientists to avoid an obvious supernatural explanation." But another Nobel laureate in physics, Charles Townes, is a Christian believer who indeed senses an air of last-ditch desperation in multiple worlds theories:

> To get around the anthropic universe without invoking God may force you to extreme speculation about there being billions of universes.... [This] strikes me as much more freewheeling than any of the church's [theological] claims.

From his vantage point at Guelph University in Canada, the philosopher John Leslie has watched this debate over fine-tuning and multiple universes as long as anyone. No Christian, he is an old-fashioned Platonist who believes that something "beyond" mandates cosmic order. This neo-Platonism has no traditional deity but is amenable to the idea that design underlies the universe we know. So Leslie was initially suspicious of the multiple universe idea as it gained steam in the 1970s. "They were arguing that our universe was one of very few that was life-containing. And this was just a matter of chance," he recalled. "I saw this as an attempt to erode the force of the argument from design." So he happily dismissed the multiple universe mania in a 1979 book.

Having fired his salvo, Leslie returned to the archives of history, and he began to change his mind. Belief in "many worlds" had a respectable pedigree across the history of religion, philosophy and science. So in 1982 he recanted. His article "Anthropic Principle, World Ensemble, Design," which appeared in the *American Philosophical Quarterly*, was a sort of mea culpa for having once derided multiple universe ideas:

> Laziness can sometimes seem a main reason for the now widespread belief in other worlds. Yet that can be very unfair. . . . There is one very forceful reason for believing in many and varied worlds: namely, that small changes in our world would apparently have ruled out Life.

In the multiple universe debate, Leslie would now take the stance that a fine-tuned world has two valid explanations, one being design and the other multiple worlds. What is *not* acceptable is the "So what?" response. He said: "The one solution you mustn't go in for is saying, 'There is no problem.' That was the sort of solution that was pushed by the standard philosophers; there is no problem here because any world has to have some laws and life results, and so what."

Back in 1982, very few scholars had read as much about multiple universes as Leslie. "That got me established in the philosophy of cosmology," he says. "Nobody was really interested in multiple universe theories, or had the time to research them." By mastering this subject, he became a visiting professor of astrophysics in Belgium and in 1998 was exchange lecturer between the British Academy and the Royal Society of Canada. Meanwhile, belief in many worlds blossomed among cosmologists. "Today it is considered quaint to assume that all of reality must be like the region visible to human telescopes."

Though an agnostic, Leslie says that theists who believe in design have as much right to use the fine-tuning argument as do atheists who want multiple universes. Either way, human existence is a surprising state of affairs. Therefore, human existence itself needs an explanation, never a "so what?" And so Leslie offers his "sharpshooter" thought experiment.

He imagines himself tied to a post, awaiting his execution by firing squad. When the fifty sharpshooters all miss, to say to oneself, "If they hadn't all missed then I would not be considering the affair" is not an adequate response; in other words, someone in that situation is required to be truly surprised that he is still alive. The analogy here is with human beings finding themselves alive in the universe: in their surprise, they are required to ask whether this outcome was designed or just the stochastic result of infinitely many possibilities. Standing alive and tied to his post amid the hypothetical smoke of fifty rifles, the philosopher concludes that "I must be popular with the sharpshooters—unless, perhaps, immensely many firing squads are at work and I happen to be one of the very rare survivors."

That alternative has been marshaled by one of Dennis Sciama's most outstanding students, Martin Rees, who in his thirties became professor of astronomy at Cambridge (and whose 1979 *Nature* article laid out the cosmic coincidences). Lecturing at Princeton in 2000, Rees acknowledged the remarkable cosmic "recipe" that made human existence possible: "The expansion speed, the material content of the universe, and the strengths of the basic forces, seem to have been a prerequisite for the emergence of the hospitable cosmic habitat in which we live," Rees said. While he would agree with Leslie that a thinking person cannot say "so what" to existence, Rees rejects any idea of design or "providence" and does not agree that we must be surprised at our existence.

The surprise is taken away, he believes, by recognizing that there *are* multiple universes, an idea that Rees hopes to make a mainstream scientific hypothesis. With a thought experiment of his own, he uses the analogy of an "off-the-rack clothes shop" to explain the proper human attitude toward existence. When the shop has a wide enough selection, he says, one should not be surprised to walk in and find a coat that fits. "Likewise, if our universe is selected from a *multiverse,* its seeming design or fine-tuned structure would not be surprising."

Over the years, Leslie has watched scientists and theologians respond to the apparent fine-tuning of the universe. Curiously, there has been relatively little movement on the theologians' side towards using it for design arguments. Perhaps their reluctance stems from embarrassment over past design claims—that angels pushed stars, for example, or, as Sir Isaac Newton maintained as he was forced to "save appearances," that God might occasionally have to adjust the orbits of planets. Says Leslie: "The standard response of theologians has been, 'We've got bloody noses by trying to run the argument from design. Let us rush in the other direction as hard as we can or otherwise we are going to get bloody noses *again.*'"

Apart from the design debate, Leslie holds that thinking people must continue to ask the metaphysical *ur*-question that goes back at least to the ancient Greeks: Why is there something rather than nothing?

Why does anything exist at all? This baffling enigma appeals to cosmologist Charles Misner, the student of Wheeler and Sciama who pioneered work in general relativity himself. As a Catholic believer since his college days, Misner does not think a design argument is very helpful. He is skeptical of how physicists "twiddle numbers" in such theories: "No one has pulled out of these theories any predictions of what set up the constants of nature."

"Someday," he wonders, "are we going to find not only a theory, but the theory that, so to speak, is the only theory that is self-consistent?" Once that is found, however, he thinks that belief in God will still elude scientific certainty. "You have to ask, 'Once there is a blueprint, how is it created?' There is a difference between the plan and the execution. That is where 'something rather than nothing' comes in."

In other words, the ultimate question of "why" the universe exists may itself be the only satisfying proof of God.

4

LOOKING FOR LIGHT

The last few September nights of 1953 were going to be particularly good for observing galaxies from Mount Palomar in southern California, where the new 200-inch telescope, the largest on earth, pierced the dark of the universe. The master of this great instrument was the astronomer Edwin Hubble. His work was tedious and physically demanding, but his program aimed to measure the luminosities of the most distant markers in the sky, one after the other, vanquishing the limits of vision and the faintness of light. The goal was to determine the rate at which the universe was expanding, its age and even its ultimate fate. On September 25, 1953, Hubble had packed for four good nights of gathering another round of data. Before he could leave his home, he died of a stroke.

Few outside of astronomy knew Hubble's name or legacy until he began to make global headlines in 1990, when the Hubble Space Telescope, named for the pioneering astronomer, was boosted aloft with world attention fixed on it. Newspaper reports brayed about the telescope's failure because of a mirror aberration; but they were to change their tune when NASA's dramatic rescue operation over Christmas of 1993 was successfully completed. Two years later, the Hubble Deep Field photographs were the highest-resolution images ever taken of the distant universe. And then came 2002 and another life-risking foray by astronauts to install even more powerful cameras. The pictures that came back amazed even NASA veterans.

With the newly installed Advanced Camera for Survey, the Hubble recorded incredibly detailed images of colliding galaxies roughly 300 million light-years away, six times farther than Hubble himself was able to see when he analyzed the blurry Virgo Cluster of galaxies. With the 2002 sightings, NASA scientists claimed the camera had glimpsed speck-like galaxies at the edge of the visible universe, 10 billion light-years off. With the confident wording expected of announcements from big science, the project's honcho told the news media, "We will be able to enter the 'twilight zone' period when galaxies were just beginning to form out of the blackness following the cooling of the universe from the Big Bang."

Such reaches were not even imaginable to Hubble himself, who insisted in the 1930s that only when technical resources, such as telescope power, and empirical findings are exhausted should the scientist move on to "dreamy realms of speculation," as he memorably put it, about the physical universe. Yet even with the Hubble Space Telescope, the human desire to measure the universe strained against limitations, and dreamy speculation on the part of cosmologists became inevitable.

THE MOUNT PALOMAR TELESCOPE, perched in a mountain range northeast of San Diego, began operating in 1948. But the story begins a few decades earlier at Mount Wilson, located in mountains east of Los Angeles.

There, using another optical masterpiece equipped with a 100-inch mirror—the world's largest at the time—astronomers confirmed an expanding universe by charting the "redshift" of light emissions from galaxies as they move away from us, stretching wavelengths toward the red end of the spectrum. Once this revolutionary new idea of the expanding universe had become conventional, the Palomar telescope, a skeletal steel tube with a massive, 200-inch mirror delicately couched at its base, and with twice the observational power of the Mount Wilson instrument, opened up new possibilities for Edwin Hubble's research program.

The impression that the American astronomer liked to leave was one of reluctance to wax philosophical about his findings. This no-nonsense approach rubbed off on his successor at Palomar, Allan Sandage. A graduate student at Caltech in the Los Angeles suburb of Pasadena, Sandage joined Hubble as an assistant, succeeding him within a few years as master of the peerless instrument.

"A real astronomer asks, 'What is out there? What is it doing? How can we determine the distance? How can we do a survey to figure out the morphological structure of the whole thing?'" says Sandage, now in retirement. He watched with curiosity as the new generation of cosmologists came on the scene in the 1960s, beginning what he somewhat disdainfully calls the "speculative cosmology of today." As Hubble's heir, he staunchly defends an empirical vision of astronomy: "Practical astronomers provide the data by which you can go back only so far, and then you reach a wall that science cannot go beyond."

That wall, though being pushed farther and farther back by remarkable new technologies, will, because of the nature of light, ultimately be an impenetrable barrier. For good reason the motto of astronomy is "Look but don't touch." What astronomers have always contemplated is a bewildering array of objects: stars in various stages of their life cycles, gas clouds or nebulae, galaxies, clusters of galaxies, quasars and so forth. The rule of thumb that "fainter means farther" works in some cases, but obviously by no means in all. Often enough, it turns out that fainter means smaller, not farther; and brighter means larger, not nearer.

Thus the quest for "standard candles" or distance calibrators is one of astronomy's most sought-after goals. One such was handed to the fraternity in 1912 when the astronomer Henrietta Leavitt, working at the Harvard Observatory, found a class of pulsating or "variable" stars. These Cepheids revealed their luminosities by the spacing of their pulses, and with their relative nearness they provided a yardstick by which the distances of more remote Cepheids could be estimated on a fainter-is-farther basis. By this method, in the 1920s the size of the Milky Way was understood, and Andromeda, a spiral galaxy now known to be some 2 million light-years distant, was determined to lie beyond our own galaxy. More distant Cepheid variables were fainter and less reliable yardsticks than the nearer ones, so the Hubble program had to use a leapfrog guessing game, estimating the distance of one shining galaxy, comparing it with others farther off, then estimating the next enormous distance.

In following the light into space, the astronomers faced two major complications: the antiquity of the light and the expansion of the universe. Though nothing in the universe travels faster than light, it still has a finite speed. Most of the universe is seen by "ancient light" emitted by objects millions or billions of years ago. This makes astronomy the only science that can directly witness what happened in the past.

Second, the galaxies are moving away from each other. In 1929, Hubble had studied these retreating galaxies (whose ebb causes telltale redshifts of their spectra), and he determined that their recessional velocities increase as they move farther apart. To explain this to a baffled public, scientists offered homely images: galaxies were compared to ants on the surface of an expanding balloon, or to raisins moving farther apart from each other in a swelling pudding in an oven. Hubble tried to pin it down in what became known as the Hubble diagram.

On his graph paper, he assembled his measurements of fourteen galaxies and four bright objects in the Virgo Cluster of galaxies 50 million light-years away. It produced an oblong swarm of dots, and the line drawn down their center represented 6 million light-years of distance (a light-year being approximately 6 trillion miles). Then Hubble asked this question: For every million light-years of distance from a given point, how much faster does an object travel?

This method of calculation was Hubble's great legacy, according to his pupil Sandage: "What Hubble discovered was the velocity-distance equation. That is the backbone of the expanding universe idea." Hubble put a number to that equation as well. According to his measurements, objects seem to move apart 550 kilometers per second faster for every million light-years of distance. Thus, his value for what would be called the "Hubble constant" was 550. With new measurements and calculations down through the century, this value would shrink dramatically and be fiercely debated.

In the expanding universe model, it was also assumed that gravity is slowing the expansion down. In the 1920s and 1930s the "Hubble program" included an effort to measure this "deceleration parameter." With the rates of both expansion and deceleration in hand, the astronomer could then estimate the age of the universe—which Hubble put at 2 billion years, the first such determination in astronomy.

Sandage would continue this project, an effort dubbed the "Sandage program." By 1970 he was still describing cosmology as the search for two numbers, the Hubble constant and the "quotient of deceleration."

But the newer generation of cosmologists were conceiving of the expanding universe in still another way. What is the density of the expanding universe in comparison with the density needed to arrest the expansion with the force of gravity? they asked. They called this ratio Omega, or the "density parameter."

The name Omega and the simplicity of the ratio would gain it great attention, especially in popular science writing. "Hubble was actually the first to get a reasonably good number for it," says astronomer and science historian Virginia Trimble. She explains that already in the 1940s this ratio was being given a value of one, or equality between the expansion and the force of gravity. Astronomy professors put it this way for their students: a ball thrown straight up with insufficient speed will eventually fall back to earth, but when thrown hard enough it will keep going; here the ratio of Omega is in favor of expansion.

Still, the slightest difference could dramatically alter the universe's ultimate fate. A universe in which the mass and expansion were equal was called "flat" and was given the Omega value of one. A universe with sufficient gravitational mass to arrest the expansion was called "closed." Here was an Omega higher than one: the universe would eventually collapse in a Big Crunch. The third scenario was an "open universe." In this case, the expansion force ultimately won out, with an Omega ratio that was less than one. Naturally, Omega would take astronomers into the dreamy realms of speculation, despite Hubble's cautions.

FOR MOST OF HIS THIRTY-FIVE YEARS at Mount Palomar, Allan Sandage could not avoid this cosmic quest, even though he styled himself "a mere bench scientist."

To do his work, he took a small elevator up to the prime focus cage of the telescope, where he had a chair and equipment to expose the photographic plates. Below him was the gigantic, 15-ton mirror, and above, the naked cosmos. "You saw the universe looking down on the mirror," he says. "I could open the top and look out at the universe." The power of the telescope brought galaxies and nebulae to the prime focus "as if the real object was right there with you." A galaxy showed up as large as a half-dollar that "you could inspect with an eyepiece as you would a page of a book." Then he inserted a photographic plate to record its image, sometimes with exposures that lasted hours.

He dubbed the two southern California telescopes the "tablets of Moses," and he knew his privileged position. He was one of only a few observational cosmologists on the planet, and the group at Pasadena had the biggest guns. Sandage called it "a monopoly."

An Iowa native, he grew up not only with a telescope but also with a religious curiosity. He absorbed a Spartan work ethic as a Caltech science student, the grim patience to perform fourteen-hour stints at the prime focus, where he hunkered down, often in the exposed cold, at least thirty times a year. More time was spent off the mountain at the observatory's Santa Barbara Street offices, where he and his assistants squinted and blinked at the plates, comparing the black smudges (on reverse negatives) that were galaxies, gas clouds called nebulae, ancient stars in globular clusters, supernovae, red giants, quasars and of course, the Cepheids.

Finding the physical truth was difficult and fraught with uncertainty. It became clearer than ever to Sandage that while science could do much, there were some mysteries it could not probe, given the size and complexity of the universe. It was a hard admission to make. "Being trained as a bench scientist, I was unsatisfied with that answer," he said. "I could not live with mystery." He nursed this feeling of "divine discontent," and daily confronted the question of the nature of the physical universe. "For forty or fifty years, I insisted I had an answer to that question. Now, I know I never will, and so I have decided that I must live with the mystery."

Hubble too had been candid about the Olympian task of comprehending the physical universe. "[W]e measure shadows," he wrote in 1936, "and search among ghostly errors of measurement for landmarks that are scarcely more substantial." Accordingly, the story of Mount Wilson, and of most astronomical cosmology to follow, would become one of data published and data revised, theories proposed and theories demolished.

The revising of Hubble's data began in 1952. Mount Wilson astronomers began to realize there were two classes or populations of variable stars, old and young Cepheids, a correction that made the universe much larger and twice as old as Hubble had theorized, now up to an estimated 3.6 billion years. Sandage later used the 200-inch telescope to make other corrections; Hubble had mistaken near stars for far, and gas clouds for galaxies. In 1956, Sandage reported a truer Hubble diagram, which shrank the distance-velocity constant from 250 to 180. The *New York Times* liked the Big Bang element in the Sandage findings, and headlined, "Birth of Universe Traced to Blast." Mount Wilson promoted Sandage to full astronomer, and Harvard invited him to lecture there in 1957.

With the confirmation in 1929 that the universe was expanding, a new question arose: where is the expansion headed? In England, astronomers Sir Arthur Eddington and Sir James Jeans popularized the idea of an ultimate "heat death," or dissipation of the universe, as it cooled and spread out into nothing. There was still the curvature of space and gravity to contend with, however, and Hubble's measurement of Omega—based on counting numbers of galaxies in volumes of space—leaned toward a closed universe that would stop expanding. But the measurements were inconclusive, and up to 1960 Sandage's annual report from the observatory said that Omega remained unresolved.

In time Sandage, like all astronomers, would have to take a position on the fate of the universe. But before that he contributed to a revolution in our understanding of the life cycle of stars, which bears directly on the question of our existence in the universe. In fact, he regards his work in this crucial area as his primary achievement.

A critical stage in the chemical evolution of stars was first identified by Walter Baade, a senior member of the Mount Wilson team when Sandage had arrived. It was Baade who divided the Cepheids into two classes; the older population was predominantly made up of hydrogen and helium, while the new had a larger share of heavy elements. Where did the newer elements come from?

Sandage had collected data on one thousand stars in what are called the globular clusters, which contained the earliest stars formed in the Milky Way. One day in 1952, a Princeton theorist visiting Caltech saw the Sandage data and, in effect, cried *Eureka!* "We had found the 'main sequence' termination point," the point at which the hydrogen at the center of the star was exhausted, Sandage recalls. This provided the critical clue for the deciphering of stellar evolution.

Sandage went to Princeton for a few seasons to use pencils, pads and calculators to plumb the physics of nucleosynthesis. The life of a star, it was realized, could be figured out from the basic principles of nuclear physics.

Sandage's data estimated the oldest stars to be 5 billion years in age, which set a minimum age for the universe as well. "The entire chemical evolution of the galaxy was being discovered at that time," Sandage says, speaking of the period from 1952 to 1963.

Another catalyst was the 1953 arrival in Pasadena of Fred Hoyle, the British astrophysicist. In his fierce defense of the steady state universe, Hoyle wanted to show that stars alone—not the Big Bang—could produce all the elements in the universe. In the Big Bang's favor, the prediction that the universe was made up of 75 percent hydrogen and 25 percent helium had always checked out. But in the chain reaction that followed, which proceeded from the simple to the complex heavier elements, the creation of carbon, a gateway to the other elements, was a puzzle. Three helium nuclei had to smash together to make carbon, and the sheer force of the collision did not seem to work. So Hoyle elaborated on a hypothesis from the 1930s that a resonance, or vibration, in the nuclear structure of carbon might allow the helium nuclei to fuse. Hoyle asked the Kellogg Radiation Laboratory at Caltech to run an atom-smashing experiment, which verified his remarkable prediction.

With Hoyle as the lead author, his team published what Sandage called a "wonderful crucial paper" in *Reviews of Modern Physics* in 1957. It outlined what would become the classic cosmic scenario: from Big Bang to the formation of stars out of the primordial gas clouds of hydrogen and helium, which in turn forged the heavy elements. The production of the elements followed an elegant simple-to-complex arrow of atomic weights, starting with hydrogen and ending with iron.

A very important discovery in all this—and later in the search for Omega—was the supernova explosion. If a star is massive enough, it collapses when the hydrogen is burned up, creating a supernova. This was the most violent force in the universe after the Big Bang, spewing the cooked-up heavy elements into space. After that, new stars formed from gas clouds would include the heavy elements. Thus, what Baade had found was "old" and "new" generation stars, the old lighter, the new heavier.

"It was a ferment in science that I've never experienced since," Sandage says. "It was really a magic fifteen years." But the wonderful evolution of stars and carbon-based life is not necessarily proof of God, even if God exists, stresses this religiously committed bench scientist:

It was exceedingly beautiful, but it had no theological implication what-soever. We don't know why that design is there, but we know that design goes through all this exquisitely beautiful science. But if you stand back from that beauty, and want to know why it is that way, then you're no longer a scientist.

Hoyle, on the other hand, was widely quoted years afterward as com-menting that the fine-tuning of carbon had seriously shaken his atheism.

When it came to proofs about God, stellar evolution held a dim can-dle to the debate stirred by the Big Bang itself. Since the era of Hubble and Sandage's early work, the Big Bang theory had stood on three empirical find-ings. First was the recession of the galaxies, as evidenced by the redshift of their spectra towards longer wavelengths. Second was the estimate that the age of the universe is roughly comparable to the radiometric age of the earth (within a billion or two years). Third was the confirmation of a hydrogen-to-helium ratio in the universe that was predicted by the theory.

The fourth discovery may be considered the most important, how-ever, and its revelation in 1965 turned the dreamy speculations of cosmol-ogy into hard science. In that year, a cosmic background radiation was discovered, an everywhere-present afterglow of the Big Bang itself.

The discovery that the universe is expanding and may have arisen from a single point of creation was a radical shift from thousands of years of sci-entific and philosophical belief. The idea, launched by speculation on Ein-stein's theory after 1917, was reinforced and much debated after the redshift findings—though until 1965 one could hardly claim that it had been "proved." But individuals like Hubble put no philosophical spin on this growing earthquake in cosmology. "We never discussed the philosophy or meaning of it," Sandage recalls. "A real astronomer does not ask about origins."

It took Pope Pius XII, in his 1951 address to the Pontifical Academy of Science, to turn that question into an international debate. The Pope spoke of how "true science discovers God in an ever-increasing degree." The Big Bang suggested that "the material universe had in finite time a mighty beginning." It showed how matter was dependent on a Necessary Being. In other words, matter had mutability and nature a teleological order. He acknowledged that there can be no absolute proof from science regarding God, and cautioned against tying faith to transient theories. Nevertheless, the evidence was looking pretty good: a religious concept of creation was "entirely compatible" with the Big Bang. Science had "confirmed the contingency of the universe.... Hence, creation took place in time. Therefore, there is a Creator. Therefore, God exists!"

Though Pius's rhetorical technique was straight out of Thomas Aquinas and other classic proofs of God, and he made no scientific mistakes in his talk, atheistic scientists were offended and not a few Catholics involved in science thought it was in bad taste. The Belgian priest and physicist Georges Lemaître, who was an early contributor to the Big Bang theory, thought the Pope had lorded it over the scientists, informing them that the Church had already known these things from Genesis. For Lemaître's part, he had used Einstein's physics and Hubble's redshift to theorize that the universe kept the same mass but had an expanding radius. By 1931 he was postulating that a "primeval atom" had started the universe off. Even before Hubble, the priest had measured a velocity-to-distance ratio for the universe of 600. But in 1951, Lemaître knew well that the Big Bang was hardly proven—the background radiation would not be discovered for another fourteen years. He knew that Christian faith should not depend on any theory of the day.

ALTHOUGH IT QUICKLY ENTERED POPULAR CULTURE and became a household term, the Big Bang theory still had only provisional acceptance in scientific circles until the 1990s. To evaluate the precise fluctuations, or "wrinkles," in the background radiation reported in 1965, NASA sent aloft the Cosmic Background Explorer (COBE) satellite in 1989. The findings, announced three years later, were an astounding endorsement of the Big Bang, explaining why its apparently smooth beginning ended up in a universe full of clumpy galaxies. The proof came none too soon, said a relieved COBE mission leader George Smoot: "Very simply, the discovery of the wrinkles salvaged Big Bang theory at a time when detractors were attacking it in increasing numbers."

When the Cambridge astrophysicist Stephen Hawking arrived at the Vatican in 1981 to address a session of the Pontifical Academy of Sciences, he did not question the Big Bang, but he may have felt he was taking on the legacy of Pope Pius. Hawking unveiled his "no-boundary theory," which used quantum physics and "imaginary time" to say there was no beginning to the universe. "So long as the universe had a beginning, we could suppose it had a creator," Hawking has said elsewhere. "But if the universe is really completely self-contained, having no boundary or edge, it would have neither beginning nor end. What place then for a creator?"

Astronomer George Coyne, a Jesuit and director of the Vatican Observatory, said Hawking embarked on his foray into theology with too little philosophical training in the matter. He was mixing up the "nothings" as used by physics and by theology. "He speaks of a quantum nothing, but that is not nothing," Coyne said, playing on words. "It has nothing to do with the nothing of Scripture—that God created the universe from nothing." In sum, "the God he excludes is not the God we believe in."

The Protestant philosopher William Lane Craig, a key player in the cosmology debate, has argued that cosmologists seem bent on proving there was no beginning so that believers cannot seize upon a creation event to cloak their faith with scientific authority. Before the Big Bang, the classical rebuttal was the steady state theory, which in the 1940s built upon the idea current since Aristotle that the universe has no beginning and no end; the theory explained the apparent galactic expansion as the result of the pressure of new atoms appearing out of the void. (Steady staters had a number for this—the creation rate amounted to one atom per cubic meter each 10 billion years.) Craig argues that the steady state theory was the most obvious and purely metaphysical attempt to avoid the concept of a beginning. Another attempt has been the "oscillating theory," which holds that the beginning, like a yo-yo, repeats again and again infinitely, so there is no real start.

A popular solution is the quantum fluctuation proposal, which suggests that the universe arose out of a flicker in the primordial vacuum—a something out of nothing event—that forever conceals the origin of cosmic matter. A "chaotic inflationary universe" has also been proposed, in which universes split off from one another like bubbles in a kitchen sink, with no apparent beginning point. In Craig's view, all these theories either have no scientific utility, or still must acknowledge contingency on something outside time and space. "These models entail a beginning of the universe," he says. Even Hawking's no-boundary idea lacks only a physical point of beginning. And when science concludes that a universe must have a beginning, argues Craig, the idea of God enjoys the support of science.

Sandage has always felt far more comfortable in the practical world of astronomy—simply "counting galaxies"—than in talk about ultimate meanings. Yet even that empirical stance cannot seem to escape the ultimate speculations of cosmology, such as the question Hubble set out to determine: how will the universe end? Sandage's participation in the discovery of quasars illustrates how hard it is to stay at the bench and avoid Hubble's "dreamy speculation." Sandage had obtained from an enterprising student a list of locations in the sky where radio astronomers had detected extremely energetic points of light far out in the universe. So he turned the 200-inch instrument in their direction.

Today, quasars are thought to be extremely dense stellar systems, perhaps galactic nuclei, that are undergoing catastrophic gravitational collapse, emitting incomparable amounts of energy in the process. Though perhaps no larger than a solar system, an average quasar is brighter than 1,000 billion suns. Quasars were a revolution in astronomy because, as ancient objects, they seemed to show the Einsteinian collapse of gravity in action. They were a portent of the black hole phenomenon (the term was invented by Fred Hoyle in 1967), and a scaled-down model of the fate of a closed universe collapsing into a Big Crunch.

Sandage's isolation of quasars in 1960, and their explanation by others, set off a flurry of new observation. Besides its strange radio signal, a quasar's high energy pushed it into the blue spectrum. By 1964 Sandage had found a thousand bluish objects. When he plugged them into the Hubble diagram, the universe appeared closed. Sandage rushed his findings into the *Astrophysical Journal* in 1965: "The clues indicate that our universe is a finite, closed system originating in a 'big bang,' that the universe is slowing down, and that it probably pulsates perhaps once every 82 billion years." The media loved it, and especially the philosophical implications. Said the *New York Times* on the front page, "Not only do these discoveries have great philosophical and scientific implications; it is hard to see how they can fail to influence the creative currents of our time."

Unfortunately, Sandage had mistaken other blueshift objects for quasars, and his announcement opened him to attack by rivals in the field. He decided to return to bench astronomy. ("I left the world in 1965 and became much more reclusive, not to emerge until 1983," he says.) During that retreat from cosmological speculation, he teamed up with Gustav Tamman, a Swiss colleague, to complete the collection of data—spectral type, magnitude and redshift—for a catalog of thirteen hundred of the brightest galaxies. He did northern skies from California and southern from Australia, and the project was completed in 1982. "It turned out to be a gold mine," he says enthusiastically.

During this time also, the revolution in astronomical technology got into full swing. Hubble had made his judgments by eyeball at the Mount Wilson Observatory and at Palomar, and so did Sandage until the early 1960s, when the first electric photometers more accurately compared the magnitudes of objects caught on film. With the 1970s came digital detectors, and the light was sent directly into computers to produce the pictures and measurements. The charged-coupled device, or CCD, pushed new limits, allowing computers to read 85 percent of the light collected by the mirror. The next horizon was using computers and optics to correct distortions caused by Earth's atmosphere.

"It's a new world than it was in my time," says Sandage. "One gets immediately colors, positions, identifications, morphological types that separate the galaxies from the stars, from a million or so discrete positions, with the electronics, data banks and computer." He likens it to military reconnaissance. A telescope can run on automatic and come up with the one type of star that researchers are looking for. They can ring up the world's largest telescope—the twin Keck 10-meter instruments atop Mount Kea, Hawaii, each of which consists of 36 contiguous 1-meter mirrors—and ask for shots of the target object. There is also the Hubble Space Telescope, with its sky-based ability to see a postage stamp's detail at 25 miles.

During this observational revolution, the Palomar telescope's prime focus was removed and replaced with a cozy control room downstairs. "The last time I had been up in the prime focus must have been about 1985, finishing up the photographic survey of bright galaxies," Sandage says. Until 1991, he continued some projects using the control room. "I remember the last night I went onto the observing floor, and I knew that I would never come back. And I said good-bye to that telescope, and I've never been back."

The novel technologies were also leading to new challenges to some of the old assumptions in astronomy—for instance, one holding that the universe is distributed evenly and everywhere expands uniformly. Hubble had operated on that assumption. But now the mass collection of galaxy data by computers could gather such large samples that it could be tested. By the 1980s, for example, one survey team had counted objects in a region of sky 100 million light-years across; it found gigantic voids that contained no galaxies at all. Another survey of 1,100 galaxies produced images of walls, bubbles and clumps—not homogeneity. Then in 1987, the evenness of the expansion was challenged by an up-and-coming group of seven astronomers, called the "Seven Samurai," whose mass surveys showed galaxies near the Milky Way drawing together and toward some center of gravity, which they called The Great Attractor.

What was closest to home for Sandage, the veteran of observational astronomy, was the ongoing "Hubble wars," as he called them—disputes over the Hubble constant. This warring of theories always seems inevitable; when Hubble's generation overturned the ideas of their predecessors, Baade noted how "the 'old boys' didn't take it sitting down" because the new findings in the 1920s "just about smashed up all the old school's ideas about galactic dimensions." Now a new group of cosmologists had arrived to smash up the Hubble legacy. Most notable was the so-called "Gang of Four," a group of younger astronomers with newly minted doctorates and a desire to challenge conventional beliefs about Omega. Because the Hubble diagram had leaned toward a closed universe, they hoped to find the opposite. They totaled the mass of the universe, then compared it with the expansion force of the universe. In a 1974 *Astrophysical Journal* article they announced that the universe is open.

Not to be outdone, Sandage was also recalculating along the new lines of the mass-velocity approach, and in a 1975 issue of the *Astrophysical Journal* he reversed the traditional Hubble stance by concluding that the expansion would never stop. (He told *Time* magazine, "It's a terrible surprise.") In the process, however, Sandage ended up with a Hubble constant of 57, plus or minus 15. And he estimated a universe 20 billion years old. Sandage would stick with these numbers for the rest of his career. "And those with higher numbers are coming down," he said in 2002.

The mid-1970s, in fact, marked the polarization of groups behind high (70–100) and low (50–60) Hubble constants. Around this time, open universe interest blossomed in much the same way that the death crunch had gained bumper sticker popularity in the 1950s and 1960s. Thanks to the launch of the Hubble Space Telescope, the 1990s became the golden age of cosmology, accented by a renewed round of debates on the Hubble constant and on whether the universe was open or closed.

Before the telescope was launched, a panel of astronomers had agreed that one of its priorities would be to settle these fiery debates once and for all. Accordingly, a small portion of the five years of Hubble observing time was given over to the Distance Scale Key Project, which came back with a Hubble constant of 80 and a younger age for the universe (8 billion years). "The discrepancy made the front pages of newspapers all over the world," says science writer Kitty Ferguson. "Scientists ground their teeth."

As ever, the key to this astronomical quest was a reliable "standard candle" with which to judge distances accurately. The new candle had become the supernova, because the physics of the exploding star was considered to be identical whenever the phenomenon occurred. Reports of supernova sightings have dotted the annals of recorded history. The Hubble telescope had systematically recorded dozens of them over a decade as a result of the devoted work of the American-led Supernova Cosmology Project, whose goal was to find the true Omega. The team spotted supernovae far and near, measured them and compared them.

An Australian-led project, the High Redshift Search Team, had been doing the same, and in 1998 the findings of both teams converged on a surprising conclusion: the expanding universe was picking up speed. *Science* magazine declared the "accelerating universe" to be the breakthrough of the year in 1998, and gushingly editorialized: "Although the nature of the universe was once chiefly the realm of philosophers, in 1998 it seems that cosmology is grounded on data, as visions of distant supernovae revealed the true nature—and perhaps the future—of the cosmos."

In the face of the usual attacks from science rivals, the theory had enough staying power to become a *Time* cover story in early 2001: "How the Universe Will End." In hypertrophied prose, the magazine reported that "peering into space and time, scientists have just solved the biggest mystery in the cosmos." Though past data had produced conflicting views on a flat, open or closed universe, "the question may now have been settled once and for all."

The most interesting aspect of the new theory, however, was illustrated by the cartoon of a surprised-looking Einstein, sucking on his pipe, on the cover of *Science*. In his cosmological theory of 1917, Einstein had added a cosmological constant, or repulsion force, to his field equations in order to counteract the collapsing pull of gravity. The new experiments seemed to provide compelling evidence for its reality. As *Time* reported, "The universe was indeed speeding up, suggesting that some sort of powerful antigravity force was at work, forcing the galaxies to fly apart even as ordinary gravity was trying to draw them together."

Long before modern cosmologists tried to calculate the ultimate outcome of the universe, of course, sacred scriptures had described that fate. The apocalypse was the dramatic end to the cosmic drama, and eschatology (from the Greek *eschatos*, "last") contemplated the end of time. The first contribution of science to eschatology was the second law of thermodynamics, formulated around 1850. The law implies that time has a direction because all systems pass from a state of order to disorder (unless energy is injected).

The second law suggested that an expanding universe would cool down and dissipate in a final "heat death." Scientists in the 1930s popularized this depressing scenario and theologians offered responses. The dean at St. Paul's Church in London was called the "gloomy dean" for preaching that only God offered eternal life in the face of such doom. A few decades later, Pierre Teilhard de Chardin, a Catholic priest and anthropologist, offered an optimistic alternative. He said that an unseen, even divine, energy was countering the second law and evolving matter and spirit toward a final state of repose, the Omega Point, where Creation and Creator united. A few decades later physicists were offering a "secular eschatology," proposing that intelligence or consciousness might conceivably survive the heat death, perhaps in the particles or quantum energy that remained.

When a group of theologians and scientists formed the Eschatology Project in Princeton on the eve of 2000, their papers, published as *The End of the World and the Ends of God,* covered all these options. But science offers religious believers only a disturbing paradox at best, the physicist and theologian John Polkinghorne explained later: "Science can do no more than present us with the contrast of a finely tuned and fruitful universe which is condemned to ultimate futility." He offered two classic Christian responses:

> If the universe is a creation, it must make sense everlastingly, and so ultimately it must be redeemed from transience and decay. [And] if human beings are creatures loved by their Creator, they must have a destiny beyond their deaths.

WHATEVER THE THEOLOGICAL IMPLICATIONS of an expanding universe, scientists were hard at work amassing data relating to its ultimate destiny. A scientific quest such as this was first-class material for a "great debate" in astronomy. So in the mid-1990s—around the time the Distance Scale Key Project was reporting its new Hubble constant—a group of astronomy boosters decided to air these stormy discussions publicly at the Smithsonian's Baird Auditorium at the National Museum of Natural History in Washington.

The first event, convened in 1996, focused directly on the Hubble constant debate by bringing together protagonists who represented the two extremes. Tamman, who was Sandage's protégé, argued for a Hubble constant of 55; he was forced to this conclusion by a complex array of data, which he presented masterfully. The astronomer Sidney van den Bergh, on the other hand, while conceding that the Tamman-Sandage model offered a beguilingly elegant and simple universe, vigorously defended his value of 80 for the constant, which gives us "a more complex (and perhaps more interesting) world."

While the Baird Auditorium debate became a sort of benchmark for the history of astronomy, it was not expected to resolve the overarching problem. Nevertheless, there is some degree of certainty, according to the astronomer Virginia Trimble, who has chronicled the Hubble wars. She said the "bottom line" is that the value of the Hubble constant is between 40 and 90; every numerical claim has a 20 percent "error bar" (plus or minus 10 percent), so most Hubble estimates overlap. But until better observational data come in, for astronomers to do their science they will have to agree on a working value to enter into their equations; she predicts that it will probably hover around 65.

By 1998, the next topic worthy of a great debate at the Smithsonian was whether, by demonstrating the acceleration of the universe, the Supernova Cosmology Project had actually revealed the Holy Grail: "Has cosmology been solved?" The particle physicist Michael Turner provocatively took the view that 1998 marked a major turning point in cosmology, and that twenty years from now cosmologists will indeed refer to it as "the year cosmology was solved." He held to a Hubble constant of around 65 and to an open universe with an accelerating expansion. This solution is called the "inflationary universe plus the cold dark matter" theory: an unseen dark energy is pushing the universe apart.

The specter of an unseen cosmic force has long been fertile ground for science fiction, and even for religion. Corey Powell, an editor at *Discover* magazine, has used the accelerating universe findings to propose a new "sci/religion." This secular faith gathers in the Church of Einstein in awe of the invisible force that Einstein called *Lambda,* and which Powell calls "God in the equation." In 1917, Einstein had added this cosmological constant to his "static universe" model to explain how the universe remains stable: *Lambda* was the cosmological repulsion force that counterbalances gravity. When Edwin Hubble showed that the galaxies were indeed receding, Einstein decided that the constant was his "biggest blunder." But Powell thinks that Einstein may actually turn out to have been a prophet who foretold a force so fundamental that it evokes religious reverence.

Nothing quite so metaphysical as this arose at the Smithsonian debate in 1998, at which James Peebles of Princeton responded to Turner's enthusiasm with great skepticism about an accelerating universe and about the notion that cosmology was solved: "We theorists ought to resist the temptation to draw large conclusions from the latest observational reports." Modesty was in order, because even the Big Bang model was on "dangerous ground" with hardly enough data for a truly convincing scientific case. And he drew the distinction Sandage had known so well, that observational science is imprecise at best, "a point that is obvious to astronomers but not always to their colleagues in physics"; and the new data on supernovae and accelerating galaxies involved extraordinarily difficult measurements. "We should stop all this talk about how the world ends," was Peebles's verdict.

Though Peebles also brings skepticism to issues of meaning or purpose in the universe, his avowal of science's limits should appeal to religious-minded people more than the Church of Einstein, with its worship of an impersonal and material, albeit mysterious, force. Traditional believers, after all, seek their personal Creator in realms of mystery that science, with its inherent limits, cannot reach.

Astrophysicist George Ellis, a Quaker, thinks a lot about the limits of astronomy and cosmology, and on purely scientific grounds. After studying at Cambridge, he returned to his South African homeland to teach and write about those limits. He stresses that there is only one universe to be observed, and that we can effectively observe it from only one point in space-time. The mathematical assumption about a smooth universe is useful, but can never be verified. Even the Hubble Space Telescope sees no farther than the "visible horizon." Brilliant calculations have taken physicists back to the Big Bang, but its reality will never truly be seen. What we *can* see is an infinitely small fraction of all there is.

Ellis agrees with Peebles that the bench astronomers know this daunting reality better than the theoretical physicists: "Observers are very, very aware of the complexity of the real thing, while theoreticians are always looking for simplified models." Often enough the theoreticians will ignore the data, and a beautiful theory will be favored for awhile; but in the end every theory has to face the data or it will lose support.

Ellis is not inclined to use science to prove God, but he believes that science's limits open the way for transcendental thinking. Ironically, in the era of the Hubble Space Telescope we are now "much clearer on the limits," he says.

> In cosmological terms, we are very clear now about these horizons. We'll never see past these horizons. We'll never get the data there. There are limits on the energies we can probe in the early universe, and so on. Science hasn't yet adjusted to this, but I think it is beginning to realize these limits.

Sandage remembers Ellis's arguments beginning in the 1970s. "He had written a series of papers on the limits to data you can obtain at the telescope," Sandage said with a skeptical laugh. The editor of the *Annual Review of Astronomy and Astrophysics* liked Ellis's tough papers because they threw a monkey wrench into much of the alleged certainty surrounding astronomical findings.

Working at the telescope every day, Sandage was getting exciting new information. But he knew the complexity of the task and of the wall beyond which science could not go. From Hubble's "shadows" in 1936 to the Hubble Space Telescope's "twilight zone" in 2002, there was always that barrier. In the early 1980s, Sandage himself became fascinated by this quest for certainty and how it expressed itself in religious faith.

He met a group of conservative Christians in southern California and adopted their faith, or at least began, as he puts it, "to try much harder to seek the divine." He was fascinated by their certainty about the Bible. "I asked them, 'How can you be sure of what you say?'" he recalls. "There are those who were born with a faith, and have the gift of faith. Then there are those who try to prove the existence of God." For him, the leap of faith to reach God is not easy, but it is far easier than trying to use science to prove God's existence. It is better that the spiritual quest remain completely separate from the project of science.

Because he is a high-profile astronomer forever caught up in the cosmological debates of the day, word of Sandage's association with a traditional faith got around. As one story goes, during the controversy over the Hubble constant in the 1980s, Sandage attended an astronomy conference where three graduate students from the University of Arizona were gossiping about his newly grown beard and (erroneously) about his having become a preacher. Because of this, they questioned his Hubble constant of 55 when a set of rival findings had just come in at 90. Sandage says, "I overheard them saying, 'Well, you heard about Sandage. He really can't be believed now. He has become a Baptist minister.'"

Perhaps he had become an evangelical Christian, but he was not even sure of that. "I was just overcome with amusement," he says of the incident.

Some of his favorite references today are to the great existential thinkers who spoke of taking a "leap of faith" (Søren Kierkegaard), having the "will to believe" (William James), or "wagering" that faith is true (Blaise Pascal). And he often quotes St. Anselm, the medieval logician, who said plainly, "I believe so that I may understand." The physical parts of the universe may indeed appear to be designed, but the scientific method has nothing to say about that appearance. What a person *may* do is take the leap of faith regardless of science, apprehending that the atoms and the galaxies work as they do because God is the inscrutable Designer.

His scientific and spiritual interests finally drew Sandage into the dialogue between science and religion as organized by the Science and the Spiritual Quest forum, a series of events that took place from 1996 to 1998. He recalls one session where a "rough and ready" fellow with a South African accent was making the rounds. Sandage caught up with him and asked who he was. "He said, 'I'm George Ellis.' It bowled me over. I thought George Ellis would have been the last person that would have been religious. We started talking religion. I realized he is deeply religious."

When Sandage was featured in the opening paragraph of a 1998 *Newsweek* cover story, "Science Finds God," he may have been flattered, but he may also have wished to alter the headline to say, "Faith Finds God."

5

THE DIALOGUE

The modern discussion between science and religion emerged from two main quarters: the heart of historic Christianity, and the world of high finance and philanthropy. The leading figures of these currents met only once and briefly, but this encounter symbolized a modern desire for rapprochement between the two realms.

On October 16 of 1978, the white smoke from the Sistine Chapel at Vatican City signaled the election of a new Pope, a Polish university professor named Karol Wojtyla, soon to be Pope John Paul II. Just three weeks later, the Wall Street wonder John Marks Templeton appeared for the first time on the cover of *Forbes* magazine. "Where the Smart Money Is Going," the headline told us, and Templeton was depicted as an owl flying over Manhattan with wads of $1,000 bills in his claws. The proverbial wisdom of the owl is perhaps reflected in one of the millionaire's remarks cited in the article: "We don't pray so that our stocks will go up," he told *Forbes*. "We pray because it makes us think more clearly."

Pope John Paul II had a world stage and a venerable institution that could boast the oldest continuous governance on earth and included the oldest academy of sciences. Templeton, for his part, had the wealth of a Carnegie, Mellon or Rockefeller; but as a Christian with an interest in metaphysics and scientific progress, he had quite a different vision from any of the robber barons.

The Pope entered the science-religion fray in 1979, when he used his first address to the Pontifical Academy of Sciences as an occasion to celebrate Einstein's one-hundredth birthday. In this important speech, he also honored Einstein's predecessor, Galileo, and acknowledged that the Italian had greatly suffered after the Inquisition tried him in 1633 for declaring that the Earth revolved around the Sun. The Pope stated that "an honest recognition of wrongs on whatever side they occur, might make disappear the obstacles that this affair still sets up, in many minds, to a fruitful concord between science and faith."

Such a reassessment of the Galileo case, and his efforts to dispel the myth that faith necessarily conflicts with science, were nearly stopped one May afternoon in 1981, when John Paul paid an open-air visit to St. Peter's Square. The assassin Mehmet Ali Agca's bullet tore into him, and at Gemelli Hospital he was given last rites. But in six weeks, John Paul was back working at his office. One of his earliest actions was to ask the Vatican secretary of state to launch the Commission on the Study of the Ptolemaic-Copernican Controversy, of which Galileo's case was a part. By July, the secretary had tapped the French cardinal Gabriel-Marie Garrone, head of the Pontifical Council for Culture, to start the project.

That same year, John Templeton began his quest to introduce "humility theology" to the world. His own belief was born of all that he was: a son of Tennessee, reared by an industrious father and mother who favored the Presbyterian Church and New Thought spirituality. The latter, similar to Christian Science, was a mind-over-matter outlook as interpreted by the nascent Unity School of Christianity. Moreover, Templeton's wife, Irene, was a Christian Scientist, to whom "mind over matter" was a fundamental belief. To these influences, Templeton himself would add thrift, salesmanship, positive psychology, love of information and a ken for technology.

Templeton summarized his outlook in his first book, *The Humble Approach: Scientists Discover God.* Published in 1981, it was a preliminary seed in an intellectual garden he would eventually cultivate with about $50 million a year, giving rise to history's most widespread dialogue on science and religion. As Templeton saw it, scientific progress could be a role model for a parallel and equally rapid progress in the gaining of spiritual information. But God's nature is infinite, and science and theology can necessarily discover but a few aspects of this infinity. A humble approach might be a good start: it could at least "develop a way of knowing God appropriate to His greatness and our littleness." In 1987, at age seventy-five, he opened the Templeton Foundation and by 1990 the "science-religion" grants began to flow.

The Pope and Templeton met only once—a brief encounter during a standard papal audience when Templeton visited Rome in 1996. They were unwitting co-conspirators, two men who made the dialogue between science and religion happen.

JOHN PAUL'S INITIATIVE ON GALILEO aimed for a closure on the case, but it gave rise to much more than that. The Pope commented on Galileo again in 1983, this time to mark the 350th anniversary of the publication of the astronomer's *Dialogues,* saying that it is by study—both "humble and assiduous"—that the Church may "dissociate the essentials of faith from the scientific systems of a given age."

At the same time in Poland, an academic conference was held on the subject of Galileo; Vatican diplomats intimated that the conference was intended to put flesh on the rhetoric of the Catholic Church's unprecedented démarche of accommodation with modern science. A formal statement the following year seemed almost incidental: Church officials had erred in condemning the arch-Copernican. Two years later, while greeting visiting bishops from Tuscany, the home of Galileo, the Pope lamented how their native son had "encountered foreseeable difficulties in biblical interpretation." Be that as it may, Galileo had still operated on "the clear premise that true science and authentic faith cannot be in disagreement, having their origins in the same author."

It was Galileo's successor in Protestant England who left behind the truly difficult problems for the interaction between science and religion. When he published his *Philosophiae Naturalis Principia Mathematica* in 1687, Isaac Newton presented a theory of a clockwork universe that ran on its own laws. Only anomalous phenomena that these laws could not explain were attributed to God's direct action. Newton posited, for example, that perturbations in the orbits of the planets were adjusted by the Creator. Ever since, the world has had to deal with this Newtonian "God of the gaps." One of Sir Isaac's rivals, the philosopher and mathematician Gottfried Leibniz, phrased the criticism in terms that continue up to the present: Nature must be just as God wants it, "otherwise we must say that God bethinks himself again." The God of the gaps would haunt the science/religion dialogue that John Paul was trying to promote.

The Polish Pope made ripping open the Iron Curtain part of his every move, and perhaps for this reason, the celebration he ordered for the 300th anniversary of Newton's masterpiece included an academic conference in Poland in May 1987. A key player in this development was the Jesuit astronomer George V. Coyne, who in 1978 was appointed head of the Vatican Observatory and who shortly afterward was made an ex officio member of the Pontifical Academy. Before the Polish conference, the Pope, working through Vatican channels, had asked Coyne about ways to memorialize Newton's classic. "We proposed that, rather than have a parade with balloons, we should have a scientific conference to address the issues in a scholarly way," says Coyne. "We didn't want to be snobbish, but serious." So another assembly was held in fall of 1987, this time at Castel Gandolfo, a picturesque site overlooking Lake Albino, just southeast of Rome, that is the summer residence of Popes and home to the Vatican Observatory.

The event drew twenty-one scientists and theologians, and its proceedings, published as *Physics, Philosophy and Theology*, became a vehicle for the Pope's agenda. He agreed to write a letter as a foreword to the book, and now the group had a world-class attention-getter, the first major papal statement on science and religion since Piux XII's 1951 speech on the Big Bang. While the Pope declared the independence of the scientific and theological methods, he shunned a "two worlds" separatism. Instead, he urged a dynamic interaction in areas of ultimate concern where science and faith overlap.

He scolded science's "regressive tendency to a unilateral reductionism," but gave the Church strong medicine, too, explaining how doctrine had become entangled in Aristotelian science along the way. He cited progress in healing the breach: in the "relationship between religion and science, there has been a definite, though still fragile and provisional, movement toward a new and more nuanced interchange." The two sides, he said, "uncovered important questions which concern both of us." For theology to have "vitality and significance," it had to keep up with science. For it is science, he added, that "can purify religion from error and superstition; religion can purify science from idolatry and false absolutes."

To increase the document's influence, Robert Russell, William Stoeger and Coyne solicited nineteen respondents, and their essays were joined with the Pope's for a 1990 book: *John Paul II on Science and Religion*. Thinking bigger now, Coyne set out to organize a decade-long series of such summits, with the main topic for discussion being simply "divine action in the world." The core group held one more meeting of scientists and theologians, and during the October 1991 session at Castel Gandolfo it became apparent that there was a deepening resolve for theology to have a more equitable relationship with scientists, because "too often science tends to set the agenda for the theological discussions."

As the project grew, so did the role of Robert Russell, an energetic physicist, who was also a United Church of Christ minister teaching theology at the Graduate Theological Union. A decade earlier, in 1981, Russell had founded the Center for Theology and the Natural Sciences (CTNS) in Berkeley, California, and had established close ties with the leading contributors to the "divine action" discussions. Now CTNS added its grant money to the Vatican Observatory's budget and the five-conference plan was launched.

The question of "divine action" was age-old and had long-established answers, even if they could not satisfy everybody. Protestant neo-orthodox theology held that God and God's action were "hidden" behind nature and behind the secular. Neo-Thomism, a Catholic perspective based on the philosophy of Thomas Aquinas, identified the Creator with the unseen primary causes of the universe. A third alternative was the outlook of "process theology," which located God within material evolution itself: God was emerging as an evolutionary reality. Coyne, Russell and the others hoped the conferences could give the issues of "divine action" much more visibility. This was the backdrop to the long-awaited final release of the Vatican's Galileo report.

The Galileo report was timed for release at the October 31, 1992, meeting of the Pontifical Academy of Sciences, at which French cardinal Paul Poupard, the commission vice chairman, would present the findings. Founded in 1603, the academy was active in the days of Galileo and up to 1870, when the political separation of the Vatican State and Italy secularized many papal institutions. The secular academy went its own way, and so Pius XI in 1936 established a pontifical branch. John Paul had reinvigorated the academy, whose primary role is to advise the Church on science. "It chiefly aims not to contribute to the science/religion dialogue, but of its very nature, it does," George Coyne admits.

The commission's report said that Galileo had actually "not succeeded in proving irrefutably the double motion of the Earth." Nevertheless, Galileo wanted to state his position as factually true; here he was going against the advice of the Inquisition's Cardinal Robert Bellarmine, who had asked Galileo to "say that we do not understand" rather than proclaim his model, which he knew was in conflict with Scripture.

Meanwhile, the report continued, "certain theologians . . . failed to grasp the profound non-literal meaning of the Scriptures when they described the physical structure of the universe." Thus, the theologians had "unduly" forced "a question of factual observation into the realm of faith."

In the Church's favor, the report said, it was able finally to treat the condemnation of Galileo as "reformable," that is, temporary. Thus the report noted that the Church gave an imprimatur to the *Complete Works* of Galileo in 1741, after the 1728 discovery of the aberration of starlight, which proved the Earth's motion around the Sun. And in 1822, Pius VII sided with a priest-scientist who was ready to publish his *Elements of Optics and Astronomy,* which backed heliocentrism.

In his talk to the Pontifical Academy, the Pope drew two primary lessons from the Galileo case, the first being the astronomer's confusion between scientific proof and philosophical argument. Galileo "rejected the suggestion made to him to present the Copernican system as a hypothesis." Hence the need for various disciplines to clarify their methods and claims. Also important was the "pastoral dimension" of the case: Galileo had challenged the authority of Scripture, and thus the faith of the ordinary "people of God," who take a long time to "overcome habits of thought."

Citing the commission's report, John Paul commended Cardinal Bellarmine for his forbearance with Galileo, who is known even by sympathetic scholars to have been an aggressive self-publicist. But the intractable fact remains that the old man was put under house arrest for heresy, a sentence that lasted the final nine years of his life.

At the end of the day, the public went away with the impression that the Church had made a mistake and was sorry. This, at least, is what George Coyne believes. But, he added, "there's a great deal of disappointment in the scholarly community." In other words, the report cast no blame on the Pope, Bellarmine, the Inquisition or the Congregation of the Index of Prohibited

Books. It erred in saying that Galileo's heliocentric views were purely hypothetical, when in fact they had been empirically derived.

"The picture given in the discourse of 31 October 1992 does not stand up to historical scrutiny," George Coyne argues. "Until we face up honestly to the historical conflict, and really admit what happened, the myth [of faith and science in conflict] is going to remain. So the Pope's very sincere and obvious desire to remove the myth, to my mind, has not succeeded yet."

And what of the conferences on the shores of Lake Albino throughout the 1990s? Five books were produced, crammed with details, documenting the proceedings. But if "divine action" had been disclosed in new areas of science, or conceived of in fresh ways, the breakthroughs were too elusive to have been trumpeted at conferences or manifestos.

WHILE KAROL WOJTYLA WAS STILL A POLISH grade-schooler, John Templeton was peddling Hearst Publishing Company subscriptions for $2 a year. After entering Yale in 1932 to study investment "because of deep interest in the difficulty of judging the value of any shares of corporations," he was awarded a Rhodes scholarship to Oxford. By 1940, he was running his own fund management company on Wall Street.

Templeton and his wife worshipped at First Presbyterian Church of Englewood, New Jersey. He helped with its fundraising, became chairman of trustees for the county YMCA, and in 1940 was elected to the ecumenical commission of the National Presbyterian Church. Soon, he was chairman of the denomination's $50 million endowment fund. To do his Wall Street work, he always carried about sheaves of reports, graphs and analyses, mountains of information that doubtless stimulated his appetite for spiritual information.

Having moved to the Bahamas in 1968, Templeton became a British citizen. According to his biographer Robert Herrmann, "the 1960s was a time of spiritual renewal for John." After helping people make fortunes on the stock market, his ambition now was to help them grow spiritually. Already in 1959 he had begun selling off assets and giving grants to religious institutions, ranging from the Princeton Theological Seminary to the Templeton Theological Seminary, which he founded in the Bahamas. As a trustee of the Princeton seminary, he noticed that theology school teaching, based on revelation, did not grow with the times by nourishing itself from science; naively, perhaps, he compared it with instruction at the medical school his son was attending. More painfully, all his well-educated and well-to-do associates were irreligious. "They thought of religion as uninteresting and old-fashioned, or even obsolete," he said.

For all these reasons, Templeton decided to put his money to work. "Since I couldn't find any organizations concentrating on progress in religion, I've undertaken that," he later said. "The first step was to offer prizes for progress in religion." His initial idea, inscribed in his will, was that after his death the estate's trustees would award a prize for progress in Christianity, much as Nobel had done for other realms. "But then I began to realize that it was a mistake for me to leave the assets for later use, because 'later' might be a long, long time away."

So in 1972 he awarded the first $1 million Templeton Prize for Progress in Religion, which went to the most beloved religious figure on the planet, Mother Teresa.

But that was only the start. Six years later, in 1978, he formed the Templeton Foundation "to explore and encourage the relationship between science and religion." Within the foundation, he established what became known as the Humility Theology Information Center, which opened with the announcement of a three-pronged research program: "utilization of scientific methods in understanding the work and purpose of the Creator," research on studying or stimulating progress in religion, and research on the benefits of religion. In 1992, when Templeton threw himself full-time into foundation work, he sold his remaining interest in the $22 billion of assets he had once managed.

Around 1996, the Templeton Foundation's science/religion work got onto a new footing with the arrival of a new executive director, Charles Harper, who had doctorates in both earth sciences and theology—and an eye for promising links between the two. By then the foundation's work had begun to expand rapidly into supporting university courses on science and religion, special conferences, research grants and fellowships.*

---

*Templeton did not so much break new ground as regenerate the old. Before him had come the Gifford Lectures, which still today offer regular forums at four universities in Scotland,

The first scientist to win the prize was the marine biologist Sir Alister Hardy. Approaching ninety, Hardy was knighted in 1985 in recognition of his Religious Experience Research Unit at Oxford, which he had inaugurated in 1969. Hardy had formerly been skeptical of the paranormal, but he had changed his views. Far from orthodox, he likened his research to a completion of the work of William James, the American philosopher whose 1901 and 1902 Gifford Lectures were published as the classic, *The Varieties of Religious Experience.*

Perhaps the chief Spinozan of the Templeton winners was the British physicist Paul Davies, who won the prize in 1995 for his popularization of anthropic ideas. Having drifted to agnosticism from his Anglican upbringing, and then struggling with the question of free will, Davies trained in physics and began to give public lectures. "Whatever topic it was, the big bang or black holes or quantum physics, at the end people would ask, 'What about God? What does all this mean, and where do I fit in?'" They were less interested in technical detail. "So I thought, 'I really should address those questions and write some books.'" His Templeton honors came for works that did not shy from using the word "design," or the slogan "mind of God," or speculating on the amazing match between mathematics and the human mind.

By 2002, the prize had been given to thirty-one recipients, twelve of whom were in the science-and-religion field. From 1999 to 2002 all the winners were in science and religion: Ian Barbour, the process theology physicist; Freeman Dyson, a speculative Princeton physicist who favored a nontheistic anthropic universe; and Arthur Peacocke and John Polkinghorne, both scientists who became ordained clergy. Indeed, by 2002, the prize had

---

on "natural religion." These, depending on which learned lecturer is holding forth, preach everything from a near-atheism to a more traditional conception of God. It should be mentioned that, since 1941, the American Scientific Affiliation had convened evangelicals in science each year, in quiet exchange, and the more modernist and Spinozan aficionados of science-and-religion, since 1954, had held annual retreats of the Institute on Religion in an Age of Science (IRAS) at Star Island off New Hampshire's coast.

Indeed, when the Templeton Prize began to tap its first recipients in science and religion, much of the pool of possible winners was in the Gifford and IRAS orbit. In its sixth year, the prize went to Templeton board member and Scottish divine Thomas Torrence, who was known for trying to make the Incarnation of Christ and the Trinity "congenial" to quantum mechanics and field theories, and for being caretaker of Polanyi's papers.

become entirely oriented toward science, redefining itself as the "prize for progress toward research or discoveries about spiritual realities."

By and large, this science/religion dialogue took place within a safe intellectual harbor where there was a willingness to clash over atheism, yet a general reluctance to question conventional science. It preferred the decorous world of orthodox science and shunned Newton's God of the gaps, an idea it identified with the creationist fringe. This was particularly true of the Templeton-funded Program on the Dialogue Between Science and Religion, which opened in the American Association for the Advancement of Science in 1995. This was not a setting that would favor, for example, the rant of the astrophysicist Fred Hoyle, who reminded colleagues about the "wages of respectability" in science and claimed that "the collective opinion of scientists [is] almost always incorrect."

When theology talked to science, there were clear risks of secularization. According to the historian Ronald Numbers, "Nothing characterizes modern science more than its rejection of God in explaining the workings of nature." As the National Academy of Sciences says, "The goal of science is to seek naturalistic explanations for phenomena—and the origins of life, the earth, and the universe are, to scientists, such phenomena—within the framework of natural laws and principles and the operational rule of testability."

Some participants in the science/religion dialogue have openly worried about science co-opting the transcendental. George Coyne, the Vatican astronomer, calls it "the temptation of the new physics." God becomes mathematics: "God is the ideal mathematical structure, the theory of everything. God is Mind." Such a view ignores God as a person. "The most important element in religious faith is a sort of humble acceptance of a gift from God. Namely God himself," Coyne says. He recalls how Spinozan friends such as Paul Davies ask why they do not experience this gift coming to them. "The real answer is, 'You have or you will, but you don't know it yet,'" Coyne tells them. "That's a little hard to take."

Coyne points to one other erroneous legacy of the author of the *Principia:* "Newton had a keen desire to establish religious faith on rational grounds. That's a corruption of religious faith to exclusively want to do that."

Peacocke, an Anglican priest, has proposed at least an "open theology" that allows science to redefine concepts of God and faith. He asks this blunt question: "Can religion learn to outgrow its reliance on claimed authorities and popular images of a God who acts and reveals by supernatural means?" Ideas of God must match "the world we now find it to be through the sciences," he says. "We require an open, revisable, exploratory theology."

This challenge to traditional faith was already laid out by John Templeton in his 1981 work that demanded humility of theology. He said that religion should "continually test and re-examine what has been passed down from before and what has been accepted in the present. Admittedly, this is a tall order for theology, which operates from the standpoint of revelation and knows little of the empirical methods of the sciences."

The astronomer Allan Sandage, who like Coyne is comfortable with leaps of faith, says that the attempt to make religion scientific is a pronounced trend in the religion-and-science dialogue. A former member of a Templeton board, Sandage was particularly taken aback by Peacocke's attempt to remold Christianity. "I wrote a letter saying, 'I believe the Templeton Foundation is trying to start a scientific religion," Sandage says. "I told them that was dangerous to traditional religion." (When Coyne heard of Sandage's protest, he said, "Good for him. I would have signed the letter.")

The other physicist-priest, John Polkinghorne, has outlined a spectrum of attitudes between those who want to accommodate more to science and those who want to stay truer to revealed doctrines. He believes that he received the Templeton Prize because his work stays with traditional Christian doctrines such as the Trinity, the Incarnation and the End of the World. "What has been happening in the science and theology area is a sort of spiraling inward," he says of the past three to four decades of the dialogue:

> It began where you'd expect it to begin, at the obvious frontier regions, like creation and natural theology. Then it moved on to this question of God's action in the world, which in the 1990s was the big topic. Now I think we're at another twist of the spiral, moving inward to more theologically grounded issues, and I think eschatology, the last things and the question of hope are where things are going at the moment.

It just happens to be the topic, moreover, of Polkinghorne's most recent book:

It's about belief in a destiny beyond death, both for individual human beings and actually the whole universe, since the universe on a much longer time scale is also going to end in futility as far as present processes are concerned. It is exploring the credibility and motivations for belief in such a hope.

One laser physicist who has his own prize to boast of—a Nobel Prize in physics in 1997—is William Phillips, a churchgoing United Methodist who teaches Sunday school and sings in the choir. He finds the science-and-religion dialogue fascinating, but the God of Spinoza and Einstein (or of Hardy, Davies and Peacocke) does not satisfy his longing for some bridge between the two. First, says Phillips, "There's always a danger that people think that because you have a Nobel Prize in something, you know something about other things." That isn't necessarily true, he says, and points to his knowledge of the science/religion discussion. "I am probably one of those people who would be characterized as having put these two aspects of my life in relatively separate compartments, without denying that there are going to be overlaps." Some have called his views, because of the neat compartments, "minimalistic."

Phillips is among those who believe that "God doesn't leave his fingerprints on the universe," and that perhaps there is evil and suffering because God wanted both free human beings and a Creation governed by laws: "In order to give us the gift of free will and relationship, something else has to happen as well; that there are constraints in the way even God can design a universe."

But natural theology and arguments from design come up short for him as descriptions of the essence of God:

> Let's just imagine that we learn a lot more, and what we learn points us to the idea of a Creator. It's difficult for me to see how science is going to point to a Creator who wants to have personal relationships with us, who loves us, who wants us to love each other, who has expectations for us that had been passed to us by the wisdom of the Scriptures, and other ways that we receive knowledge about God.

No offense to science, of course. But, for Phillips, "those are the things about God."

MOST OF THESE SCIENTISTS—Sandage, Peacocke, Polkinghorne, Phillips and nearly 120 others—participated in one of the biggest science/religion events of the era, the Science and the Spiritual Quest conferences I and II, held respectively in 1998 and 2001.

Funded by Templeton and organized by Robert Russell's Berkeley center, the SSQ I project had begun earlier by recruiting sixty believing scientists representing the three great monotheistic religions. Once the group was selected, they were interviewed at length and the printed transcripts of their lengthy personal reflections shared with all the others.

The interviews were like confessionals for scientists who often kept their religious inklings private, or a sort of "coming out," and some of the private narratives were later published. "I have no problem with scientists saying there is no God," says Arno Penzias, who won the Nobel for co-discovering the cosmic background radiation. "But for them to say 'This is God' annoys me. It is blasphemy.... They haven't got a clue what God is." Biologist Pauline Rudd of Oxford says: "It's as if religion and Christianity have evolved with human thinking. And it continues to evolve with my thinking. That's part of what I think of as the inspiration of the Holy Spirit." The man who shared a Nobel Prize for discovering the laser principle, Charles Townes, links God to free will: "Science acknowledges no free will in the usual sense at all. And yet, I believe I have free will. I sense it very strongly.... In much the same way, I sense the presence of God and His influence."

The interviewers tended to focus on belief in God or purpose, and how spirituality related to science. After these benign interrogations for SSQ I were completed and sent around for confidential review by all the scientists involved, they met each other for the first time in the spring of 1997 and again later in the year. Then in June of 1998, what had transpired behind closed doors was made public in presentations by twenty-three speakers at the Science and the Spiritual Quest public conference, which was held on the Berkeley campus of the University of California.

In opening that assembly, Russell said that many scientists find that the universe is its own answer. But those who had gathered felt that a "truly adequate account requires language about the God whom Jews, Christians and Moslems praise as the Creator." He said the "objectivity" of science had softened, while theology had acquired a harder edge. The upshot was that religion now included the data of science, and scientists could "share their experience of science as a spiritual journey." To some, the Berkeley event came off as a series of philosophical or scientific lectures, and to others as the oblique religious confessions of scientists. If materialists called SSQ an invasion of religion on science's turf, the more traditional theists came away feeling that talk about God had hardly played a part.

Unlike the "divine action" conferences, which held to academic discourse, SSQ programs emphasized personal disclosure and a deepening of friendships. "Because of SSQ I became aware that Charlie Townes is a man of faith," says William Phillips, who participated in the SSQ II events. "I've known Charlie for years, but I didn't know about this aspect of him." During the private SSQ meeting, "only one person said, 'Gee, I've never had these discussions with my scientific colleagues. This is really neat.'" On the other hand, "Nobody said, 'I can't believe you idiots are talking about this spiritual crap.'" Both SSQ I and II were in the main attended by older scientists, not the young—who might face tenure battles or peer criticism. Both produced reports of scientists feeling liberated, returning to Harvard, MIT or Carnegie Mellon to cast off taboos on science-and-faith talk, and urging others in science to come out of the closet.

The first SSQ ran on a budget of $4.1 million and generated a mountain of news reports, and partly because of this publicity the Templeton Foundation "was eager to receive an application for a renewal grant," as one organizer said. Accordingly, SSQ II was charted as a four-year, $3.5 million follow-up project. It was essentially a repetition of the first SSQ, again using a format of sixty (new) scientists, the sharing of personal interviews, and then two collegial workshops for each group. As a new twist, SSQ II included scientists of all faiths and none. The public event—again, a series of talks and panels—was held in fall of 2001 at Harvard University's Memorial Church. Then it went on the road with similar private and public forums in Paris, Jerusalem, Bangalor in India, and Tokyo. By its end in 2003, a total of 130 scientists are expected to have been spiritually enriched by SSQ II. But while its Berkeley predecessor made the cover of *Newsweek* and rang media bells around the world, SSQ II was eclipsed by the September 11 terrorist attacks on America.

"Because of the SSQ gatherings, the science and religion discussion has gained credibility years earlier that it might have," says Philip Clayton, an evangelical and a philosophy of religion scholar who helped organize both conferences. "A discussion of this sort, with its inherent risks, requires a critical mass of participation, of visibility, of theoretical options. The large influx of Templeton funding has created that critical mass years earlier than would have occurred otherwise."

While a young student at Westmont College in Southern California, Clayton began his quest with a struggle over how Christianity could make its claims rational. He felt compelled by the camp of science, with its privileged knowledge, and asked, "What reasons could be given for using scientific knowledge as a basis for the credibility of Christianity?" He later studied at Yale and then in Germany with Wolfhart Pannenberg, who like Thomas Torrence was trying to reconcile Christian dogmas with modern quantum physics. Clayton returned to California in 1991 to teach at Sonoma State University, and with his background in science and religion gave a few talks at Russell's center. Then in 1996, he conducted half of the interviews with the sixty scientists, and SSQ became a full-time pursuit for him.

"There's something about that phrase, 'science and the spiritual quest,' that has an openness to science and theological traditions," he says of recruiting top scientists. "That got them into the program."

For the first SSQ, many of the participants were theologians, added as "advisers" to clarify what the religious traditions were saying. But looking back, he says there was perhaps too much theology—which was hard for the scientists to talk about in their normal vocabulary and categories. So the second SSQ brought together only scientists. "I saw these poor theologians in SSQ I, who would trot out the old theological distinctions, and the scientists would be nonplussed or outright bored." The second time around, however, "the questions were ones the scientists found crucial in trying to interpret their results and lives." Still, he believes scientists on this quest must tackle "the hard issues," not just mush. He wants them "to talk about design, to talk about consciousness, to talk about how human and animals are alike and unalike."

Scientists of all persuasion agreed that the spiritual questions had to include ethics and justice. After that, the easiest fields with which to reconcile the concept of God's action in the material universe were physics and cosmology, which do not have to find deity in the details. As history testifies, however, God and biology is a far more contentious issue. In those workshops, Clayton says, "the differences between theists and nontheists are much more pronounced and problematic." There it leads to a heated debate about whether Darwinian evolution is sufficient to account for all things that exist. "The theists inevitably say 'no,' the naturalists inevitably say 'yes.'"

As an arbiter of the project, Clayton tries to stay above the fray. When his SSQ hat is off, however, he speaks as a fairly traditional Christian who assumes a supernatural God who is free to communicate with human consciousness. "There is no problem with divine communication with a free conscious being," he says. "You break no physical laws in doing that."

The world of science, he says, has experienced three revolutions: the heliocentric system, Darwinian evolution and finally genetic determinism. There have also been three anti-Copernican revolutions against the principle that downgrades human uniqueness:

> We have the distinct history of the universe with the red shift, the big bang, the big crunch or eternal expansion. That's one uniqueness. Then there is the anthropic principle [and uniqueness of human perception]. Finally we have the uniqueness of the human person and the uniqueness of human language, which snowballs into the uniqueness of human rationality, morality and I'm going to want to say, spirituality.

All of these reinforce the human identification with God.

But Clayton does not depend on the proofs offered by natural theology; he is more comfortable with a humbler approach. "As a good Templeton scholar I should be humble," he says. The picture he offers of the Christian God as the Creator arises from his espousal of Christian *panentheism,* which differs from pantheism. As a reviewer described it, "The world is God, but God transcends the world." In other words, both pantheism and panentheism define the laws of nature as God; the latter also sees God as the transcendent Supreme Being of biblical faith.

The debate on divine action brought Clayton to this view: "I believe that God is in every act of physical law, and every object that moves in accordance with physical law is a direct expression of God." Accordingly, he likens

God's law-like nature to the autonomic nervous system in humans, which keeps the body going without people controlling its functioning. But God also acts intentionally, just as the human mind does: "Those are the acts of God to the consciousness of the human person."

For monotheists in general, Clayton has compiled a sort of scorecard of where the science/religion debate stands. While physics had long been hard on Christian belief, he proposes, it was finally coming around because of theories involving the Big Bang and the fine-tuned universe: "Now, we can say physics has shown us the kind of universe that we would expect if God had done what we believe he did." But in neuroscience, the transcendental is losing ground as big science throws its weight at explaining not just the brain's physiology, but consciousness and the "soul" itself.

Another crucial battle-line is the origin of life. "That is on hold as we debate whether science can supply the answer," Clayton says. Evangelicals have had to concede much to the mindless processes of evolution. "But the place where we have built our Alamo is the origin of life. There, surely, Genesis requires us to say, 'God was involved to launch the whole thing in the first place.'"

6

LIFE'S ORIGIN

One September morning in 1969, a meteorite fireball exploded over Murchison, Australia, hurling stone fragments across a five-mile area. Malodorous alcohol and bluish smoke tinged the air. When the sonic boom hit that Sunday morning around eleven, most of the townspeople were attending church.

For the Gulburn River Valley, nestled in southeast Australia, the meteor was one of the most exciting events in recent memory. For pure extraterrestrial drama, however, it paled next to the Moon landing of Apollo II just a few weeks earlier. One important objective of the moon mission was to bring back samples of rock in order to probe them for signs of ancient life. NASA's Ames Research Center in northern California had prepared a new quarantined laboratory for this delicate task.

But the astronauts returned with only lifeless rock samples, while the meteor crashing down in the Australian farm fields delivered what a billion-dollar space program could not. For amid the debris of the carbonaceous chondrite meteorite, a seven-kilogram fragment had both survived the blast and escaped contamination. The Ames lab found it to be 4.5 billion years old—the age of the solar system. And it contained amino acids, the building blocks of life. Over the coming years, the Murchison meteorite became the most studied of all space rocks.

While the quest to understand our origin has always sent the human gaze skyward, Charles Darwin was pondering a more earthly chemistry when, in 1871, he famously speculated whether life arose "in some warm little pond, with all sorts of ammonia and phosphoric salts, light, heat, electricity, etc., present." The modern search for origins is required to keep the solar system as an ever-present backdrop, since the atmospheric makeup of the early Earth is clearly central to the problem.

In a 1924 pamphlet, the Russian biochemist Alexander I. Oparin proposed that the central ingredient for life was hydrogen, entailing that a hydrogen-rich environment was necessary for the start of life. Also helpful would have been methane. The enemy of this environment, on the other hand, would be oxygen, which destroys organic molecules.

Oparin first proposed the famous "reducing," or oxygen-free, atmosphere that would become the focus of origin-of-life research throughout most of the twentieth century. In England, the biologist J. B. S. Haldane asked whether the life-giving primordial soup of the earliest chemicals could have been the wide ocean itself, a laboratory where the ultraviolet rays of the Sun bound lifeless elements into the first organic compounds and organisms.

As organic—that is, carbon-based—chemistry advanced in its knowledge, the ocean idea was soon discarded. A higher concentration of these chemicals was needed, and this pointed back to Darwin's idea of some tiny pond. So by midcentury, lagoons that could theoretically concentrate the amino acids, fatty acids, sugars and other components that constituted life were favored as the likely cradles of life. Other means were also considered, such as the repetitious structures of clay that, functioning as pattern-setting environments, might arrange amino acids in the order required to produce a functioning cell. Soon enough, the chemicals of life—compounds of carbon, hydrogen, oxygen, nitrogen, sulfur and phosphorus—were detected outside the solar system. As the Nobel Prize-winning chemist Christian de Duve has put it, "The final demystification of organic chemistry has been achieved by the exploration of outer space."

Outer space had also been a key interest of another Nobelist, Harold C. Urey, who in 1951 wrote a book on how the solar system formed. After a career that included friendship with Einstein and the making of atomic bombs, Urey focused on the abundance of hydrogen in outer space. That abundance must also have been true for the early Earth, he believed. He further argued that the early oceans contained 10 percent organic materials, and that the Earth was not too hot—maybe 100 degrees Celsius—when life arose. It would take one of his graduate students, however, to turn his speculations into a classic experiment.

Teaching at the University of Chicago, Urey gave an October 1951 lecture on his early-Earth scenario of hydrogen, methane, ammonia and water. Conceivably, he said, a spark of energy might have turned this chemistry into life. He challenged any student to try the outlandish experiment, and newly arrived Stanley Miller took up the gauntlet. "So I went to him and said, 'I'd like to do those experiments,'" Miller has recalled. The professor worried that the uncertain project might derail a promising doctoral student with only limited time at his disposal, so they gave it six months. As it turned out, Miller obtained some preliminary results in a matter of weeks.

Afterward, Miller would call the amino acids he produced "the first laboratory synthesis of the organic compounds under primitive Earth conditions." For the experiment, he filled a sphere with methane, ammonia and hydrogen—Urey's supposed primitive Earth atmosphere—and then swirled them in hot water vapor and zapped them with electricity, as if with ancient lightning. As a result, a newly formed hydrogen cyanide and some aldehydes dissolved in the water along with the ammonia, and their reactions with each other produced an apparent miracle: amino acids.

That result was so astounding that it might not have been published except for Urey's good name. It was reported in *Science* a month before *Nature* published the Watson-Crick discovery of the double helix of DNA. Now, it seemed, both the origin and the structure of life had been established. The elegantly simple Miller-Urey experiment, diagrams of which proliferated on textbook pages and became routinely described in high school science classrooms, gave life to a new field of "abiogenesis," the chemical origin of life.

The original Miller experiment ended up producing slightly more than half of the twenty protein-producing amino acids of living organisms. Later, prebiotic laboratory experiments went further, producing nineteen of the twenty. All five nucleic acids in DNA and RNA and many of the sugars needed for life were also synthesized by similar experiments. Yet if the Miller experiment seemed to simplify the study of origins, others made it more complicated.

Between the amino acids and the living organism was a middle stage: the production of proteins, enzymes, membranes and memory molecules.

The proteins were believed to have been simple units, but then in 1958 proteins were found to be extremely complex chains folded into bizarrely irregular shapes. More clearly than ever, the first stage of amino acid production was only a small first step in developing a complete theory of abiogenesis.

Despite the difficulties the field faced as a science of past events and despite its solid grounding in chemistry, origins research received its share of knocks. A *Nature* editorial in 1967 revealed a "deep suspicion" of its speculative tendencies. "Some attempts to account for the origin of life on Earth, however ingenious, have shared much with imaginative literature and little with theoretical inference of the kind which can be confronted with observational evidence," the editorial said.

What is lacking in the abiogenesis field is fossils. But that is what the Australian meteorite finally provided in 1969. The fragment contained seventy-nine amino acids, some of them found in all proteins but others not found on Earth at all. When this was discovered in the NASA laboratory, the news caused a sensation among origin-of-life researchers. The meteorite, which was 12 percent water, also contained fatty acids, which are capable of forming a cell membrane. As Stanley Miller recalled years later, "They were the same kind of amino acids you get in prebiotic experiments like mine. This discovery made it plausible that similar processes could have happened on primitive Earth, on an asteroid, or for that matter, anywhere else the proper conditions exist."

Miller eventually went on to become a famous researcher in the chemistry department at the University of California at San Diego, a coastal home also for the Scripps Institute for Oceanography. The history of the institute was colorful. It had begun before the turn of the century in beachside tents. A permanent home came with the 1907 purchase of the land that became the city of La Jolla by Ellen Browning Scripps and her brother E. W. Scripps, both British expatriates. During the 1950s, Harold Urey had moved there. In the next decades, many of the leading origin-of-life researchers also migrated to the San Diego region, including the British chemist Leslie Orgel, who in 1965 joined the beachside Salk Institute for Biological Studies.

When NASA announced the findings from the meteorite, Miller was not the only one to take notice. At Scripps, a bright oceanography graduate student named Edward Peltzer also understood the significance of the rock. "This was the first chemical fossil that was found; the first to be recognized as legitimate and free of terrestrial contamination," Peltzer recalls. "But no one bothered to analyze the meteorite for hydroxy acids." In the Miller experiments the hydroxy acids were a byproduct of amino acid production; if the hydroxy acids on the Murchison rock were the same as in the Miller experiment, a link between possible prebiotic chemistry on Earth and in space would be established.

Peltzer's instructor at Scripps in the spring of 1973 was Jeffery L. Bada, a protégé of Miller's, and he knew of the hydroxy acid link. He challenged someone among the graduate students to check it out. "So I said, 'I'd like to give that a try,'" Peltzer explains. "Jeff was ready to go. But first I had my qualifying exams. And I was getting married." Peltzer was back in a month and work got under way.

Over the years, Miller's dynasty of graduate students had refined his 1952 experiment—the typical electric discharge experiment—to an art. They knew most of the kinetics, thermodynamics and chemical reactions. What was more, the reaction always traveled down the same "pathway" (sequence of chemical reactions), which was known as the Strecker-cyanohydrin synthesis, and the question was: Had the pathway operated in outer space? The only way to know was to find the reaction's byproducts, the hydroxy acids.

"It took me three years to develop the analytical method for finding the hydroxy acids in the meteorite," Peltzer says. "When I got one that seemed to work, Jeff said, 'Okay, Ed's ready.' So we went up to Stanley Miller's lab." They obtained some broth from his discharge experiments, and the Peltzer method worked with flying colors. Finally, Bada obtained a chip off the Murchison meteorite from a colleague at Scripps. Peltzer ground it up for the test. "At that point the Miller prediction was confirmed," he says. "The Strecker pathway was the source of the simple amino acids on the meteorite." An earthly link had been made with an amino acid reaction in space: "We could think about it as the possible pathway for reactions on the early Earth."

The finding was probably quite as important as the original discovery of the meteorite's amino acids, he argues. "It didn't get the same kind of fanfare in the popular press as the first NASA announcement. But scientifically, it was a big deal."

AT THE OUTSET OF THE ORIGINS RESEARCH, even Miller had assumed that the production of living matter was a result of chance. This seemed to be the law of Darwinian evolution, and it was formalized by the French Nobel chemist Jacques Monod when he argued that the origin of life was based on "chance and necessity," that is, randomness and law. "The universe was not pregnant with life," Monod said. Life arose by an accident that might not happen again.

The mathematicians who were skeptical of sweeping Darwinian claims had already argued that chance could not possibly have produced complex living organisms. At the famous Wistar Symposium in Philadelphia in 1966, this was the argument made by mathematicians Murray Eden of MIT and Marcel P. Schützenberger of the French Academy of Sciences. Two years later, the chemist Michael Polanyi wrote similarly in *Science* that if the DNA molecule were explained as random chemical bonds, "then such a DNA molecule would have no information content. Its code-like character would be effaced by an overwhelming redundancy."

Despite these mathematical challenges, Darwinian theorists believed that time was on their side: given enough time, random chemicals could fall into place. When Miller was making his experiments in 1952, the available time for such a process to occur had seemed almost infinite. In fact, in 1954 the Nobel Prize-winning biologist George Wald claimed that this factor had made life on Earth inevitable. During the fifties all the data pointed to an origin for cellular life of about 2.5 billion years ago—coinciding with the appearance of iron oxides in rock, algae fossils in southern Rhodesia and fossils in Canadian shale. Though the line between chemical and organic life was still arbitrarily defined, according to the journal *Evolution,* "complex chemical systems, such as algae and bacteria, apparently capable of photosynthesis, were present over two billion years ago." Wald subtracted that from an Earth age of 4.5 billion years and came up with a vast period available for life's appearance. "Given this much time," he said, "the 'impossible' becomes possible, the possible probable, and the probable virtually certain."

But that picture of boundless time began to change around 1967. In South Africa, carbonaceous rocks with cell-like fossils and signs of photosynthesis were dated to 3.1 billion years old. The window for the origin of life was further narrowed by signs of microorganisms found in Greenlandic rock, some dated to 3.8 billion years. In the new equation, once the molten Earth had cooled, life had no more than 170 million years to appear. "I always say it took between 15 minutes and 100 million years, but it's a relatively short time," says biophysicist Harold Morowitz.

At most centers of origin-of-life research, the reducing atmosphere proposed by Oparin and Urey had become a pillar of the theoretical work. As with the previously assumed generosity of time, it turned out that the reducing theories were also too generous. It is now believed that they overestimated the abundance of hydrogen, which produces quick reactions, easy energy and easy amino acids. Scientists must allow for a different kind of setting, an early Earth atmosphere that may have been "neutral"—composed mostly of nitrogen, carbon dioxide and water. A neutral atmosphere is lethargic: it absorbs energy and most easily produces ammonia, nitric acid and formaldehyde—not amino acids.

A third option also had to be conceded. In this scenario, deadly, life-decaying free oxygen had filled the primitive atmosphere. Oxygen may have been belched out by volcanoes or separated from water molecules. As the Oparin theory was losing ground in the 1970s, geologists who explored sedimentary layers openly doubted "that an oxygen-free atmosphere has existed at any time during this span of geological history." Given the equal odds for a reducing, neutral or oxygenated atmosphere, in 1984 one group of critics called the Oparin-Urey-Miller theory "the myth of the prebiotic soup."

With the odds narrowing, theories of chance plus time were being sidelined. "Since 1979, articles based on the premise that life arose through chance random reactions over billions of years are not accepted in reputable journals," said one report. Hence, researchers in abiogenesis began to speak of how life "seems inevitable," as Miller put it, or how it arises from "highly deterministic" processes, according to de Duve, who explained:

A single, freak, highly improbable event can conceivably happen. Many highly improbable events—drawing a winning lottery number or the distribution of playing cards in a hand of bridge—happen all the time. But a string of improbable events—the same lottery number being drawn twice, or the same bridge hand being dealt twice in a row—does not happen naturally. All of which leads me to conclude that life is an obligatory manifestation of matter, bound to arise where conditions are appropriate.

By the time de Duve made those remarks, he was a convert to the "RNA world," a theme first promulgated in 1986. Origins research had a classic chicken-or-egg puzzle. For life to exist, DNA, RNA and the proteins that structure life had to exist all at once. "By what series of chemical reactions did this interdependent system of nucleic acids and proteins come into being?" Leslie Orgel asked in a 1994 *Scientific American* article. Since they had to come together spontaneously in the same place at the same time, "one might have to conclude that life could never, in fact, have originated by chemical means."

One way out, scientists then argued, was to assume that RNA arose first. RNA is the active enzyme-like agent that copies and transmits information from the DNA code. It seemed to be the most versatile first player. Accordingly, Harvard chemist Walter Gilbert proposed the RNA world in 1986. "RNA molecules [were] a sufficient set of enzymes to carry out all the chemical reactions necessary for the first cellular structures," he argued. As Orgel explained, "If RNA invented protein synthesis . . . the main task of origin of life research then becomes explaining how the RNA world came into being." The RNA world would pretty much become the only game in town.

This search produced ideas about crystal-like fabricators of the first RNA. Or there might have been different kinds of pre-RNA as "alternative genetic material." Another idea was that chemical polymers built RNA backbones. A number of computer-assisted models were also generated and put forward as proposals. "Whether RNA arose spontaneously or replaced some earlier genetic system," Orgel said, it was "probably the watershed event" in life's evolution. Yet the evidence of *how* it was a watershed remained fragmentary at best. Orgel considered that the puzzle was unlikely to be cracked "in the near future."

Whatever the obstacles, de Duve said a decade after the RNA world was proposed that "today it is almost a matter of dogma that the evolution of life did include a phase where RNA was the predominant biological macro-molecule." He added, "Some form of abiotic chemistry must have existed before RNA ... protometabolism (which could have developed with time) was in charge until metabolism took over."

Not everyone in biochemistry was as optimistic as de Duve. One sci-entist who began optimistically was Dean Kenyon, who had worked in the laboratory of the Nobelist Melvin Calvin. In 1969, he co-authored a book that was the epitome of the "life is inevitable" school of thinking. Titled *Biochemical Predestination,* it theorized that chemicals where naturally attracted to each other in the DNA molecules. Their complex folded shapes charac-terized that mysterious attraction. Three decades later, however, Kenyon had rejected his determinist theory, and was now willing to accept that the ori-gin of life was so beyond law, chance or determinism that an intelligent force, namely a Creator, must have played a role.

The key flaw in origin-of-life research, Kenyon argued, was that the experiments were intelligent—unlike anything found on the primitive Earth. He cited one project that produced RNA in a test tube. The result prompted an adviser to ask bluntly whether the RNA would have "emerged sponta-neously without the gentle coaxing of a graduate student desiring a com-pleted dissertation." Another pair of research professors joked along similar lines: typical abiogenesis experiments "claim abiotic synthesis for what has in fact been produced and designed by a highly intelligent and very much biotic man."

Kenyon elaborated further in his 1995 essay, "Re-creating the RNA World." He explained, "In vitro RNA selection does not demonstrate that com-plex ribozymes could have arisen naturally in prebiotic soup, because the in vitro experimental conditions are wholly unrealistic." Such experiments are con-taminated by "intervening intelligence." What is more, Kenyon wrote, every-thing science knew about RNA was summed up in two rules: "According to those rules, RNA does not arise from its chemical constituents except (a) in organisms, and (b) in laboratories where intelligent organisms synthesize it."

NEVERTHELESS, THERE WAS THE GOOD NEWS of the Murchison meteorite, which had been subject to no investigator interference for four billion years and was living up to its reputation as the most-studied fossil ever. Every few years a new claim of prebiotic evidence was generated by a laboratory probing a Murchison sample. Despite setbacks in abiogenesis theory, the meteorite stood tall. "Although the primitive atmosphere is no longer believed to be as rich in hydrogen as once thought by Urey," de Duve explained, "the discovery that the Murchison meteorite contains the same amino acids obtained by Miller, and even in the same relative proportions, suggests strongly that his results are relevant."

Today, Peltzer looks back on that period of his Murchison meteorite research with mixed feelings. He relished the cutting-edge research and enjoyed the excitement of discovery. But he is nagged by doubts as well. "Whatever excitement we had quickly faded," he recalls of the March 1978 publication in *Nature* of finding the Strecker pathway, which produced amino acids, on the ancient meteorite. For a career in science, working with rare meteorite falls did not strike him as having much of a future. So he began his research career at the Woods Hole Oceanographic Institution in Massachusetts. He returned to California in 1997 to join the research team at the Monterey Bay Aquarium Research Institute (MBARI), which has three ships and two unmanned submersibles docked across the street from the main laboratory building. His primary project, working with Peter Brewer, has been to investigate how carbon dioxide, the main effluent of industrial machinery, might be dissolved in a deep sea setting without skewing the ocean's ecology.

Reared a Catholic in Baltimore, Peltzer has never felt a conflict of faith and science. ("As long as God is the first cause, the mechanism wasn't important," he says.) Despite years of studying under skeptical science faculty, Peltzer took an interest in the evangelical faith. He joined La Jolla's largest Presbyterian church. In New England he sampled Congregational, Episcopal and Baptist congregations. After moving to Monterey, he and his wife settled into a Mennonite Brethren congregation with an Anabaptist tradition.

Peltzer began to think about what the Murchison findings really meant. "Stanley Miller had said, 'Wait a minute. Maybe the Earth was bombarded with carbonaceous chondrites and this is what brought the amino acids here,' [based on the premise that] the meteorite was a window back to the early solar system." Peltzer knew that half of good science is asking the right questions, and that the questions asked heavily color the results. He wondered why the meteorite was important at all. "I asked myself, 'Why is a meteorite that is 4.5 billion years old, with processes that went on for perhaps millions, if not billions, of years, so similar to an experiment that a graduate student can do over a weekend?' Something else is happening here and we are missing it." He began to see that the main attraction of the Strecker pathway was another byproduct; perhaps in both cases, the amino acids were a sideshow.

> Sure, in Miller's experiment we make that first step. But in the meteorite, there's so much more time there. Shouldn't there be some evidence of going the second step, or the third step? And it suddenly hit me. Why should the two look anything alike at all? The Miller experiment was stopped after a week or ten days. Nobody stopped the meteorite. It had ample opportunity to go much further. Yet the two are virtually the same.

The real Murchison story, dull as it might be, was not the amino acids but another entity in the space rock: a complex mixture of organic molecules called melanoids. They are red-black and their formation stops amino acid accumulation in its tracks. Melanoids are formed by the Maillard reaction, a condensation reaction of amino acids with sugars. "It suddenly hit me," Peltzer says. "In the Miller experiment the melanoids were immature, red and oily. In the meteorite they were much more mature, black and tarry, far more condensed." Indeed, Miller's prebiotic soup came out pink. "There was lots of red goo in the flask. While this experiment was hailed as the key to the formation of life, its major products were oils and tars, not amino acids."

Peltzer went back and read Miller and Orgel's book on their research. They identified the melanoid problem, but they minimized it by positing a cool Earth. "They know that if it's a hot early Earth the melanoid reaction is going to consume everything, and you've got nothing but black tar." Sugars react quickly with amino acids. "It's a competing reaction," Peltzer explains. For the origin of life, sugars are as big a problem as oxygen.

Peltzer has also doubted the relevance of some of the early origins research. Sidney Fox, for example, began with a neutral atmosphere hypothesis. Then he added a heat element to simulate "the flow of volcanic gasses through fissures or 'pipes' of hot igneous rocks of lava." This "thermal synthesis" approach was announced as promising in the 1960s. But again Peltzer asks the question: how does that get around the sugars? Fox got around it by boiling pure amino acids in a sugar-free environment. "That's cheating," says Peltzer. And it proves the point that Kenyon also made: that laboratory experiments are difficult, if not impossible, to do in a relevant fashion.

Still, Peltzer gives credit to Miller: "He used fundamental compounds that you can find throughout the universe." He added energy and stood back. "It was an elegant and simple test of the first step in that molecules-to-man scenario. To go beyond that, they have to start contriving things"— refinements such as concentrating the amino acids or finding ways to avoid the melanoid counterreaction. "It becomes an exercise in getting things just right, just so," he says. And that is not how nature works.

PERHAPS IT WAS ALIEN INTELLIGENCE that made it work so well. This was a serious proposal made by Orgel and Francis Crick of DNA fame in their 1973 paper, "Directed Panspermia." This paper revived speculation about life drifting onto Earth from outer space but questioned the old-fashioned "nineteenth-century mechanisms" of transport in favor of something far more effective: spaceships. It said that "organisms were deliberately trans-mitted to the earth by intelligent beings on another planet."

The idea was not so new. Oparin in 1957 had spoken of such an "infec-tion" from space; Fred Hoyle had written books about the idea;* and astro-physicist Thomas Gold speculated in 1960 that life could have originated from the garbage left behind by space aliens. These musings had even ear-lier origins. In 1908, the Swedish scientist S. Arrhenius proposed that spores were flushed into the solar system by the light force of a different star, and Lord Kelvin looked to meteorites as the bearers of the first life. "Neither of these theories is absurd, but both can be subjected to severe criticism," Crick and Orgel wrote.

---

*Among Hoyle's books on the subject is *Astronomical Origins of Life: Steps towards Panspermia*, with co-author N. C. Wickramasinghe.

The principal objection is that cosmic radiation would have destroyed so delicate an organism. That a meteorite could escape from the gravity of another solar system seems equally unlikely. Furthermore, turning to outer space, it has been said, just locates the abiogenesis problem elsewhere—and puts it beyond science. Nevertheless, said Crick and Orgel, "For all we know there may be other types of planets on which the origin of life *ab initio* is greatly more probable than on our own." Advances in technology "will permit location of extrasolar planets within the next few decades."

At one time, de Duve saw despair in all this star gazing, but now he believes it has calmed. Science has rallied around a necessary assumption—that life "must have arisen fairly quickly, more in a matter of millennia or centuries, perhaps even less."

NASA HAS JUST OPENED THE ASTROBIOLOGY INSTITUTE to promote research on the origins of life. The new target is the "extremophiles," microbes that have been found alive in deep rock shafts, frozen in arctic caves, and by volcanic vents on the deep ocean floor. A few decades earlier—a time when the biophysicist Harold Morowitz served, alongside the likes of Carl Sagan, on NASA's planetary biology subcommittee—the focus had been on the big targets: Mars, Mercury, Venus.

Says Morowitz, "I have no doubt that there's life out there." But he is not sure that researchers have to look that far, given his own theory about abiogenesis. Morowitz says he has never been a member of a school of thought in the origins debate. "I was never part of the Miller group, the La Jolla gang. My ideas have always been somewhat idiosyncratic, out of the mainstream." But he happens to think they are the most fruitful for research.

"If I had to make a prediction, I'd think we'll find the origin of life in the citric acid cycle, the Krebs cycle." This is the cascade of molecular reactions in a cell that produces the energy molecule ATP (adenosine triphosphate). Because the early arrival of DNA or RNA is so improbable, says Morowitz, he posits that a living cellular entity arose first, informed by a primitive citric (also called Krebs) cycle that now pervades biological organisms. The DNA came along later. As Morowitz has cleverly phrased it, "metabolism recapitulates biogenesis." In other words, the metabolic cycle is the clue to the origin of life.

Over decades of research and teaching, Morowitz has built his reputation as a cutting-edge biophysicist, theoretically taking apart cells and microorganisms, molecule by molecule, long before the Human Genome Project cataloged the codes on the human DNA molecule. He has been called a pioneer of genomics, and his physics made him a "hard-nosed reductionist." A year before Miller's experiment, Morowitz received his doctorate. His first work was on how ultraviolet radiation affects bacterial spores. Viewing life as a biophysical machine, "we were trying to think of a quantum mechanical solution to the entire cell, or some hubris like that," he says.

He once had focused on space origins, but Morowitz had never settled in with the abiotic soup, DNA or RNA approaches. Instead, he went with his theory of metabolism. In 1951, he tried to determine the "information content" of a bacterial cell, and continued the pursuit at Yale in 1955:

> I was trying to learn enough about the cellular chemistry so one could model a bacterial cell. And then in the early 1960s I decided that the way to approach this was to find the smallest living cell and see how simple a cellular system could get. That began fifteen years of work on mycoplasma [the smallest living cells]. We were looking at the number of atoms in the cell, then we got to the amount of DNA in the cell, and the amount of information, and how many proteins it could encode, and so forth and so on.

This work opened a new field called information theory in biology. The goal was to assess the number of bits of information encoding the proteins, a problem that could be handled in the age of computers. Morowitz took both a piecemeal and a holistic view of his organisms, and in 1968 published on the question of whether life could have evolved by chance. His book *Energy Flow in Biology* recounted how he conceptually took apart the simplest single-cell bacterium to determine how long reassembling it would take in a state of equilibrium, a state where energy is equal to entropy, or disorder. The odds that it would reassemble were one in $10^{100,000,000,000}$ (or 10 followed by 100 billion zeroes). "It is always possible to argue that any unique event would have occurred," Morowitz wrote, but "this is outside the range of probabilistic considerations, and really, outside of science." With these odds, five billion years was totally inadequate, and he asserted "the impossibility of life originating as a fluctuation in an equilibrium process."

Morowitz might as well have said that life was a numerical "miracle," and creationists in the United State liked his numbers most, since they appeared to support the necessity for God to have created the first life. But Morowitz said the creationists did not get his main point: it was impossible at a state of equilibrium but doubtless had happened at disequilibrium, a state when the energy input, or "negentropy," dominated the system or environment. In his famous book *What Is Life?* the renowned physicist Erwin Schrödinger coined the term negentropy, describing it as the force or energy that halts the decay of entropy. Morowitz, like scores of other origin-of-life researchers, took note of and inspiration from Schrödinger, and then went further. For cellular life to develop, he realized, it needs new information. "Work is required to get information," Morowitz wrote, and that meant disequilibrium, or a movement of energy.

He doubts that the necessary conditions could have been possible in Miller's abiotic soup model, though he credits the experiment with showing that organic compounds can precipitate from a random world of chemicals. "In the end, it involves a free radical chemistry, and I don't think we can go down that pathway toward living cells," Morowitz says. "But I thought it was interesting."

Morowitz also questions the probability of an RNA world coming out of nowhere. "What the RNA people do is require that there be a world full of RNA, and for that to happen without living cells, I just think is so massively improbable," he says.

The new systems of thought he was encountering moved him away from a mechanistic approach, away from what he calls "naive realism"—the wish to measure everything at face value. His books on biological dynamics—*Entropy for Biologists* and *Foundations of Bioenergetics*—moved him into the fields becoming known as chaos, complexity and emergence theories. In time, Morowitz began calling himself a "mystical scientist." He sat on the board of the cutting-edge Santa Fe Institute, which had opened in New Mexico to use mathematics and computers in an effort to understand complex biology and physics. And he became editor of the journal *Complexity.* "Science has changed at a deeply epistemological level," Morowitz explains. "It changed because of computer science, and complexity theory and emergence."

Whereas once Morowitz had hoped simply to add up all the parts of an organism, he now conceded the "combinatorily explosive" nature of life. In the new complexity, organisms are viewed as following gamelike rules, expanding what wins and pruning away what is not used. "'Pruning rules' and 'design' mean the same thing," Morowitz says, suggesting that this is design without a Designer. "Novelty is there. You don't know what's going to come out. The emergent properties are novel. And that makes science different than it was before."

As part of his Krebs cycle theory—holding that a chemical energy cycle arose before the advent of DNA—Morowitz needed a source of energy to counteract entropy, and that is why he favors the deep sea vents. In an address on the origins of life to a gathering of U.S. Catholic bishops, he used metaphors:

> The energy for life fell from heaven or bubbled up from hell. I am embarrassed to admit in this company that I have switched from being a "heaven" theorist to be a "hell" theorist. The great bulk of energy driving nature's cycle today comes from the sun; heaven has won out. But I'm still betting on hell as the source of energy for the origin of life when the Earth was young.

The vents from hell became a new area of research in the early 1990s. There was pressure, heat and conditions conducive to rapid reactions. "The thermal gradient is very steep. You go from 4 degrees up to 600 degrees, down where the lava hits the water," he explained. Organisms cannot survive directly in the heat. "But chemicals may bubble up from that vent that might be the right set of chemicals for the origin." He told the bishops:

> It appears from certain experiments now in process that the proper sorts of molecules could have been formed with relative ease in deep rift zones of the ocean floor. At 500 atmospheres of pressure and 500 degrees centigrade of temperature, reactions occur that seem to have produced the principal molecules that stand at the base of the metabolic chart.

Critics of abiogenesis still wonder how energy could have sparked the first nascent life, when the odds seem high that in so fragile a state it would have been destroyed.

Though reared in a Jewish family, one day at New York's Grand Central Station in the 1960s, Morowitz picked up a copy of a new book, *The Phenomenon of Man,* by the French paleontologist and Jesuit priest Pierre Teilhard de Chardin. "That was a turning point," he recalls. Teilhard wrote about two levels of energy, which Morowitz takes as the dual aspects of nature: its deterministic chemical laws on the one hand and its emergent, higher-level properties on the other. "What he was saying for the first two-thirds of the book made a lot of sense."

He says that Teilhard foreshadowed Schrödinger's "negentropy," the anti-entropy force that empowers life. Biologists rarely had a good grasp of these laws of thermodynamics; but in his poetic way, Teilhard did understand them. All this added up to a strong developing intuition about emergence as complementary to reductionism, which analyzes nature down to smaller and smaller pieces. Emergence shows how nature moves to higher levels by selecting out what works and pruning away what does not.

"When we begin to understand the selection rules in emergence, then we are going to have a better understanding of how novelty comes about in the world," Morowitz says. "And this is going to, I think, open dialogues between science and religion, among other things." His 1987 book, *Cosmic Joy and Local Pain,* was subtitled *Musings of a Mystic Scientist.* Once, when Morowitz was asked specifically about his beliefs, he opted for a system to which many scientists turn when, averse to the idea of a personal God, they still seek meaning or design in the universe. "And that was a moment of truth," Morowitz recalls. "So I said, 'Well, I'm a pantheist in the tradition of Spinoza.'" Or at least that was the closest to a formal system he felt able to commit to.

"I do think of the universe and the divine as being somehow the same or overlapping," he said from his offices at the Krasnow Institute for Advanced Studies, in a Virginia suburb of Washington, D.C. "Emergence goes from universe, to life to consciousness. I tell my religious friends, 'Well, that's how the word becomes flesh.'" His latest book, *Emergence of Everything,* ends with, "In the words of the Talmudist, 'It's not up to you to finish the task. Neither are you free to cease from trying.'"

Comfortable with encounters between science and religion, Morowitz says that in his science he must take a deterministic origin-of-life stance just like de Duve, because it is required "if we wish to undertake a *scientific* study of the origin of life." Where most biologists just see chance, however, he looks for the phenomenon of emergence. On occasion, he has recognized the relationship between emergence and design.

For Edward Peltzer, the biochemist and Christian believer, design takes on a different meaning. The limits of science and origins research leave open the possibility of God's intervention. If Morowitz began a stage of his spiritual journey in science by reading Teilhard de Chardin, Peltzer's deepened when he began to give talks on science in the Santa Cruz area, not far from the sandy coastline where the Monterey Bay Aquarium Research Institute's research vessel lies anchored. He says people don't ask *how* nature works, but *why* it is there. The answer to the latter requires faith, and science doesn't go there.

Peltzer's public talks on the origins of life describe how the research field bristles with varied approaches. Some start from the first elements and build up, others from cells and then work backward, as in reverse engineering. Some see life emerging slowly on a relatively cold earth; for others, heat is the catalyst. But the fact remains, says Peltzer, that no prebiotic organic fossils remain. With no concrete evidence to work on, science has no way to constrain its imagination, and it can easily make detours into fantasy. In such a situation, he says that it is best to make a choice: "When it comes to the origin of life on Earth, there are only two possibilities: one is that life was purposely created, the other that it arose naturally."

As biochemists like Peltzer increasingly find life more complex and irreducible than they ever imagined, "the idea that it was purposely designed is becoming ever more apparent."

7

THE MOVEMENT

Convictions about design in nature are old and hard to eradicate, and criticisms of Darwinism have been rampant since the publication of *On the Origin of Species* in 1859. The Darwinists more than held their own. But by the 1970s, a new cultural and scientific climate gave rise to a freshly conceived attack on materialist evolution; it was called the intelligent design movement.

Its ancient antecedents notwithstanding, the movement gained a contemporary flair and intellectual sophistication. It built upon how Michael Polanyi's seminal work in the 1950s questioned reductionism in biology; how mathematicians such as Marcel Schützenberger in the following decade asserted that it is impossible for chance, even with the aid of natural selection, to produce complex novelty in biological systems; and how the distinguished French zoologist Pierre Grassé launched his "frontal assault" on the efficacy of natural selection. In the next decade, the British biochemist Michael Denton, an accomplished writer, brought the hitherto little-appreciated problems of molecular evolution in Darwinian theory to a wide audience.

If this critique constitutes one wing of the new anti-Darwinism, a second contributes the movement's most notable feature: the idea, held by some of its most active proponents, that design (not ignoring its theological implications) can be rationally and scientifically argued as an alternative to Darwinism. It is for the most part a negative argument: random chance cannot explain a world such as ours.

While that was design's ancient proposition, the new argument comes richly illustrated with science's latest findings, which are revealing nature's incredibly complex but effective arrangements in unprecedented detail. With an emboldened political will and armed with an array of academic degrees, the design protagonists took two decades to climb into public prominence. In April 2001, they made the front page of the Sunday *New York Times* under the headline "Darwin vs. Design."

The design revival was largely shaped by Christian intellectuals in science. One of them was Charles Thaxton, a native of Texas, who began his adventure around 1970 on a flight to Switzerland. Thaxton had just finished his doctorate in chemistry at the University of Iowa. His destination was the picturesque town of L'Abri, where the Protestant thinker Francis Schaeffer, who was advocating a Reformed (that is, modern Calvinist) "worldview," had set up an intellectual community of evangelicals.

By worldview, Schaeffer meant that every sector of life, including the arts, politics and science, came under God's sovereignty, so God-thinking people had to master the various secular disciplines and get involved in the cultural debate. Before Schaeffer, chroniclers have said, the more conservative Protestant traditions had preferred to withdraw from the world, to be separatist and uninvolved. In contrast, many who left L'Abri were eager for the fray.

On his trip over, Thaxton had picked up a hot new book on biochemistry, *Biochemical Predestination,* by San Francisco State University biologists Dean Kenyon and Gary Steinman. The authors theorized that the earliest chemicals on earth had congealed into the first DNA and hence to the first replicating cell. Thaxton was taken by the scientists' statement that "implicit in this assumption is the requirement that no supernatural agency 'entered nature' at the time of origin, was crucial to it, and then withdrew from history." Thaxton was already a Christian believer, so he was skeptical that life could arise without God. But he read the Kenyon-Steinman book with enthusiasm because of its scientific quality.

One evening in Switzerland, Schaeffer asked Thaxton to give a talk on his specialty. Citing the Kenyon-Steinman theory of chemical predestination he was studying, Thaxton argued that the theory still made the speculative assumption that mindless chemicals could organize the biological information that produces, for example, the human brain. His listeners at L'Abri were enthusiastic; an encouraged Thaxton wondered whether he should pursue further research on the science/religion topic. Not yet contemplating a design argument per se, he considered a worldview approach: the reconciling of Christianity with modern science. He decided to renew his studies by going to Harvard for a postdoc in the history of science.

At Harvard, he met the visiting professor Reijer Hooykaas, a Dutch science historian in the Russian Academy and Dutch Royal Society, who was soon to deliver the Gifford Lectures, the world-famous lecture series on natural theology held regularly in Scotland. Hooykaas was an eminent researcher, a master of original sources, and a Christian who, while holed up during the Nazi occupation of Holland, had studied the deism and the methods of Enlightenment scientists. He is best known for a history of the Christian roots of science, in which he took the position that Puritan thinkers isolated divinity from nature, which freed them to analyze nature's parts and processes.

But when Thaxton met Hooykaas, it was the Dutchman's 1970 book on the history of geology that was gaining attention. Hooykaas showed that despite an idealized uniformitarianism in geology—the doctrine that "the present is key to the past"—uniform laws had nevertheless produced a record of repeated geological catastrophes. A meticulous scientist, Hooykaas had not lost interest in the question of how or whether God actually intervenes in the regularities of natural law. "He operated within the standard framework of geology and brought criticism to it," Thaxton recalls. "One of the things I learned from him was that, if you want your scientific arguments to penetrate the market, you'd jolly well better do your research up front. So I began to speculate or contemplate on the origins question." And he did research, both at Harvard and later at the biochemistry laboratory at Brandeis University, where he completed yet another postdoctoral stint.

Besides the laboratory work, Thaxton built on the ideas of the world-class chemist Michael Polanyi. He had read Polanyi's "Life Transcending Physics and Chemistry" around 1967, when it was first published, and was taken by the Polanyi metaphor that the information in DNA could no more be reduced to the chemicals than could the ideas in a book be reduced to the ink and paper: something beyond physics and chemistry encoded DNA. The Polanyi piece, says Thaxton, "was one of a half-dozen articles that shaped my whole thinking."

On Thaxton's return to Texas, he worked on a publication for Probe Ministries, started in 1972 by Jon Buell, another Texan. Buell had published some of the most intellectually accomplished essays in natural science by conservative Christians. Now he asked Thaxton, Walter Bradley of Texas A&M University and industry researcher Roger Olsen to collaborate on a booklet on the origin of life. The project took seven years to complete.

A parallel approach was being taken by a student group at the University of California at Santa Barbara. Beginning in the mid-1970s as a creationist fellowship, in 1977 it became Students for Origins Research (SOR). "As we watched the origins debate play out on the university campus, we wanted to make this a science versus science discussion, not a science versus Bible discussion," says founder Dennis Wagner. When they organized SOR, it was "a little tongue-in-cheek," according to Wagner. After all, at that time the best-known student organization in the country was the bomb-throwing Students for a Democratic Society.

The SOR students began to produce a newspaper that became known for its reliable documentation of current developments in the origins debate. They built the first computer database of relevant articles. In 1991, after the Internet revolution had begun, the organization morphed into Access Research Network, the preeminent information vehicle for challenges to naturalism and for work on design theories.

Meanwhile, Thaxton was probing the scientific minutia of origins research. "I went to origin-of-life conferences, talked to many of the principals," he says. "I mentioned a lot of the criticism we were going to use in the book [he was writing with Bradley and Olsen]. Almost everybody acknowledged, 'Oh, yes, those are big problems.'" What struck Thaxton most, however, was that apparently no one in the science community dared raise the question of information. Much as a written page suggests an author, complex chemical information in DNA suggests the work of a mind—a key argument that was to be developed in the intelligent design movement. Leslie Orgel had mentioned the information puzzle in a footnote and used the term *specified complexity* to explain why the DNA codes were so different from redundant crystal structures. Says Thaxton: "Orgel was trying to define or describe what he meant by these 'informational molecules.' He didn't put it in the text, but in a footnote. That was the first use of the term 'specified complexity.' It never went anywhere with him. But it fit exactly what we needed."

Nobody talked about DNA as "information" because it smacked of intention, not of chance and law. "If you are a materialist, well, by definition there can't be any other source of the 'information' besides material processes," Thaxton says. "That prevented people from recognizing the significance of the information question." So he studied the topic and made it a central issue in his overview book *The Mystery of Life's Origin,* co-authored with Bradley and Olsen and published in 1984 by the Philosophical Library. Carefully researched and skeptical, the book was unique in laying out all the current origin-of-life theories and how they fell short. Dean Kenyon, the author of the equally seminal *Biochemical Predestination,* wrote the foreword, and the book opened a new debate.

The Mystery of Life's Origin offered the opening shot of a design proposal for the origin of material life. "We wanted the epilogue to include the thought of intelligent causation, a concrete alternative," Thaxton says. "And the book laid the groundwork for that idea." *Mystery* also spoke plainly about the tainting of origins research: human control of the procedures "accounted for the successful experiments." This was not fraud; it was the unavoidable result of intelligent bias in the effort to replicate the nonintelligent origins of life. The irony is palpable: though no superintelligent intervention is allowed in explaining life, scientists possessed of intellect—and with intellectual commitments—regularly intervene in their own experiments.

Thaxton would popularize the argument that what was at issue in the origins debate was not a "supernatural" force, which smacked of religion and gave scientists veto power over the idea. The issue, Thaxton believed, was intelligent intervention in nature, because the results should look different if intelligence is at work as opposed to when law and chance exclusively rule the material world.

One of the young scientists attracted by the ideas in *Mystery* was Stephen Meyer, a geophysicist working for Atlantic Richfield in Texas. The year of *Mystery,* Thaxton helped organize a Dallas conference on atheism and theism in modern universities. The British atheist Anthony Flew spoke, and Kenyon addressed the origin-of-life topic as "Going Beyond the Naturalistic Mindset." Meyer met them both and talked with Thaxton, and his

imagination was stirred. The next fall, Meyer secured a scholarship to go to
Cambridge University for a doctorate in the history and philosophy of science, focusing on the idea of how life originated.

While Meyer was getting his start, Kenyon was heading into one of
the era's most celebrated battles over academic freedom and evolution. A
tenured professor at San Francisco State University in the early 1980s, Kenyon
faced hearings and was stripped of the right to teach biology courses because
he criticized some aspects of neo-Darwinian theory. "The first people who
break from a dominant research program are always ostracized," Meyer
observes. "But they provide inspiration for younger people. That's where
the future lies. It's very much like a political campaign." Rather than be
daunted by what had happened, Meyer enthusiastically distributed *Mystery.*
Thaxton calls him the "Johnny Appleseed" of the intelligent design movement.

In addition to the ferment taking place around Thaxton, Kenyon and
Mystery, there was an unexpected boost from Australia. There, the British
biochemist Michael Denton, who worked in a laboratory and taught at a
university, published *Evolution: A Theory in Crisis.* Denton's mastery of biochemistry, molecular biology and anatomy allowed him to make the most
effective case against neo-Darwinism since French zoologist Grassé's work
in 1973. Denton criticized the central tenet of Darwinism: that random
genetic changes are capable of producing complex organisms. Though a
kind of evolutionist himself, Denton said that genes did not show clear transitions from one phylum to another and that the simplistic comparisons of
bone shapes and arguments about the tree of life did not match the evidence—and the experts knew it, even if it was not popularly advertised. The
"crisis" was that they could find no scientifically acceptable alternative: "After
a century of intensive effort biologists have failed to validate [Darwinian
theory] in any significant sense." When Thaxton organized a conference of
Darwin-doubters and others in the science/religion debate in Tacoma, Washington, in 1988, the topic was "Sources of Information Content in DNA"—
and Denton was there.

In this growing movement, thinkers such as Denton had no use for
the word *design,* and others eschewed it for its historical religious baggage.
Thaxton came to terms with the design terminology in December 1988,
when he gave a lecture to a class at Princeton University. In his overhead

visuals, he included a news article with a photo that the Viking I spacecraft had taken of a sphinx-like face on Mars; a scientist was quoted as saying that the Mars formation suggested "intelligent design," not just a random Martian surface. The phrase went over well with the class, and Thaxton decided it worked well for him too. He seized upon it in the nick of time.

Jon Buell, who had commissioned *Mystery,* was just about to publish a supplementary textbook for high school biology teachers on the origins and evolution debate. On a tight deadline, the book had to settle on a term for the alternative theory to evolution. When *Of Pandas and People: The Central Question of Biological Origins* was published in 1989 (with Kenyon as an author, Meyer a contributor and Thaxton the academic editor) it espoused the concept of intelligent design, which its glossary defined as:

> Any theory that attributes an action, function, or the structure of an object to the creative mental capacities of a personal agent. In biology, the theory that biological organisms owe their origin to a preexisting intelligence.

While the book's critical analysis of Darwinian evolution was fairly standard, it all came in an accessible classroom idiom. Attacking the book became a pastime for evolutionists in public education and the American Civil Liberties Union. Still and all, it sold in the tens of thousands to school boards and individual teachers.

Soon after that project, Thaxton traveled to Eastern Europe and received an appointment to teach biochemistry at Charles University in Prague. He began making the international trek from his home near Atlanta in 1993, to teach a course in Prague twice a year.

IN DECEMBER OF 1993, the new rumblings of the origins debate and Dean Kenyon's academic dispute over Darwinism were noticed in Seattle. One Monday morning, Bruce Chapman sat in the Discovery Institute, a think tank he had co-founded a few years earlier, flipping through the day's *Wall Street Journal.* The headline, "A Scopes Trial for the '90s," caught his attention. It was an opinion piece by Stephen Meyer on Kenyon, whose academic freedom battle at San Francisco State University had flared into a full faculty senate vote (which Kenyon would go on to win). "Mr. Kenyon knows perhaps as much as anyone in the world about a problem that has stymied an entire generation of research scientists," Meyer wrote in the *Journal*. "Yet he now finds that he may not report the negative results of research or give students his candid assessment of it."

After returning from England, Meyer became a professor of philosophy at Whitworth College in Spokane. Chapman noticed the proximity: over the mountains, in the eastern part of the state. Discovery staff member John G. West Jr., soon to be a political science professor at Seattle Pacific University, remembers the day Meyer appeared on their radar screen: "Bruce said, 'Save the article and give this guy a call.'"

From its founding, the Discovery Institute was interested in regional and national public policy. It would pursue topics such as the political vocation, regional transportation, the future of technology, religion and civic life, and reform of the military. It leaned libertarian, was technologically optimistic, and described itself as a secular institute interested in natural law theory and supportive of the Judeo-Christian moral tradition. It had one other defining characteristic: "We've been pro-science from the beginning," Bruce Chapman says.

After graduating from Harvard in 1962, Chapman had headed for Washington, D.C., pursuing the career of a political writer and idea man. Catching the Potomac fever along with him was one of his good Harvard friends, George Gilder. In Washington they formed a short-lived progressive Republican journal called *Advance: A Journal of Political Thought*. "That was a wonderful, interesting period," Chapman recalls. They worked together on racial desegregation policy and Chapman took a particular interest in a volunteer military service. He later went to Manhattan to write editorials for the *New York Herald Tribune*. Then he moved to Seattle. In 1971 he was elected to the city council and four years later appointed, and then elected, secretary of state, a post he held until 1981, the year he made an unsuccessful bid for governor.

Chapman was a longstanding Republican moderate, but the charisma and ideas of the GOP candidate in the 1980 presidential race confirmed his own move to the right. "To my amazement, I found myself cheering Ronald Reagan's campaign," he says. As secretary of state, Chapman had been the state's ex officio statistician. During his time in office, he wrote a booklet comparing state statistics. The new Republican administration took note, and Chapman was tapped to head the Census Bureau from 1981 to 1983. He learned a lot about the science of statistics, especially in a political pressure cooker like Washington, D.C. Statistics was indeed a science, falling, for example, under the advisory purview of the National Academy of Sciences. And science, Chapman found out, was easily twisted for one political end or another. He left the capital with a healthy skepticism about the "pretense of science."

By the time he returned to Seattle in 1990, after an appointment as ambassador to the United Nations in Vienna, Chapman hankered to fulfill a college-days dream of opening a think tank. He began by establishing a Northwest branch of the Hudson Institute, a conservative think tank based in Indianapolis. But its Midwest roots (and its reach to Washington, D.C.) did not fit the Pacific mood and environs, so he and his old friend George Gilder and a couple of others broke off and started the Discovery Institute. By then, Gilder had been a best-selling author for a decade on topics ranging from economics and marriage to the new technologies. It was his 1989 book, *Microcosm,* in fact, that took the two pragmatic Republican friends across a secular divide toward a more spiritual awareness of science.

In *Microcosm,* Gilder argued that microtechnology had revolutionized economics, politics and even the spiritual outlook of modern man. In an age of quantum physics, Gilder spoke of the "materialist superstition" that was a hangover from an older scientific milieu. His closing chapter was called "The Death of Materialism." It was a theme the Institute would build upon in a series of lectures, to include forums on topics such as C. S. Lewis's writings on moral sensibility in human nature.

In its new environment, Discovery decided to support the first platform of the intelligent design movement, which emphasized criticism of orthodox Darwinism. "The foremost thing is to demolish the Darwinist superstition," says Chapman. "All our people can get along on that. What they don't agree on are the alternatives, such as the theory of design." The essence of the Darwin critique was to analyze the weaknesses in its scientific logic, challenge its evidence in sectors such as the fossil record, and show in technical studies (using math and biochemistry in particular) the improbability of random evolution producing seemingly designed natural objects.

Whether an organ like the human eye was "truly" designed (by an intelligent agent) or just "apparently" designed by a force yet unknown was a robust debate within this anti-Darwinian movement.

During the first years of Discovery, however, Chapman was chiefly occupied with the decline of politics as an honorable vocation. "We exalt democracy but disparage its practitioners," a perplexed Chapman says. He and John West, a political scientist with a doctorate from Claremont Graduate University in Southern California, mulled some of the root causes. Chapman's thinking took him back to the early twentieth century, when politicians became enamored of "scientific governance." Modern governance, with its excessive use of science, regulation, expertise and ethics enforced by laws, was a revival of the methods of the ancient Greek Sophists, who used artful, sometimes devious rhetoric to win excruciating arguments.

> They want to quantify the governance of a polity. Aristotle warned against trying to exert more exactitude in governance than a subject allows. Governing is an art. And you don't use a law to try to make people virtuous after they hold authority. The question is how to find virtuous leaders to start with.

From the day Discovery opened for business, it was skeptical of all kinds of utopianism, including scientific utopianism. Chapman takes the view that "since science became fashionable, people sometimes make claims with it that aren't true." The goal was to support science, but also to ask science advocates and philosophers to take a more modest role in society. "At Discovery, we say that the deposit of Western thought and morality is guidance for our future." Based on a culture of belief and virtue, science is a greatly helpful product. "Now, some people are trying to say that science is not only a product but that it will dictate back to the culture what culture must be. That has an air of tyranny about it."

That was why Chapman took note of Stephen Meyer's article in the *Wall Street Journal* in the first place: it had to do with free speech, or dissent in the face of science. Each summer, Discovery brought in university students as fellows, and Meyer was asked to give a talk on freedom of speech. John West recalls how Meyer went quickly from the Kenyon case into an argument about DNA. By then, he had his argument down pat for popular consumption, and it built upon Thaxton and Kenyon: the information in the chemical codes on the DNA molecule that produced proteins (and thus all biological life) was too complex to have arisen purely by chance or law, but rather reflected something akin to intelligence. Recalls West, "It was a case for design from DNA and the argument from information. Where does information come from?"

West had studied the role of social science in government and modern policy-making. He knew the general debate about free will and responsibility, the issues of crime and punishment, and how these played out amid the arguments for the influence of environment versus the influence of genes. But now, the perspective on the DNA problem that Stephen Meyer so ably elucidated seemed to open a new policy angle: "For years we had seen how scientific materialism had demanded all these cultural changes, and now here was an argument about how outdated, how bad, some of that science was." The determinism of science had shaped public life by dismissing ideas of free will and the efficacy of belief. "So we fused all this together. There was an issue of academic freedom. And there was a social policy connection to what Meyer was saying about DNA." That put it on Discovery's agenda.

After that summer's talk, West drove Meyer to the airport when he was going to Cambridge for a conference on much the same issues. Meyer explained that the biggest obstacle for design-oriented graduate students was an absence of research grants. As dissenters, they lacked bona fide affiliations and publishing outlets. The idea resonated with Chapman when West told him about the conversation. A few years later, in August of 1996, Discovery opened what would become its largest single project, the Center for the Renewal of Science and Culture. Its mandate was to "provide a rigorous critique of scientific and philosophical materialism and [promote] a broadly theistic understanding of the origin of the natural world and the nature of human consciousness," and Meyer was appointed its director.

Meyer also had the most experience in making grant requests, and what he brought in, working with West, underwrote the first year of operation. They relied mostly on two underwriters of conservative intellectual causes, a funding institute of Howard F. Ahmanson Jr. and his wife, Roberta, and the Stewardship Foundation, created by C. Davis Weyerhaeuser, an heir to the wood products company. Weyerhaeuser was interested in the science/religion debate and he had taken a liking to Meyer's chutzpa. Thanks to annual grants ranging from $750,000 to $1 million raised from Ahmanson, Weyerhaeuser and others, the Discovery Institute's Center for the Renewal of Science and Culture attracted forty research fellows (agnostics, Jews and Christians) in its first few years. Many of them, like Kenyon, had attached to the center while holding teaching posts at universities. They all worked on scientific challenges to orthodox Darwinism, and some looked for design alternatives.

Bruce Chapman is reluctant to take any credit for these developments, pointing instead to Meyer and West. And all three acknowledge a new player on the Darwinian scene: Berkeley law professor Phillip E. Johnson, whom Meyer had met in England in 1988 and whose book *Darwin on Trial* appeared three years later. "Phil Johnson was a crucial catalyst in all this," Meyer says about the man who is credited with transforming the technical debate over Darwinian science into a public debate over Darwinism's core philosophy, which Johnson calls philosophical naturalism.

There were a few superficial parallels in the lives of Chapman and Johnson, both of whom were natives of Illinois and just a year apart at Harvard. But while Chapman threw his lot in with the Rockefeller Republicans, Johnson was attracted to the Democratic liberalism of the Roosevelt-Kennedy era, whose aura seemed to dominate Cambridge. It was a kind of "end of history" period, Johnson recalls, when liberal notions of the state and benign activist governance seemed to have brought America to the best of all possible worlds.

The Darwin Centennial of 1959 came and went without Johnson noticing. Darwinian evolution was a given in academia and, as such, not much discussed. "Freud was more ideologically important than Darwin at the time in marginalizing Christianity," recalls Johnson, who had become committed to agnosticism in his early student days. Still, what grabbed his attention as an English major in 1959 was *The Lord of the Rings,* the fantasy epic by J. R. R. Tolkien imbued with Christian themes that was beginning to acquire a cult audience. Captivated by Tolkien, Johnson went on to read *The Chronicles of Narnia* and most of C. S. Lewis's other fiction, and his Christian nonfiction as well. "Lewis and Tolkien did not convert me to Christianity," he says. "But they prepared my imagination for everything that came later."

What came immediately after was law school at the University of Chicago. ("My father always wanted me to go to law school, and eventually I ran out of reasons not to do it," Johnson says.) The contrast to Harvard could not have been more marked. Chicago harbored famous conservative intellectuals such as Milton Friedman, who introduced a conservative revolution to economic thinking. "People like him demolished the stereotype that all smart people are liberals," Johnson recalls. "That started me thinking outside the box."

By 1965, Johnson was married and serving as clerk to the chief justice of the California Supreme Court. The next year, when his daughter was born, he began a term as clerk for Chief Justice Earl Warren of the U.S. Supreme Court. He was learning about the real world, but his real education would come not so much in Washington as in his next career post as law professor at the University of California.

At age thirty-eight, after getting divorced, Johnson remarried and became a Christian, attending a Presbyterian church near the university. "I was a careerist who expected to climb the institutional ladder of the university or the legal profession to a high position," says Johnson. "I now count it as providential that I narrowly missed being appointed to the federal appellate bench, an honor I coveted for the wrong reasons. I am much happier as an outsider making a cognitive revolution."

Having watched the demise of such "scientific" edifices as Marxism and Freudianism, Johnson had his suspicions about Darwinism in the 1980s. But it was reading Michael Denton's *Evolution,* together with Richard Dawkins's *Blind Watchmaker,* that gave him the confidence to start writing himself.* The opportunity came in fall of 1987, when he traveled to the University of London as a visiting professor. He visited the Darwin home and museum at Down and dropped by the British Museum of Natural History, the so-called citadel of Darwinism.

While in England, Johnson also made another crucial connection: he met Stephen Meyer through a mutual friend, a Presbyterian minister. From

---

*Johnson also read an earlier work by the lawyer and skeptic Norman Macbeth, who published *Darwin Retried* in 1971. Macbeth argued that Darwinian evolution by natural selection was a tautology—that which survives, survives—making it a theory that could be neither proved nor disproved.

Meyer, Johnson learned of Thaxton and the early intelligent design advocates, and in 1990 in Portland, Oregon, some of these activists met Johnson to size him up and hear his ideas, which were to be published in *Darwin
on Trial* the next year. "I wasn't really part of the group at that time," Johnson says. "They held a special meeting to meet me, find out if I was for real,
how seriously they could take me." He welcomed the friendly skepticism:
"There are a lot of people who have 'big ideas' in this area, but they aren't
necessarily so big once you get to know about them." In this case, however,
Johnson's natural leadership abilities left an impression.

As expected, *Darwin on Trial* rapidly became a lightning rod for the
origins debate. Like Thaxton's *Mystery,* Johnson's book spurred conferences
and created networks. The year after *Darwin on Trial,* the Texas publisher
Jon Buell organized a debate at Southern Methodist University between a
cadre of the new intelligent design thinkers, including Johnson and Meyer,
and five leading naturalists over whether Darwinism was "science or
philosophy."

A newcomer to the Johnson-Meyer network was Michael Behe, a biochemistry professor and evolutionist who taught at Lehigh University in
Pennsylvania. After grappling with the macromolecular world in laboratories for a decade, Behe had come to doubt whether natural selection could
produce the complex cellular mechanisms in the smallest realms of biology.
He was helped in his skepticism by reading Denton's *Evolution: A Theory in
Crisis.* And at the Southern Methodist University debate, the Darwinians
argued that science had to be philosophically materialist. Behe cited mathematical theories and experiments that showed how unlikely it is for "functional proteins" to originate out of random chemical codes on DNA. "Oddly,
all the scientists gave philosophical arguments," Behe remembers. "They
didn't give scientific arguments. In fact, I think I was the only one there with
a scientific argument. So, we thought to ourselves, 'Yeah, we could do this.'"

WHAT HAPPENED IN 1993 AT PAJARO DUNES on Monterey Bay (ninety miles
south of San Francisco) became a sort of smalltime Manhattan Project for
the intelligent design movement, high-level and hush-hush. During a weekend in the glass-walled resort building buffeted by Pacific breezes, a gallery of

scientists, some still keeping a low profile at their universities, pondered the question of how to break the neo-Darwinian hold on science. Kenyon's academic freedom battle, then unfolding, added an urgency to the occasion.

To Phillip Johnson, the idea of design in nature was not really opposed to scientific evidence, but rather to a science institution that was dominated by "normal science," to use historian Thomas Kuhn's phrase. The normal science of Darwinian theory was filled with anomalies, but it institutionally squelched any new approach. It would suppress dissent until the dissent was great enough to oust the old order, a sea change that Kuhn called a "paradigm shift."

As a former courtroom prosecutor, Johnson felt that a little pressure was in order, and as a longtime inside player in a large university, he was not intimidated by how the big academic systems worked. Science was one of those academic encampments that had become comfortable ridiculing non-naturalistic concepts of the world. "One should never be fooled when they say, 'Oh, we're just talking about the rules of a game called science,'" Johnson says, explaining how at first blush it seems fair enough. "Then they will say, 'Oh, you can play in another game if you want.' But you see, for these people there is only one game. The other games are just fantasy. They have the only game of reality, and anything that is not science is fantasy."

Johnson believes that these rule-makers have already recognized the problems with Darwinism. They know that many thinking people would opt for a classic solution, Christian or otherwise, that allows design, or the mind of a Creator, to compensate for the anomalies. But they need to frame the issue in psychological rather than strictly objective terms. "Then they will say, 'If that makes you feel good, then okay, provided you don't mistake belief in God for how things really are.'" The upshot is that science can side-step the need for overwhelming evidence under these rules, which have been rigged to ensure that it wins the game and continues its hegemony. Science thus becomes "applied naturalistic and materialistic philosophy," which fixes things so that one particular theory about nature will always win: "They cannot really grasp what you're talking about when you discuss intelligent design in biology."

In the scientific culture, the judgment of the scientific authorities is final, he points out. "You can fight individuals within it, but you do not fight the culture itself. Any scientist, even a very eminent one, can be broken for that. And so the expectation all the time was, of course, 'We will make the rules and you will accept them.'" The design movement was refusing to do that, and by sheer persistence had found a place at the academic table where legitimacy is bestowed. That cut off the Darwinists' last line of retreat: "They have to fight and die where they are."

The reception of *Darwin on Trial,* and then the Pajaro Dunes gathering in 1993, were all part of an encouraging reaction, Johnson thought. "Someone said, 'Well, I notice you guys aren't bowing and scraping anymore.'" But they were in an open confrontation with established science, and the attacks on the design cadres could be fierce.

Because the debate was so focused on the definition of science and the closed nature of the scientific peer review system, opponents of the intelligent design movement at first objected on those grounds. They said that it was arguing for supernaturalism, which science does not allow, and that it was a political game. Indeed, the activists would not deny this aspect of their strategy: a philosophical and political rampart had to be breached, either with a battering ram or by finding an alternative door somewhere. The naturalist philosopher Robert Pennock, for example, accused Johnson of being just one more antiscience postmodernist, pointing out how his book had once been entitled *Deconstructing Darwin,* using the codeword for the new postmodern analysis, which at its extreme says truth is only opinion, and most often the opinion of those in power.

Johnson is familiar with this line of thought. He focused on it one year when he was asked to be a contributor to a Stanford University symposium on the "Critical Legal Studies" movement, which imported deconstructive European postmodernist ideology into American law. "This experience turned my interest to fundamental assumptions, i.e., to metaphysics," Johnson says. He employed a deconstructionist tactic "playfully" in his early writings on Darwinism, but ended up switching to garden-variety scholarly analysis. His sin, he believes, was to do this to Darwinism, which was not a "politically correct" thing to do.

IN TIME, MICHAEL BEHE WOULD COME OUT with *Darwin's Black Box,* perhaps the most extensive argument made by a design thinker as to why specific "irreducibly complex" biochemical processes—from blood clotting to the chemical unfolding of vision—looks so much more like the product of intelligent design than of piecemeal evolution. Its year of publication was 1996, and that became a turning point for the new design movement.

More was to come. In August, the Discovery Institute launched its Center for the Renewal of Science and Culture. Two months later, others who had been part of the Pajaro Dunes summit in 1993 convened a national conference at Biola University in Los Angeles titled "Mere Creation" and drawing two hundred mostly Christian thinkers, mainly in the sciences. They came from fifty-two colleges and universities. A graduate student in astronomy who was there, Guillermo Gonzalez, says, "I had never been to such a meeting. It took 'interdisciplinary' to a new level." He was impressed by the scientific quality of the discussion. "In my opinion, this meeting marked the true beginning of the intelligent design movement."

As professors, Meyer and Johnson still had teaching loads to carry, so others in the movement had pulled the event together. Still, Meyer was in the wings and Johnson, as the movement's titular leader, summed up its agenda at the end of the three days of sessions. The *New York Times* did not show up to report on the ferment; it took another five years for the practical effects of the movement—such as debates in school boards about textbook orthodoxy—to finally put intelligent design on its front page.

Though just opened itself, the Center for the Renewal of Science and Culture at the Discovery Institute had its brochures ready to pass around at the Mere Creation conference in Los Angeles. As the new center would describe itself, "Fellows do more than critique theories that have materialistic implications. They have also pioneered alternative scientific theories and research methods that recognize the reality of design and need for an intelligent agency to explain it." As for the conference, recalls West, "We got injected into it, but late."

The conference proceedings, published two years later in a book titled *Mere Creation,* opened with an elegant dedication to Marcel-Paul Schützenberger, the French mathematician and pioneer critic of Darwinism who died in 1996 at age seventy-six. Chapman wrote a postscript for the book acknowledging forebears and colleagues in the movement, which now was making remarkable progress. He lauded the students who began the origins research work and later the Access Research Network (ARN), and praised the tenacity of Buell, who published Thaxton and launched the early debate that drew many graduate students into the intelligent design movement. Based on the foundation they had built, he said, the Center for the Renewal of Science and Culture was there to serve, as was shown by the fact that "fifteen out of the twenty-two scholars who contributed to this volume are now affiliated" with the center.

The center was still an outsider when it came to peer review journals. Some of its fellows gave papers at scientific meetings, but not on design. The print forum became *Origins and Design,* a quarterly journal. Yet the Darwinists kept up their attack on the design movement, arguing that it was primarily political because it appealed to public sentiments rather than the editorial boards of science journals.

West, who knew academic protocols in social and political science, said that this argument was either naive or invidious. First, editorial boards or department cabals often block scholarship they don't like. What is more, it was Darwin and Huxley themselves who wrote the book on how to appeal to the public so as to undermine entrenched science. West remarks:

> Darwin gave papers, but he finally wrote *Origin of Species* for public consumption, not just for the scientific community. Think about how Darwinism came to be accepted. He was a master rhetorician. He and Huxley raised public arguments to open the closed scientific community to their ideas. They took their argument to the public and to the next generation. And they raised a very public battle, and that's one reason why they triumphed.

Yet West and his comrades could not deny the power of the criticism, "Where is the science in intelligent design?" Four particular design thinkers—Behe, Meyer, Gonzalez and mathematician William Dembski—were among those who hoped to answer that question, both by redefining the logic of science and by experimentally investigating design in nature.

8

BY DESIGN

The task of modern science has been called the pursuit of the very large, the very small and the very complex. The last two categories are the focus of biochemist Michael Behe, an intelligent design theorist teaching at Lehigh University.

In his 1996 book, *Darwin's Black Box,* Behe deals with the complex world of cells and their internal molecular processes. This is a world Darwin knew nothing about, Behe points out, so his theory of natural selection has come up short in explaining how such complexity came about. For molecular mechanisms that seem "irreducibly complex," an alternative to Darwinism is needed, and for now at least, design is Behe's choice.

One of Behe's favorite slides at his public speaking engagements is of a 1998 issue of *Cell* magazine. Under the heading "Macromolecular Machines," it reviews the innards of these remarkable organic structures. References to protein machines, mechanical devices, transporters, engines, and splicing or assembly mechanisms abound. "The entire cell can be viewed as a factory that contains an elaborate network of interlocking assembly lines, each of which is composed of a set of large protein machines," wrote cell biologist and National Academy of Sciences president Bruce Alberts, introducing that issue of *Cell.* Why call them machines? "Precisely because, like the machines invented by humans to deal efficiently with the macroscopic world, these protein assemblies contain highly coordinated moving parts."

As this realm of molecular biology has become better understood, Behe argues, the Darwinian explanation of how a functioning system of "highly coordinated parts" arose is not successful. What is demonstrably true in Darwinian theory, he says, is the simple fact that useless parts and unfit organisms are eliminated (natural selection). But when a system is said to be "irreducibly complex," every single subsystem has to be useful and fit from the beginning—or the system won't work. In short, irreducibly complex systems have the marks of being engineered. Such a design concept is anathema to Darwinism, but Behe thinks the Darwinian premise must be rethought:

> If biological systems strike scientists as machines invented by humans, then why don't we actively entertain the idea that they were designed by an intelligent being? We don't do that, of course, because it would break "the rule."

The rule he refers to is the insistence by modern science that no intelligent cause may be admitted in nature; undirected natural causes alone have made everything that exists.

Behe has become one of the best-known members of the intelligent design movement. Though critics call his design idea a "science stopper" (arguing that if a designer is presumed, many questions about origins are settled by fiat), Behe keeps up his research. With a doctorate from the University of Pennsylvania, Behe is a professor of biochemistry, operates a laboratory with graduate students, and has done postdoctoral research at the National Institutes of Health. In the long term, he wants to elaborate on how to identify irreducible complexity in molecular processes. It is clear to him that many molecular processes *have* evolved by the Darwinian model: chance and gradual building up by natural selection. But some molecular machines or processes—the bacterial flagellum, the chemical process of sight, blood clotting—strike him as simply too fine-tuned for explanation by routine Darwinian schemas.

Another natural miracle is the protein, a chain of amino acids that folds and curls into a rather irregular three-dimensional shape that is distinctive for each kind of protein. Proteins do just about everything: give structure to organisms, catalyze their living processes, and transmit information necessary for the running of the vast array of molecular machines. In one promising area of his research program, Behe is testing the way that two proteins, given the opportunity for an advantageous evolutionary adaptation, might bind to form a new complex of proteins with a beneficial new function. He said:

I'm trying to simulate how long it would take for different features of proteins to develop by random mutation and natural selection. And I'll try to show that relatively modest things will take inordinately long periods of time.

Such research seems to have primarily a negative or critical aim—namely, to show the inadequacy of the mutation/natural selection model as a mechanism for the natural creation of complex organisms. This ambitious goal once achieved, the design alternative may have an opening. Meanwhile, Michael Behe seeks methods or principles for judging whether some biochemical process or molecular machine is so complex that it could not, in fact, have evolved step by step—in which case the presumption will be that it must have been designed. If so, all that's left is to find out how the thing works, not wasting time with futile, unanswerable questions of "how did it evolve?"

Design may find its own critical methods as well, asking whether some innate power coiled within the helixes or the laws of physics causes a designed entity to fall into place at the appropriate time. Perhaps understanding of such a power must lie forever beyond human ability, and will remain the Designer's alone.

Behe does not doubt the reality of evolution at the animal and plant level, conceding that their forms change over time and flow from common ancestry. But his doubts about evolution at the molecular level have galvanized molecular biologists into a frenzy of refutations. One group of Darwinians calls his design proposal a religion, and therefore not testable by science; another says that design is indeed testable and that tests have proved it wrong. "One cannot say both," Behe observes, pointing out the obvious contradiction.

Overall, Behe thinks science should "lighten up." It should not fear design theory because it *is* testable, and in fact more testable than Darwinian evolution.

To make his point, Behe turns to Darwin's famous challenge regarding how complex organisms arise. "If it could be demonstrated that any complex organism existed that could not possibly have been formed by successive slight modification," Darwin said, "my theory would absolutely break down." A prime candidate for achieving that "breakdown," according to the intelligent design movement, is the hairlike bacterial flagellum.

The flagellum is thought to be the only structure in nature that has a rotary motion. It is an organelle, or specialized part of a cell, that rapidly rotates, acting as a highly efficient propeller that drives a bacterium forward or backward. It is typically made up of about fifty proteins, and builds itself from the inside out. Its precision motor is powered by the movement of protons, with a drive shaft, equipped with a cylindrical bushing, that pokes through the bacterium's membrane; the paddle-like filament bends at an angle. It reminds scientists of an outboard motor, only it is far faster and more energy-efficient. And if a single part were missing, it clearly would not work. The question for Darwinism is, by what conceivable gradualistic series of step-by-step mutations could this amazing machine have evolved?

Behe thinks this is a good question: "In the flagellum, we have a serious candidate to meet Darwin's 'breakdown' criteria." He is aware, however, that in the real world the flagellum will never satisfy Darwin's challenge, because the challenge is so cleverly phrased. In effect, Darwin asks his opponents to prove that something could *never* happen—an obvious case of "proving a negative." Behe is well aware that this is logically impossible, so his response is to point out the perversity of Darwin's challenge: it's rather like eliminating your team's goalposts so that scoring a point against you is impossible.

In contrast, design theory has reasonable constraints. The flagellum could be extensively tested to see if it is irreducibly complex—that is, could it still operate without one part or another? To answer Darwin's challenge, however, scientists would have to disprove each and every one of *all* the possible ways that a flagellum *could have* fallen into place within the available time window—however massively against the odds each one of them is. As Behe more simply states it, "One would have to show the system could not form by any of a potentially infinite number of unintelligent processes." Because that is impossible, Darwin's challenge throws science out the window; if this is the criterion of its truth, Darwinian theory fails to pass the test of being testable science.

Brought up a Roman Catholic, Behe never had a problem reconciling his faith with the evolution theory he absorbed in the course of his academic career. His first doubts arose after reading Michael Denton, who detailed Darwinian theory's apparent failures or half-truths at every level. It was a very private reassessment, he recalls, though he did offer a seminar at his university that compared the arguments in Denton's book with those made by the British Darwinist and atheist Richard Dawkins in *The Blind Watchmaker: Why the Evidence of Evolution Reveals a Universe without Design* (1986). By 1992, Behe had stated his doubts in public debates, and in his own book, *Darwin's Black Box* (1996), he declared his openness to intelligent design theory. At this point, the Darwinians, some of whom pointed out Behe's Catholicism, initiated a strategy of ridiculing the kind of God that design theory might point to. The biologist Kenneth Miller, for example, a fellow Catholic, has dubbed Behe's God of design a "mechanic," a lowly grease monkey who cobbles parts together. From Miller's perspective, this hardly glorifies an omnipotent God who, more appropriate to his rank, can fashion universal laws and let them unfold uninterruptedly.

Professor Behe's doubts about the evolution of irreducibly complex molecular machines derive from his science, including long practical experience in the lab, not from his religion. So he wonders why he is the target of theological potshots, even from unbelieving scientists. "They seem to think, 'Yeah, everything in the world is running on its own. Then God takes out a screwdriver and hammer and nails and makes a flagellum.'" If they are serious about the question of God, he considers this criticism an impoverished view of the Creator and the universe: "If God interacts with all of the universe all of the time, which is typical Christian theology, then the laws aren't running on their own."

This sustaining aspect of God imbues many, perhaps all cosmic processes with a design that might not be quite so obvious as the flagellum's: "There might be a lot more design going on in some areas than we can tell. If we can detect design, or think we can in certain features, that's what we have to go for." He acknowledges that science has to go for what it can measure and that it can ascertain only what technology will reach, "but that's not to say there isn't more going on, which we just can't see."

When Behe thinks about a possible research program for design theory, it might begin by asking what things are so complex that they need to have been designed, and what things might easily have evolved. This is not unlike the question Einstein asked: did the laws of physics have to be that way, or could there have been many other ways? Could God have done it any other way? When Behe hears scientists chiding his "mechanic God," he recalls another Einstein story: Einstein was so set on having deterministic laws ("God does not play dice," he declared) that quantum physicist Neils Bohr blurted out, "Stop telling God what to do!" That works for Behe. "My advice to critics would be, 'Don't tell God what to do.'"

IN AN EARLIER DAY, SCIENTISTS WERE HABITUATED to the Newtonian metaphor of the universe as a great machine. In an age of quantum physics, with its fields and probabilities, the astronomer James Jeans said the universe looks more like a "great thought" than a machine. Whichever metaphor works best, astronomer Guillermo Gonzalez looks through his telescope and has inklings that what he sees was designed. Advances in science are telling him so.

One of the most dramatic findings is the galactic habitable zone in the Milky Way galaxy. The galactic zone is a band midway from the center of the rotating, disklike galaxy—which would be as thin as a phonograph record if it were scaled down to that size. Perhaps only 20 percent of the stars in the galaxy travel this path. As the home of the Sun, it is protected from gigantic explosions and collisions at the dense core of the galaxy, making life possible on Earth. At the outer edge of the galaxy there would not be enough heavy elements to form a habitable planet; the zone provides them, while other parts of the galactic disk are more vulnerable to cosmic bursts and harassing comets.

For Gonzalez, this is one piece in a puzzle that suggests Earth is not as blandly ordinary as the Copernican Principle has long demanded. The evidence of Earth's special habitability has become overwhelming, beginning with the attributes of its star. The Sun is among the top 9 percent of the most massive stars in the Milky Way; its light burns evenly; and it has more heavy elements than three-quarters of the stars of its own age. "Much of this has been known for a couple of decades, but astronomers still make statements like, 'The Sun is just an average star,'" Gonzalez says.

The Milky Way is among the top 1 percent of luminous galaxies nearby, which is crucial because a galaxy's luminosity correlates with the average amount of metals present. Without sufficient quantities of metallic elements, Earth and the other planets could not have formed. The Copernican world of astronomers, who are still inclined to believe in better habitats and higher intelligent life elsewhere, are having to adjust to this apparent specialness of the home turf. "They don't know what to make of these evidences," Gonzalez says. "They don't deny the data, but they don't quite know how to fit it into their worldviews."

The new puzzle owes its birth not only to advances in astronomy but to the new field of astrobiology, which tries to make sense of Earth's biological life in the context of galaxies, suns and solar systems. Astrobiology is still driven by the Copernican Principle—that Earth has no special properties above and beyond other bodies in the universe—and its researchers, often funded by NASA, are still eagerly looking for other planets as possible homes to intelligent life. Gonzalez, however, has taken a different conceptual path. He says that the "metaphysics of mediocrity" has stunted the thinking of astronomers, but has also made a metaphysics of design just as plausible: perhaps an intelligent Designer gauged the laws of physics to allow a habitable planet.

An assistant professor of astronomy at Iowa State University, Gonzalez said that a shift away from dogmatic Copernicanism has been aided by the "rare earth hypothesis" of two of his former colleagues at the University of Washington, where he earned his doctorate in stellar evolution. In 2000, geologist Peter D. Ward and astronomer Donald Brownlee—both key players in NASA's astrobiology program—published a book, *Rare Earth,* enumerating the ways in which the Earth was unusual, and its subtitle was telling: "Why Complex Life Is Uncommon in the Universe." Gonzalez's research has added to that list, and he has co-authored with Ward and Brownlee, who are nontheists, a *Scientific American* article on the galactic habitable zone.

The rare earth hypothesis proposes that Earth-like planets capable of supporting complex life are not as common as many astronomers have believed. The reasons are many. According to the hypothesis, the Earth, besides finding itself in the habitable zone, has a unique balance of chemical and plant life, experiences ice ages that produce ideal atmospheres, and is located in a solar system where a giant planet like Jupiter deflects meteors. The Moon stabilizes the tilt of Earth's axis, regulating the seasons. Had the Earth been formed a few billion years after it was, there might not have been enough internal heat to maintain 4.5 billion years of plate tectonics, the movement of continents that builds up the landmass necessary for life.

Though Ward and Brownlee gave a thumbs-down to the hypothesis of intelligent life in the universe, which distressed fellow astrobiologists, they did argue for an omnipresence of "extremophiles," the microorganisms that science has recently found living in extreme environments—by volcanic vents on ocean floors, in solid rock hundreds of feet down, and under the most frozen sectors of the planet. A rare earth demands a new environmental ethic, Ward and Brownlee concluded. Gonzales would amend that: "While I agree this is a worthwhile implication, it is hardly the most significant one. The most important implication of this rare earth hypothesis is that the cosmos is fine-tuned for life."

Since the 1980s, the debate over the fine-tuning of the physical constants of the universe has been in full swing. The anthropic side of this debate has weaknesses, says Gonzalez, since the argument is always vulnerable to the charge of circularity. Because skeptics can always say that human observers are liable to fool themselves when they call something a coincidence, a "tiebreaker" is needed. That is, the scientist needs a reason to think that biological life is not just superbly adapted to the environment in which it arose, but also inevitable and somehow unique. In 2000, at a conference at Yale University, Gonzalez first proposed his tiebreaker, suggesting a "correlation between habitability and measurability" on Earth.

"Starting in 1998, I noticed that certain phenomena are better observed on Earth's surface than from other places in the solar system," Gonzalez said. In *Astronomy and Geophysics* he published on the odd fact that while the solar system had 64 moons, only Earth's caused a total solar eclipse: the Moon and Sun match up in size. Though the Sun is 400 times larger than the Moon, it is also 400 times farther away from Earth. In the evolving solar system, the size matchup began 150 million years ago and will last as long again. The timescale parallels the appearance of intelligent life on Earth: we happen to exist in a window of time when it is possible to see total eclipses, which allow astronomers to study the Sun's fiery corona as it is revealed by the occulting Moon. The popular press loved Gonzalez's report; *Discover* magazine made it a "weird science discovery" of 1999; and a few cynics joked that solar eclipses were now being used as proofs of God.

Gonzalez attributes his ability to find more examples of measurability to the expanding field of astrobiology, where correlations between nuclear astrophysics, interstellar chemistry, planetary climate stability, the chemistry of life, celestial dynamics, climatology and biological life are endless. Within the naturalistic framework, the scientist must ascribe these correlations to chance. Using the design premise, however, Gonzalez can test the idea that not only does a rare biological species like *Homo sapiens* exist on Earth, but the species has been given natural tools to measure and explore the universe: habitability correlates with measurability. He believes this correlation is an authentic tiebreaker, and adds boldly, "If we are right, then ours is the strongest empirical evidence for purpose in the universe to date." And what is that purpose? "The universe was designed for scientific discovery by intelligent life."

Born in Havana, Gonzalez fled with his family to Florida in 1967, when he was four. His earliest memories stretch back to pondering the dark sky and obtaining his first telescope. When he was about fourteen, his father helped him erect a small sliding-roof observatory in their Miami backyard. "I'm one of the relatively few amateur astronomers who stuck to astronomy from childhood to a Ph.D.," he says. His doctoral studies made him an expert on older stars, and he has experience on some of the best telescopes in the world.

By suggesting that Earth is special, Gonzales has broken the sacred Copernican code, or what he calls the "metaphysics of mediocrity"—the credo among scientists asserting that humans are nothing special in the universe. He had taught the history of astronomy at the university level, however, and his readings of Kepler and Galileo strongly assured him that the discipline was born of belief, not of nihilism, and that the idea of God even stimulated scientific investigation. Presuming a lawgiver, Kepler and Galileo "were strongly motivated to search for simple laws governing the universe." The galactic habitable zone is another example, he believes, noting how in the past the presumption of mediocrity prevented astronomers from evaluating the rare attributes of Earth. Here Gonzalez deftly turns the tables and suggests that naturalistic metaphysics can be a science stopper.

Such comments have drawn genteel contempt in the journals *Science* and *Nature*. Gonzales has already been attacked in print by extraterrestrial life advocate David Darling in his book *Life Everywhere*. Though Gonzalez is aware he is risking his career, he awaits a vigorous debate on his privileged-planet hypothesis: "I know there are astronomy students and professionals out there who agree with my views, but they are keeping quiet for fear of ridicule. My closest colleagues are taking a 'wait and see' approach to find out if my ideas pan out."

Though a lifelong believer in God, for much of his career Gonzalez had no reason to buck conventional astronomy. That changed as he began studying Earth's climate more closely. The variables for life are exacting, and other planets having even remotely appropriate conditions are few if not nonexistent. "This helped to break my long-held assumption that Earth was average, or at least not too uncommon," Gonzalez says. Like many in his field, he was also taken by the new arguments about fine-tuning, the anthropic principle and multiple universes.

His epiphany that an obvious design alternative was being intentionally overlooked came in 1996, when he participated in the Mere Creation conference at Biola University in Los Angeles, a gathering of mostly Christian thinkers in the sciences. Within a few years, Gonzalez's science journal reports on eclipses, the low probability of extraterrestrial life, and the kinds of stars necessary for planets to produce life were being picked up by popular magazines such as *New Scientist*. The Discovery Institute noticed his work and invited him to be a science fellow.

One occupational hazard for the astronomer is wrestling with notions of cosmic humility, a key part of the Copernican revolution, or the Principle of Mediocrity. Gonzalez has done his share of mulling on the topic while he gazes at what seems like infinite space and time with its countless galaxies. "The idea that we and our home planet are somehow privileged is repugnant to moderns," he says. "They seem to think that anyone who holds to this view is guilty of great hubris and arrogance."

But he divides humility into false and authentic categories. Much humility in science is lip service, he says:

> A truer humility is to take the world as it presents itself to us and admit our inability to force it into a simple picture. And, yes, the brain's ability to figure out our place in the cosmos seems far beyond the ability of nat-

uralistic science to explain. The humble approach would be to admit to that truth.

At this stage in his research, Guillermo Gonzales is not worried about humility on the question of extraterrestrial intelligence. "It does seem to be a contradiction to be an astrobiologist who is skeptical of extraterrestrial life," he says. "But it really isn't. An astrobiologist is just someone interested in learning about the conditions required for life." What he calls the SETI (Search for Extraterrestrial Life) lobby has come to dominate, insisting that scientists must believe in extraterrestrial intelligence. The design argument, he believes, will keep astronomy healthy by arguing the contrary.

NOT ALL DESIGN ARGUMENTS ARE THE SAME. Over time, a distinction was made between those *teleological* arguments that infer a purpose in natural things, and those that simply assert the evidence for design, as if by a mind, in nature.

In *Natural Theology* (1802), William Paley wrote that a "watch must have had a maker" who "designed its use," and so the purpose of things often reflected the wisdom and beneficence of God. According to one reading of history, however, this early-nineteenth-century emphasis on natural theology was a detour from centuries of Christian thinking that had posited God's existence as a matter of revealed truth. "The argument for God's existence from design in creation was something of an aberration in the history of Christian theology," says biologist Jonathan Wells, a design theorist. More typical, he said, was the logic of John Henry Newman, the Oxford churchman and intellectual: "I believe in design because I believe in God, not God because I see design."

This is obviously a premise of some design theorists, just as the Darwinians usually begin with the premise that God does not exist or work in nature. But trying to be scientific in approach, the intelligent design theorists tend to stay away from purpose and focus on evidence of intelligence. It is an attitude expressed by British scientist James Clerk Maxwell when he said molecules have "the stamp of a manufactured article." That makes sense to Michael Behe:

This is object-based rather than grand-purpose-based design. We some-times think we see the purpose, but it's the purpose of the machine. The bacterial flagellum has a purpose: to propel things through the water. What greater purpose the designer intended for the machine is not some-thing we look at.

Another way design theorists phrase the problem is whether "nature points beyond itself." Cognate to this is whether Darwinian naturalism can give plausible explanations for the Big Questions: consciousness, the origin of life, the remarkable effectiveness of mathematics at modeling the physical world, and the fine-tuning of universal constants are just a few of the prob-lems that critics have claimed are not amenable to purely naturalistic expla-nation. Two of the design camp's most active exploiters of this naturalistic weakness are William Dembski, a mathematician and philosopher, and Stephen Meyer, a philosopher of science specializing in origin-of-life research.

With two doctorates (mathematics and philosophy), a theology degree and a postdoctoral stint at the Massachusetts Institute of Technology, Dem-bski is not only an academic; he is also a newsmaker and unwitting contro-versialist as a result of his organizing activities. When he founded the Polanyi Center at Baylor University in 1999, for example, nothing might have seemed more natural than to ask for an office and a couple of salaries for intelligent design research at a university built by Southern Baptists. Nevertheless, the faculty balked. Many of them were theistic evolutionists, or naturalists, and they protested the establishment of the center without a faculty vote. Per-haps most of all, they worried that a Trojan horse for creationism—the pre-ferred view of the conservative Southern Baptists whom the Baylor faculty had been battling for three decades—would be brought onto campus. Dem-bski lost the center but retained his research contract.

His successes have meanwhile been as a prodigious writer and speaker, especially in laying out the context of the design debate. While design argu-ments vary, he says, they all "look to some aspect of nature exhibiting 'the marks of intelligence.'" What is more, a useful design argument must have "empirical content," not a just a poetic sense of harmony in nature. So William Paley was on the right track when he got specific enough to ask about a watch and a watchmaker. The flagellum, unknown in Paley's day, is a similar empirical case.

The opposition to such thinking has been monumental, even in Christian circles, where the embarrassments of so many failed "God of the gaps" arguments are not forgotten. Blunders have ranged from believing in the demonic origins of illness to saying that God adjusts planetary motions (as Sir Isaac Newton said). Yet the sustained argument that design is dead, begun with Darwin's *On the Origin of Species,* has seemed to soften as physics and biology reveal nature's tremendous complexity, and as former critics of design confess that it may now have its scientific uses.

One such skeptic of design, and especially its creationist versions, has been Calvin College philosopher of science Del Ratzsch. Because of the varied uses of the word *design,* and how it was frequently obfuscated in the battle between creationists and evolutionists, Ratzsch set out to survey all possible meanings of the term and presented them in his book *Nature, Design and Science.* He concluded, "Whether design theories should prove to be ultimately scientifically successful or not, there is little to be said for a prohibition that forbids even the attempts to pursue whatever potential there might be."

In trying to frame a scientific concept of design, the intelligent design movement has repeated a few basic themes over and over. One is that in science, the question is not between finding natural causes or supernatural causes, but between natural or intelligent ones. A second motto goes thus: nature is not just chance and necessity (law), but chance, necessity and agency (or intelligent causality). Finally, as Meyer has stated the case, science has heretofore spoken of matter and energy, and said that these two sides of a single coin give rise to biological complexity. Now that the matter-energy account is looking weaker, he says, science must add a third factor and speak of matter, energy and information (which again suggests an intelligent agent writing the instruction book). Intelligence, agency and information—these are related terms for what Dembski, Meyer and their allies mean by design.

Dembski's main contribution has been to propose a method to investigate nature. He calls the method the "explanatory filter." Though it conjures the image of a kitchen appliance that strains food or coffee, the "filter" is rather the three stages of thinking that a scientist ideally may have to traverse in order to evaluate the cause or origin of a natural phenomenon, whether it is a rock formation or the human brain.

The first stage looks for "regularity," or natural law, at work in a phenomenon. In discussing the movement of billiard balls according to Newtonian physics, for example, or the formation of crystals by chemical rules, the first filter is quite sufficient; these phenomena are explained by repetitive and predictable laws.

A weather pattern is a different matter, however, and science is required to forsake regularity and move to the second filter: chance. This is the realm of probabilities. Here, scientists may try to use probabilistic methods to predict a hurricane pattern, for example, or estimate how water will flow or calculate the vibration effects of a high-speed train system.

But some complex realities in nature surpass even these kinds of mathematics, especially when the complexity and coordination of parts in nature are seen to carry out a very specific function. Agreeing with Behe, Dembski would say that the chemical process of vision in the human eye is one such supercomplex system, as is the flagellum. At this point, when neither regularity nor chance can explain a system, science must be allowed to move to a third screen in the filter: design.

The new design theorists have preferred to avoid metaphors of the past, such as Thomas Reid's phrase "marks of intelligence." Instead, they have adopted the naturalistic terminology of origin-of-life studies, particularly Leslie Orgel's concept of "specified complexity." Orgel wrestled with how information was set up and passed on by a DNA molecule. The code was not only complex, but specific in its coding mission; it was also just one of many coding molecules that complemented each other. For design theorists, specified complexity was the closest allusion that natural science could make to intelligence—to a mind writing a message.

In proposing his filters, Dembski was careful. When approaching the third screen, he did not say that science could prove design in nature, but more modestly, that it could only make an "inference to design." Indeed, natural science was already in the habit of doing that. When confronted by a complex natural phenomenon, naturalists had resorted to what they called an "inference to the best explanation."

Since intelligence was not an empirical handle that design theory could hold onto, the next best thing was its product: information. In the age of computers and electronics, "information theory" was a booming sector of science; with its mathematical obliqueness, however, it was often used imprecisely in science, and for the layperson it was a tricky concept to grasp.

Indeed, nothing seemed more slippery in modern science than this new field, since at first blush almost anything (a book, a molecular structure, someone's body language, a bird chirping) might be regarded as information. Specifically, however, the scientific discipline arose out of efforts during the Second World War to crack enemy codes by using probabilities to reconstruct encoded or degraded information. Applied to peacetime communications, the question was how to send a complex signal over a constricted channel, not only because of limited space, but because the signal deteriorated during transmission. Information theorists sought ways to restore information at the receiving end.

The term was applied to the DNA code soon after its discovery in the 1950s. Once Watson and Crick had deciphered the double helix of DNA, Francis Crick produced his successful "sequence hypothesis" that four chemicals, each one a nucleotide, were like an alphabet that gave instructions to produce proteins. As a diehard naturalist, Crick said the DNA "information" is nothing more than the "precise sequence" of the four chemicals, arranged by law and chance alone.

For intelligent design theorists, the question was: How is it that this information in nature is able to perpetuate life, and create ever more complex life, without the information becoming degraded? Even the more liberal theists and metaphysicians in the science/religion dialogue liked the idea of information as a metaphor for the source of nature's order and creativity. In one intelligent design book, *Of Pandas and People,* information theory was defined innocently enough: "a branch of applied mathematics which provides a measure of information in any sequence of symbols."

But science critics could see that information theory was being corralled for the kind of God-talk that science had traditionally not allowed. One chronicler of the DNA revolution, the historian and journalist Horace Freeland Judson, objected to the use of information theory by the intelligent design movement. The information found in DNA and by the

Allied cryptographers in enemy transmissions was not applicable to biology, Judson protested. "Biological information is not thought about in that way. I want to warn against the imprecise usage of the word information as if it's going to get you to design because it is somehow something that only humans, or only an intelligent source, can actually design."

According to Dembski, however, there is something in the real world called "complex specified information," or CSI. It exists in nature and in the scrambled security codes on credit cards. Natural causes such as chance and law "are incapable of generating CSI," he says. "Chance generates contingency, but not complex specified information. . . . Laws at best transmit already present information or else lose it." In other words, "chance and law working in tandem cannot generate information"—only an intelligent agent can. Information produced by intelligence, moreover, does not deteriorate, as in electronic signals, nor does it mutate into something else. Thus, Dembski proposes a "law of conservation of information."

Design theorists are not in lockstep when it comes to how CSI works itself out in nature. Denton and Behe hold that CSI is embedded in nature and played out over time. For Dembski and Meyer, CSI emerged "with no evident informational precursors, and thus through discrete insertions over time." In the history of design theory, Dembski explains, "this debate is not new." But by inferring the role of information, they were all at odds with Darwinian naturalism.

Since the days when Stephen Meyer began his public advocacy—starting with his Cambridge University studies on the origin of life, his work on the book *Of Pandas and People,* and finally as director of the Center for the Renewal of Science and Culture at the Discovery Institute—he has presented complex specified information as the key to most of the physical world. Information can explain molecular machines, signals in cells, and the fine-tuned forces and elements in the universe. Because the Cambrian explosion produced the basic body plans of life with their accompanying DNA, "you might think of this as an informational phenomenon," Meyer says. "To build new organisms in biology, you have to provide new information."

Much of biological science is historical and seeks the best explanation for past events. "If you're a philosophical naturalist, and want to explain some biological feature, you have to limit yourself to chance or necessity or both," Meyer says. "I think this leaves us with a truncated historical science."

Perhaps the most seminal appearance of information was the rise of the first DNA molecule and the cell in which it replicated. This is a favorite topic of Meyer's work. Meyer was a boxer in college, and some of that tenacity comes through in his debates with naturalists. He is also a young father and appears at lectures with a magnetic board and colorful plastic letters borrowed from his children. The point, Meyer says, is that the chemical codes stick on the backbone of DNA just like the letters on the board, a letter having no organic relationship with the board or with the other letters. Indeed, Francis Crick spoke of movable newspaper type on a plate. So how do the letters get in place and how do they work together?

In asking this question, Meyer has revived Michael Polanyi's challenge to science. An accomplished chemist, Polanyi argued that the information arrangement was not tied to physics or chemistry but to something beyond. Writing in *Science* in 1968, Polanyi explained that if the code arose from random chemical bonds, it would appear as a repetitive crystal: "Its code-like character would be effaced by an overwhelming redundancy."

Building on this, Meyer likes to portray for his readers and listeners the sheer complexity and precision of even the first DNA code. The code gives instructions to the cell to make amino acids, of which there are twenty that make up the basic proteins for life. The amino acids must link together in a chain, and then fold into an exacting, irregular structure called a protein. The chance of each amino acid finding the correct bond is one in twenty; the chance of one hundred amino acids hooking up to successfully make a functional protein is one in $10^{30.}$ The exact sequencing is crucial, Meyer says: "Amino acids alone do not make proteins, any more than letters alone make words, sentences or poetry." What is more, a linear code of chemicals has somehow succeeded in building a three-dimensional protein, what Meyer has called "a twisting, turning, tangled chain of amino acids."

Naturalistic scientists know as well as Meyer does how incredible this operation is. And despite the low probability that law and chance alone could make it work, that is their theory.

Like Behe, Meyer believes that science must change the rules. When a computer runs a program, the program works because complex and specific information targets a function. "Those are real properties that need to be explained, and the best explanation is an intelligent programmer," he says of the computer example. Why should it be any different in the biological world? "Information, in our experience, is invariably a result of intelligent agency. This is not a recourse to mysticism. This is something that we know. This is based on our own experience."

While the work of the design theorists has received grudging praise from some quarters of naturalistic science, others go back to the kind of problem Behe has called the materialists' double standard: design must be proved, while evolution may be assumed.

The philosopher Elliott Sober, a naturalist who enjoys sparring with the design theorists, says that the nineteenth-century natural theologian William Paley presented a far more straightforward hypothesis than Dembski's filter. "Dembski needs to supply an account of what he means by design and how it can be caused by something other than intelligent agency," Sober maintains. "His vague remark that design is equivalent to 'information' is not enough." Sober is a pluralist about evolution, recognizing that it could be driven by many different forces, but his premise is naturalism. To win the day, he says, Dembski has to show that intelligent design is the only alternative to Darwinian evolution. Since that is impossible, design has to present concrete proof: such-and-such a thing in nature is designed.

That is exactly what Behe, Gonzales, Meyer and others thought they had been doing. And they sense in Sober's protests a whiff of Darwin's mischievous challenge to "prove a negative." But Sober continues: "If defenders of the design hypothesis want their theory to be scientific, they need to do the scientific work of formulating and testing the predictions that creationism makes. . . . Dembski's Explanatory Filter encourages creationists to think that this responsibility can be evaded." Dembski disagrees, of course, saying his mathematical science is as concrete as theoretical Darwinism. But he credits Sober for writing elsewhere that the design argument "is worth considering" and that in the past it was "not the fantasy of crackpots but the fruits of creative genius."

Paul Davies, the Templeton Prize-winning physicist, is more at ease with the design thinkers than Elliott Sober has been, though Davies does not buy the personal God of many design theorists. First of all, he thinks "information" is a perfectly good metaphor for science, which operates on metaphors, from energy and matter to the world as organism or the cosmos as machine. The idea of information "is now routinely applied to nature," Davies points out. "In fact, some people are saying information is the foundational stuff from which the universe is built; that matter is something secondary." The scientists saying this are not design theorists either, and that is why Davies is attentive even to the design-minded work.

His naturalistic colleagues see design as a covert operation that is ardently Christian and politically conservative. Such suspicion would be logical, of course, since Darwinian science often enough has an agenda that is anti-Christian and politically liberal. Paul Davies makes the crucial point:

> Dembski's attempt to quantify design, or provide mathematical criteria for design, is extremely useful. I'm concerned that the suspicion of a hidden agenda is going to prevent that sort of work from receiving the recognition it deserves. Strictly speaking, you see, science should be judged purely on the science and not on the scientist.

THE HUMAN DIMENSION

9

THE WAR OF WORDS

The Nature of Nature conference in 2000, which matched theists and atheists in three days of debate about God and science, was a cordial enough affair. Yet the April gathering at Baylor University, organized by the intelligent-design Polanyi Center and partly funded by the Templeton Foundation, had enough fireworks to illustrate the contemporary clash over "the role of naturalism in science."

The conference, organized by design theorist William Dembski, was a remarkable mix of naturalists and theists, both moderates and hard-liners, including overt Christians and agnostic Nobel laureates. Atheism was represented by the 1979 Nobelist in physics, Steven Weinberg, who pulled no punches: whatever naturalism is, he said, it is better than religion, which is tantamount to belief in fairies. (Weinberg had famously said a few years earlier, "I am all in favor of a dialogue between science and religion, but not a constructive dialogue.") Science has tended to destroy religion and has allowed intelligent people to reject God, asserts Weinberg, adding, "We should not retreat from this accomplishment." As more of life is naturalistically explained, religion is forced down three escape hatches: denial, surrender or compromise. What Weinberg saw at the conference—arguments for God in a fine-tuned universe—was "an enormous retreat" from the bad old days when God was seen everywhere.

Yet for all the prowess of science, Weinberg found the Nature of Nature forum "rather alarming" because it was trying to "turn naturalism into a philosophical dogma, which has a right to equal time, but no more so than theories of fairies." The attack on science won't work, he argued, because ordinary people know that naturalism is more reliable than faith, just as weather reports are preferred over prayers for rain. "It's really scandalous how naturalistic the weather bureau has become," he said with heavy sarcasm.

As host to the event, Dembski was gracious but pulled none of his punches either. His Polanyi Center was under attack by evolutionists, even at the Baptist university, and given the controversy he had barely pulled off the event, one of the most diverse and high-level of its kind. The four-day conference featured twenty-five principal speakers at ten plenary sessions, and three periods of more specialized forums. The major topics ranged from naturalism and irreducible complexity to the origin of life, cosmology, the source of human ethics and the frontiers of neuroscience. Noting that the center's namesake, Michael Polanyi, had decried how science was subverted by Soviet authoritarianism and ideology, Dembski said that the conference also opposed the suppression of ideas: "It's in this spirit that we host this interdisciplinary conference."

Dembski's hint that a totalitarian Darwinist ideology existed at Baylor was not lost on some of his listeners. In the following months, the dispute over the presence of the Polanyi Center on campus continued to grow until the administration, under faculty pressure, shut it down.

As that episode illustrates, the battle over God and science frequently leaves the ivory tower and becomes political, social and literary. At this level, the ambiguous love-hate relationship between science and theology spills into the public realm. Ordinary folks may not catch the subtleties of all the arguments, but they can recognize that a war is being fought.

THE SCIENCE-AND-RELIGION DIALOGUE, which attracted the liberal Protestants, Catholics and Jews who sought God in science, proceeded with an awareness of a potential clash with the materialists. One of the dialogue's leading thinkers, the physicist and theologian Ian Barbour, in his 1989 Gifford Lectures (*Religion in an Age of Science*) laid out four possible ways that science and religion could interact: conflict, separation, dialogue or integration. While Barbour advocated the last two, events would soon prove that conflict had not become obsolete.

Philip Clayton, who helped to organize the Science and the Spiritual Quest (SSQ) conferences, thinks the conflict intensified when some influential people began to link Christianity and science in their writings. In 1983, for example, the Cambridge priest-theologian John Polkinghorne wrote the first of his books for a general audience as "an attempt to say more about what motivated my Christian belief than was possible in half an hour over a cup of coffee in the laboratory canteen." More books on God and science followed. Clayton says that "When Weinberg listens to these believing scientists, it drives him batty. That led him and his friends to be increasingly vocal in their responses."

Since 1992, religious believers who worked in the sciences could receive funding for projects under dozens of programs set up by the Templeton Foundation, which had about $50 million a year available for grants. Indeed, some of that grant money underwrote the Nature of Nature conference, and secured Nobelist speakers such as Weinberg and Christian de Duve. Despite this plethora of Templeton grant outlets, the two Templeton projects that reached most deeply into establishment science, and thus stirred the most debate, were the Science and Religion Course Program and the SSQ conferences.

The course program, which began in 1994, took the science/religion debate to the heart of university science. "When a course is taught in any department outside of science with a title such as, 'science and something,' the science departments get concerned," Clayton says. "So there can be resistance." To begin the national course project, a Templeton research team scanned the courses at U.S. colleges and universities and found 950 on science and religion. Questionnaires were sent to the instructors, and of those who responded, five were awarded $5,000 each for the best course outlines. Like a grant, the money could be used for research and for course materials. These best five course outlines were summarized in the science/religion journal *Zygon,* in hopes that other university professors might be similarly inspired. In the next phase, Templeton awarded $10,000 for a proposed course that the foundation's panel considered academically sound, with half of the prize going to the university as an incentive. Between 1996 and 1997, the Templeton Foundation invested nearly $2 million to train a hundred faculty who attended workshops on how to teach such courses, and as more teachers became interested, workshop sites were opened in Berkeley, Chicago, Boston, Tallahassee, Oxford and Toronto

This expansion into academia drew a swift reaction. Two months after *Zygon's* September 1995 issue with its outlines of exemplary courses, the feisty academic journal *Lingua Franca* zeroed in on the Templeton Foundation. While foundations bearing family names have forever offered money to academics, universities, chairs and research agendas, Templeton's plan "is the boldest ever hatched by a philanthropist seeking to control the curriculum," in the opinion of history professor Jon Wiener. He criticized one of the courses for assigning a book that John Templeton himself had written, titled *The God Who Would Be Known* (even though the course challenged the book's thesis that science was proving God's existence). Edward B. Davis, a science history professor whose course at Messiah College won an award, said Wiener had offered "a flippant, deliberately misleading account."

As the brouhaha over Templeton's influence on campuses grew, the *Chronicle of Higher Education* weighed in with a 1997 story about a "little-known foundation" that was funding a "controversial scholarly discipline." The story also noted that the American Association for the Advancement of Science had taken Templeton money to open a science/religion project, eliciting a grumbling reaction from scientists. But a *Chronicle* essay in 1999 by physicist Lawrence M. Krauss made him the Paul Revere of secularists as he warned of Templeton "carrots" invading the campus. Admitting his own weakness for cash grants, Krauss in this case inveighed against a "rush with too little thought to the trough." He said, "Templeton's overall program is ill conceived, and so is the field of study that he wants to promote." Not only did science and religion "have virtually nothing in common," but scientists were being cowed. By letting theologians onto their turf, they had to accommodate religious sensibilities. "Some sensibilities need to be offended," Krauss said, especially since "the driving force behind the effort is not the strength of ideas, but one man's money, compounded by the misplaced enthusiasm of some religious zealots." Early the next year, the American Association for the Advancement of Science gave Krauss its annual Award for Public Understanding of Science and Technology.

If the Templeton course project was a slow intrusion of theological concerns into university science, the grand "coming out" was the media splash created by the Templeton-backed Science and the Spiritual Quest conference in Berkeley in June 1998 and the SSQ II meeting at Harvard in

2001. To the degree that Templeton projects were big successes, they were big targets too, and it was hard for the materialists not to attack them. "What we are hearing is not the voice of a growing majority of scientists, but the well-funded, growing voice of a decreasing minority," the skeptical physicist Victor J. Stenger wrote. "The Berkeley meeting was a kind of 'Premise-Keepers' rally for academics seeking to keep alive their premise that God exists, while science continues to operate successfully with no need for that premise."

One noted science writer, George Johnson of the *New York Times,* also fixated on the Templeton money and the overreaching of believers who "seem more eager than ever to step over the line, trying to interpret scientific data to support the revealed truths of their own theology." Such critics had not attended the SSQ events; those science writers who actually participated were more likely to comment on the lack of doctrinal allusions—or even mention of God.

Harvard paleontologist Stephen Jay Gould did not attend SSQ either, but he read the newspaper reports and added his commentary at the end of his book *Rocks of Ages,* which prescribed a rigorous separation of science and religion. He called the gee-whiz news reports of Templeton's efforts "vapidly uncritical," and sneered: "At least we can now be certain about one of God's attributes; he sells newspapers and magazines." Yet even Gould's separation of science and religion—with the higher station held by science—was too kind for zoologist Richard Dawkins, who might not have called Gould vapid, but clearly thought he was naive: "It is completely unrealistic to claim, as Gould and many others do, that religion keeps itself away from science's turf, restricting itself to morals and values.... Religions make existence claims, and this means scientific claims."

AS THE TEMPLETON-FUNDED PROJECTS began to go public, the intelligent design movement was hitting full stride. Its growing power would be seen in a protracted confrontation between Stephen Jay Gould and Phillip Johnson, the Berkeley law professor who came out with *Darwin on Trial* in 1991.

A decade earlier, Gould had played a central role in the war between Darwinians and advocates of creation science who took a literal view of the

Bible. In 1980, the creationists had begun to succeed in passing laws stipulating that "creation science" must be taught whenever "evolution science" is taught in public schools. By the next year, a federal judge had ruled that such a law in Arkansas was unconstitutional, and *Discover* magazine named Gould "scientist of the year." The Supreme Court confirmed this triumph of evolutionism in 1987 by upholding a Louisiana ruling that went against creation science. After this final victory, Gould might have hoped for a *pax scientifica,* but it was not to be. He quite unexpectedly met Phillip Johnson.

They came face to face at a December 1989 forum called "Science and Creationism in Public Schools," an event organized by a group of evangelical lawyers that convened at the Jesuit Campion Center outside Boston. When Gould was persuaded to attend, he had no clue who Johnson was; the law professor's *Darwin on Trial* had not yet been published.

They agreed that public schools were not handling the topic well, though Gould warned that teachers should not be led to believe that it is up for grabs. They discussed how either side could "open the discussion without giving away the store," one participant recalls, and about the "limits of certainty" in both science and religion. Still, when the discussion framed science as the solution, and religious students and parents as the problem, Johnson staged a mutiny. Given the disagreements, the group urged that Johnson and Gould hold a debate.

Johnson vividly recalls sitting around a large conference table, exchanging arguments with Gould, but neither went away with memories of an amicable encounter. "It was not a memorable success," Gould said. He conceded that American students must learn about religion—but not in a science class. "Although I'm not a practicing religious person, religion is just so important in human history, you've got to study it."

For Johnson, turning the tables, the evolution debate was not about religion but about the philosophical assumptions of science. He characterizes Gould as "horrified" by how the meeting developed. "He was very, very nervous and aggressive and he talked too much." It amuses him that Gould defended orthodox Darwinism in the debate, even though his writings buck that orthodoxy. "Everybody agreed that the debate was a draw, and to me a draw, given the circumstances, was pretty good," Johnson says. He told Gould to his face that he was really not a Darwinist. "He is a metaphysical naturalist and materialist who really doesn't feel a need for a mechanism [for evolution]. He just takes for granted how everything popped out of the void."

Yet Johnson is also sympathetic to Gould (who died in 2002), admiring his erudition, literary pizzazz and willingness to dissent from his establishment peers. "The man is in a difficult position," Johnson says today. "You can mine Gould's writings, and he, at one point or another, has denied in print every tenet that is important to Darwinism." He disavowed evolutionary gradualism, admitted the fossil record was poor, and argued that science was frequently the biased and self-interested opinion of elite scientists. When creationists capitalized on Gould's disclosures, the Darwinians lambasted him for writing as he did. Gould's response was to come out stronger against the creationists. This is the dynamic that had resulted from Gould's "difficult position," Johnson claims. "I think one reason he's had to take a very aggressive stance is because he is vulnerable himself."

The sparring between the two men rose to a higher intensity when Johnson loaded his book *Darwin on Trial* with Gould quotes. For example, after citing how Gould told readers to "suppose" things about a specific case of evolution, Johnson says, "We have to do all this supposing, according to Gould, because it is just too hard to 'invent a reasonable sequence of intermediate forms . . . between ancestors and descendants in major structural transitions.'" Elsewhere he describes the fight between Gould and the British zoologist Richard Dawkins over whether abrupt mutations cause evolution: "Gould supposes what he has to suppose, and Dawkins finds it easy to believe what he wants to believe, but supposing and believing are not enough to make a scientific explanation." Taking on Gould's three proofs for evolution—microevolution, nature's imperfection and fossils—Johnson comments, "Nobody needs to prove [the fact] that apples fall down rather than up, but Gould provides three proofs for the 'fact of evolution.'" And of course he quotes Gould's more famous disclosures, including that "the extreme rarity of transitional forms in the fossil record" is the "trade secret of paleontology." When it became clear that a third of the pages in Johnson's 220-page book cite Gould, a friend of the Harvard paleontologist said he should have gotten credit by having his name on the book cover.

In turn, *Scientific American* commissioned Gould to pillory Johnson's work in a feature-length book review. Primarily, he excoriated him for importing legal tactics into science: "We operate with probabilities. The law must often traffic in absolutes." He credited the book's popularity to its emanation "from the symbolic home of California 'flower power,'" adding, "The press loves an oddity." Finally, he criticized Johnson for not giving credit to a hardworking, honest science profession. "A profession finds the very best evidence it could, in exactly that predicted form and time, and a lawyer still tries to impeach us by rhetorical trickery," Gould complained. "No wonder lawyer jokes are so popular in our culture."

Two venerable institutions of the American intelligentsia—the Public Broadcasting System and the *New York Review of Books*—soon took notice of the gathering storm.

One windfall of the Microsoft empire was the decision of Bill Gates's co-founder, Paul Allen, to start a film company, Clear Blue Sky Productions. In December 1999, it announced it would be funding WGBH/NOVA in Boston to produce the "first American series on evolution." The seven-part extravaganza, which opened with a Hollywood-quality drama about the life of Charles Darwin, had also geared up for distribution of film segments to American classrooms with teacher guides and audio-video aids.

Early in 2000, the producers contacted a Discovery Institute fellow and asked if he would participate in on-camera interviews for the final segment of the documentary, *What About God?* Before agreeing to participate, Discovery sleuths did some research and found that the producer for that segment had done an earlier, critical documentary on Protestant fundamentalism. That was a red flag. "We discussed whether this would be a good opportunity," says Discovery's Mark Edwards, director of the institute's public relations. "We got back and said, 'We'd love to be in the science part.'" But that was not an option for the filmmakers, and in the final version intelligent design was not discussed, except to have one evolutionist deride it as a highfalutin version of creation science.

After the contact, Discovery kept an eye on the Clear Blue Sky project. "We realized how large it was going to be," Edwards says. "So we tried to get tapes." A few weeks before its showing, they had obtained all eight hours, or seven episodes, from "various sources," including PBS affiliates. A number of Discovery scientists sat down and watched them, furiously taking notes. In the past, Johnson had engaged in Internet debates when sim-

ilar programs on evolution had made prime time television. This time, they
had plenty of criticisms. They thought about press releases. Then they decided
to subject some of the claims in the TV series to critical research.

The result, which was on the Discovery Institute website a week before
the PBS national showing, became a 120-page book, *Getting the Facts Straight:
A Viewer's Guide to PBS's Evolution.* As advertising, Discovery bought two
million pop-up banners for the *New York Times* web page's front page and
sections on science, national news, editorials, and TV and arts. The banners, which were scheduled for the week beginning September 18, read, "A
Critique of PBS's *Evolution.* Get the Facts Straight. Get Our Viewer's Guide."
Soon after, WGBH lawyer's contacted the *Times* demanding that Discovery's use of the website address pbsevolution.com be stopped, so it was
changed to reviewevolution.com. "We just wanted to be up and on line and
public," recalls Edwards.

In unequivocal terms, the viewer's guide said the program concealed
the incoherence of the evidence for evolution, showed no dissent, and focused
tendentiously on religion—despite claiming to avoid "the religious realm."
And in sending out advocacy packets to teachers' groups and others, PBS
had abused its publicly funded status by promoting political action. "Imagine, for a moment, that PBS created a seven-part series on abortion that was
designed to 'co-opt existing local dialogue' about abortion legislation," the
viewer's guide said. It pointed to a pre-program publication by
WGBH/NOVA called *The Evolution Controversy: Use It or Lose It,* which
said the broadcast could set a mood for upgrading evolution teaching in
public schools. What was more, the pro-evolution National Center for Science Education (NCSE), a private lobbying group, was an official spokesman
for the PBS documentary.

According to the Discovery viewer's guide, the first episode, a drama-
tization of the life of Darwin, "promotes the scientist-vs.-fundamentalist
stereotype." Discovery also protested elements in the "Why Sex" episode,
which frequently showed apes copulating while a voice-over narrator speculated on whether, if humans had stayed closer to the apes, "we might have
evolved to be a totally different, more peaceful, less violent, more sexual
species." The viewer's guide asked, "What is 'Evolution' trying to teach students here?"

There were plenty of details to fight over, but the guide especially protested how the program tended to "lump intelligent design theory with creation science in order to keep it out of science classrooms where it might otherwise be included in discussions of Darwinian evolution." In a burst of rhetoric it stated: "This is not education. This is not good science journalism. This is propaganda."

The NCSE did not take any of this lying down, and a battle of press releases ensued, mostly by e-mail and on websites. First, the NCSE organized its own counterproposal, "Setting the Record Straight: A Response to Creationist Misinformation about the PBS series 'Evolution.'" It contacted scientists whose ambivalent statements about orthodox Darwinism had been used by Discovery in the viewer's guide, and these scientists distanced themselves from the Discovery Institute's use of their comments, saying they were quoted "out of context."

While several creationist organizations had weighed into the debate during the week of the PBS airing, the anti-Darwinian Discovery Institute ranked as top activist, said the NCSE's network project director, Skip Evans. The Discovery Institute "evidently regarded 'Evolution' as a prime opportunity to make a splash of its own, pouring time and money into its effort to discredit it." Other organizations on "the political and religious right" used Discovery materials, Evans reported. But if the mini-controversy made no splash in the major news media, neither did *Evolution* receive much news coverage.

Still, there might have been something like a national debate if the news media, and the entire nation, had not been overwhelmingly distracted by the terrorist attacks of September 11.

For *Evolution,* the poor timing was a letdown after two years of buildup. To try to recoup some of the lost momentum, PBS aired the series again in June 2002, and a classroom video package was released. As another rejoinder to *Evolution,* the Discovery Institute ran advocacy advertisements in the *Weekly Standard,* the *New Republic* and the *New York Review of Books.* They listed over a hundred notable people in science who dissented from a statement in the *Evolution* promotional materials that "all known scientific evidence supports [Darwinian] evolution" as does "virtually every reputable scientist in the world."

In reaction, the NCSE charged Discovery with adding the bracketed "Darwinian" to skew the documentary's claim about the truth of evolution in the broadest, generic terms. It is true that mainstream evolutionists constantly debate the accuracy of Charles Darwin's theories. "Arguments within the scientific community about how evolution occurs should not be confused with arguments—conspicuously absent from the scientific community—about 'whether' evolution occurred," Evans said. Despite the furor, a central theme of the PBS series was how plenty of people adapt their religious beliefs to the fact of evolution, and how this bodes well for détente between science and religion.

As might be expected, the *New York Review of Books* was not so sanguine. It commissioned the brilliantly polemical Frederick Crews, emeritus English professor at the University of California at Berkeley, to write a two-part, nine-thousand-word article critiquing twelve science-and-religion books. Crews began his career as a Freudian literary critic, but ended up renouncing Freud and psychoanalysis "root and branch" in 1992. With penetrating documentation, he strove to unmask Freud as a purveyor of pseudoscience, and his series on the subject in the *New York Review of Books* influenced court rulings on the new claims about "repressed memory syndrome," which had a Freudian air to them. Crews went on to deflate student rebels, literary critics, the sex-obsessed novels of John Updike and, as he allied himself with the skeptic societies, all the hokum of the day, from Zen Buddhism to UFOs. The only thing left was creationism. In October 2001, he had his chance to kneecap the movement in his "Saving Us from Darwin."

His masterful essay, however, is the two-edged sword of proverb. One blade nicks the creationists, but the other draws just as much blood from softhearted evolutionists and Christian Darwinists who, having suffered a "failure of nerve," in Crews's phrase, write friendly books on science and religion. Every overture to build a friendship between science and religion will "prove to have adulterated scientific doctrine or to have emptied religious dogma of its commonly accepted meaning." The "waffling and confusion" only hurt science, and for a misguided motive: "The problem, once again, is how to make room for God."

The militantly anti-Freudian Crews takes the intelligent design thinkers to the couch for a little therapy, looking for the psychological factor in the controversy. The new creationists have "recruits and sympathizers among intellectual sophisticates, hard-headed pragmatists, and even some scientists," he lamented. "Intelligent design is thriving," he further laments, "in cultural circles where illogic and self-indulgence are usually condemned." But in a time of moral gloom and "a cascade of appalling fears," even smart people will fall for religion. Creationism succeeds because "the Darwinian revolution remains incomplete," and that goal is only slowed when Darwinism is prettified to avoid offending society.

Crews thinks that by conceding the reality of microevolution, the intelligent design people have already conceded all of evolution. Existing organisms obviously derive, by a series of small variations, from "more fundamental types," the English professor says dismissively. "The whole business requires a bookkeeper, perhaps, but surely not a God." And he latches onto another admission by Phillip Johnson, who says that if there is no God, then naturalism and Darwinism surely make sense. For Crews, this is a surrender of the first order: "The intelligent design team has handed argumentative victory to its opponents before the debate has even begun."

Crews is a writer's writer. He also has a "penchant for rhetorical overkill," according to English professor Elaine Showalter of Princeton. She remarks that he cannot simply say an opponent is wrong, but must condemn his character as "furtive," "glib" or "limp." In the Darwin essay, Crews describes theists as "triumphalist," "crude" or merely "professional-looking." They use "sleight of hand." Their arguments are "obtusely impressionistic," filled with "absurdity" and creating a "ludicrous spectacle." Smart people follow the intelligent design creationists because the latter are "well-funded" and "shrewd and media-savvy people."

Worse still, their God is strange. This Almighty, "dispenser of wrath, absolution, and grace," is also "a curiously inept cobbler of species." In this implausible story, God has "frittered away thirteen billion years, turning out quadrillions of useless stars, before getting around to the one thing he really cared about, seeing to it that a minuscule minority of earthling vertebrates are washed clean of sin and guaranteed an eternal place in his company." Instead, Crews pays homage to the Principle of Mediocrity: "The time has run out for telling ourselves that we are the darlings of a deity who placed nature here for our convenience." The true story is Darwinian, and its telling "could be the first step toward a wider ethics commensurate with our real transgressions, not against God but against Earth itself and its myriad forms of life."

Though the intelligent design movement would hardly get equal space to respond, Johnson gave an unofficial rebuttal on a web page called "Weekly Wedge Update," where friends and enemies regularly read his reports and commentary. A former campus colleague of Crews, and just as clever, Johnson analyzes why the retired English professor was asked to do the "demolition job" when the *New York Review of Books* has a stable of science icons who could say the same things. Having a scientist weigh in would lend credibility to the intelligent design books, Johnson surmises. A literary torpedo was the alternative, but either way there were indications of a "desperate counterattack" showing that "Darwinism is in serious trouble."

Johnson writes that Crews's article consists "mainly of standard scientific materialist putdowns that could have been stitched together from handouts distributed by any of the so-called 'skeptic' societies." He gives "Fred" credit for his forthrightness: "One thing I can say for Crews is that he is relatively candid about the entwined relationship of Darwinism and atheistic materialism." When it comes to the question of which side has the advantage, Johnson considers that the materialists are on the defensive, and that such Crews-like bombardments are "the best the materialists will ever do, and their best effort conflicts with the evidence."

Most significant, Johnson continues, was the way that Crews negatively portrayed Christian Darwinists and soft-peddling evolutionists, suggesting that "those church councils are composed of fools, and the scientific bodies, of liars." By scorning both, Crews was actually proving Johnson's own point that "the manipulative metaphysicians of big science" have "religious dupes." Crews demonstrates that Darwinism is indeed equivalent to atheism, the very thing Johnson has been trying to prove for years. Johnson concludes by saying that he was going to present Crews with an autographed copy of his latest book, *The Wedge of Truth,* which argues that Christians who embrace Darwinism end up agnostics or nihilists.

While this open but civil warfare between professors on the Berkeley campus was taking place, another skirmish was developing in the larger domain of public policy.

EVOLUTION BECAME A PUBLIC ISSUE in Ohio after the state legislature called for the upgrading of all education standards—in math, English, social studies and science—by the end of 2002. Local school boards were free to ignore the new state standards, but only at the students' peril: information in the standards would be in achievement tests and in a tenth-grade exam required for graduation from high school.

In previous years, a small creationist group had lobbied to modify the treatment of evolution in the science standards, and the term *evolution* had been avoided. While a review of all states by the Fordham Foundation research group awarded Ohio a *B* for its science standards, a follow-up report by the staunch evolutionist Lawrence Lerner gave the same Ohio material an *F* because it lacked the E-word (though not the concept of evolution).

The nineteen-member Ohio State Board of Education had no incentives to wrestle with the topic of evolution once again. Half were appointed by Governor Bob Taft, a moderate Republican, and in an election year Taft wanted to avoid the subject. As fate had it, however, five of the eight members on the smaller Standards Committee were very interested in the evolution debate and wanted to review possible alternatives to straight Darwinian evolution. "That's why it had gotten this far," says Robert P. Lattimer, a research chemist from Cleveland. "The chairman was against it, but he didn't have a majority on his side."

Lattimer was appointed to the Science Standards Writing Committee as what he called "the token conservative" among forty-one members. He had followed the creation-vs.-evolution debate for years and had allied himself with the intelligent design movement. Before the writing of the standards began in fall of 2001, Lattimer attended an Intelligent Design Network conference in Kansas. When the Standards Committee met in January, his proposal to bring in an intelligent design advocate had been approved. The January session set off the official alarm bells; both sides organized for battle. "They started to realize that this thing was going to get big," says Lattimer, "and it's been going ever since." In opposition to the alleged "flat Earth" mentality of the "new creationism," the pro-evolution Ohio Citizens for Science was formed. Meanwhile, supporters of the intelligent design alternative organized Science Excellence for All Ohioans.

The upshot was an extraordinary "information session" on intelligent design for the state school board. It convened on a cold March morning at the Veterans Memorial Auditorium in downtown Columbus. Spectators took up more than a quarter of the four thousand seats, to hear two teams arguing pro and con. Joining physicist Lawrence Krauss in defense of an unadulterated evolution curriculum was Kenneth Miller, the Brown University cell biologist and Christian Darwinist whom Crews had both pilloried and praised. On the other side, arguing for possible inclusion of intelligent design, were two Discovery Institute fellows, biologist Jonathan Wells and science philosopher Stephen Meyer. As the *New York Times* coyly reported, the audience patiently sat through "abstruse arguments about the bacterial flagellum and the peppered moth before one of four clashing scholars finally used the G-word that had attracted the crowd in the first place."

Krauss, chairman of the physics department at Case Western Reserve University, was the second presenter, but the first to say "God" as he warned of a latent religious agenda in the push for intelligent design theory. "The real danger is in trying to put God in the gaps," he said of the design argument. "What they're really attacking here is not Darwinism but science." He protested as unfair the format of the hearing, since he and Miller, bona fide scientists, were paired off against intelligent design theorists. "They're not a part of science," he claimed. "If this debate were fair, there would be ten thousand scientists versus one representative of the Discovery Institute. There is an agenda here, no matter what you hear, to replace materialistic explanations with a theistic understanding of nature."

Indeed, Wells and Meyer did argue that science should be defined more broadly. They said it should look at all the evidence in nature and allow an array of logical explanations, including design. They also contended that this approach made science more interesting in the classroom.

Wells, who was first up, projected his PowerPoint images onto a gigantic screen, as the others did, to make his case that a scientific controversy was raging over the evidence for Darwinian evolution. "Should teachers be permitted to tell students about the controversy?" he asked. Two years earlier, Wells had written *Icons of Evolution,* a book that listed ten evolutionary "icons"—from peppered moths and finch beaks to horse fossils and life's creation in a chemistry flask—that were either misleading or fraudulent. The icon he used to capture the school board's attention was Ernst Haeckel's drawings of embryos, which the German evolutionist had faked a century earlier. Embryologists today know just how different embryos can look, even among vertebrates, and Haeckel's fabrication of look-alike vertebrate embryos may go down as one of a handful of great frauds in modern biology.

Running short on time, Wells asked whether Ohio teachers are permitted to tell students about the textbook problem, and then moved on to the toughest sell of the day: study of intelligent design in science class. It was not crazy to see design, he said. Charles Darwin had seen design, but called it illusory. The modern biochemist Michael Behe looks at the utter complexity inside a cell and sees design that probably requires an intellect. "Is the design that we all see real or merely an appearance?" Real design can be known by "inference from the biological evidence," Wells said. "We can only speculate where the designer came from."

As for Krauss's expelling him from science, Wells suggested that his own credentials made him as much a biologist as Krauss was a physicist. Meanwhile there were students and taxpayers who stood for something in the debate as well. That was a point Meyer also pressed, citing a recent Ohio poll showing that by a 71 percent majority "voters overwhelming favor teaching the controversy." A part of the controversy, he said, is who decides the rules of science: "The methods of science are part of the debate." Scientists already use design inferences, as when archaeologists decided the Rosetta Stone's hieroglyphs were human writing, not the scratches of naturalistic forces such as wind and erosion. For this reason, design advocates want science to look for the best logical explanation from the evidence, not just a naturalistic explanation as demanded by the science establishment.

As the March session took place, a first draft of the Ohio science standards had been written, closely following the National Science Education Standards. The Science Standards Writing Committee declined to add any of Robert Lattimer's proposed changes, including his recommendation that "the standards should state that some scientists support the alternative theory of intelligent design." In Veterans Memorial Auditorium that day, the polarized school board believed that public demands for such changes were still the policy issue on the table—until Meyer gave them an escape hatch.

Meyer proposed a compromise measure that would jettison local efforts by Ohio design activists to put intelligent design in the teaching curriculum, and instead adopt a science standard that says teachers may criticize Darwinism if they wish to. In other words, he said, allow teachers to "teach the controversy." Let teachers also have the freedom to cite the design concept as one alternative. "Let's not persecute teachers," said Meyer.

While school board members breathed a sigh of relief that, with Meyer's proposal, a direct battle over mandating intelligent design might now be avoided, the Ohio newspapers played the "compromise" as a retreat. The *Columbus Dispatch* said the "surprise move" signaled that the design advocates had "abandoned their fight in Ohio . . . for now, anyway." Said the *Dispatch*, "[Meyer's] proposal could shift to local school boards and even teachers the debate over the validity of Darwinian evolution and whether intelligent design—the idea that life couldn't have begun or developed without some unidentified designer—is merely a guise for biblical creationism."

Cell biologist Kenneth Miller watched the debate evolve. When it was his turn, he warned that the design advocates were using politics to get into the science game, not peer-reviewed channels. As a peacemaker, Miller first said that teachers must tell students that science can't do everything. "Let them know science has limitations," he conceded. The last thing he would want in the science class was that students feel forced to choose between science and religion. This said, Miller shifted into battle mode and declared that there was no "scientific controversy" in biology. The design interlopers were "propped up from outside the scientific community"—namely, by pressure politics on legislators and school officials.

In truth, the politics were there, but not always plain to see. When President Bush signed the "No Child Left Behind" education spending bill in January 2002, the language of the accompanying report showed how far the design movement had come. The report, which interpreted the bill and explained its history, affirmed: "Wherever topics are taught that may generate controversy (such as biological evolution), the curriculum should help students to understand the full range of scientific views that exist, why such topics may generate controversy, and how scientific discoveries can profoundly affect society." Darwin critics such as the law school professor Phillip Johnson were instrumental in drafting the short text.

Once it had been included in the legislative package, however, nobody could agree on who had won the political battle and what the language entailed for states taking federal money. According to people in Meyer's camp at the Discovery Institute, what had been achieved was beyond their wildest ambitions. When Senator Rick Santorum introduced the report on the Senate floor as a "sense of the Senate" resolution, it passed overwhelmingly, as most resolutions do. But whereas most such resolutions are thrown out when the House and the Senate reconcile their versions of a particular bill, in this case some Republican lawmakers fought to keep this advisory, nonbinding language on science in the legislation's report; that way, it was on the record and highly symbolic.

The national intelligent design strategists said they were delighted that the resolution got as far as it did, but in the heat of political debate, some partisans went to extremes. Some who liked the language thought it was legally binding. Those who detested the language said it was not even in the legislation (meaning that the report, in their view, was not part of the bill). The latter claim was made by biologist Kenneth Miller in his Ohio School Board presentation. Miller had loaded the entire education bill onto his laptop computer and showed it onscreen by PowerPoint projection. He told the school board members that he was about to employ a word search tool to find "evolution" in the bill, and as they watched, the computer finally made a loud beep—the word had not been found.

That was beside the point as far as Stephen Meyer was concerned, because the report's language was advisory. He emphasized that it was a statement by the U.S. Congress, and it backed the notion of "teaching the controversy." From the design movement's point of view, the real problem lay in how the American Civil Liberties Union and the National Center for Science Education, which had promoted PBS's *Evolution* series, threatened to sue school boards or districts if a teacher criticized Darwinism in a biology or earth science class. But now, Meyer believed, schools had three legal supports in such cases: the federal report language about teaching science critically, a law review article by a Discovery Institute fellow explaining why intelligent design passes constitutionality, and finally the 1987 Supreme Court ruling against creation science, which nevertheless concedes that "teaching a variety of scientific theories about the origins of humankind to schoolchildren might be validly done with the clear secular intent of enhancing the effectiveness of science instruction."

A few days after the showdown in the Veterans Memorial Auditorium, Senator Santorum's office published an op-ed piece saying the report language was binding, and the next day Senator Edward Kennedy rebutted his colleague, saying that while he was for critical thinking in science, he was not for design. To try to clear the matter up for Ohio, two of its lawmakers routed their opinion to the State Board of Education. "The language is now part of law," wrote Representative John A. Boehner, a Republican and chairman of the House Education Committee, in the letter. And it "clarifies that public school students are entitled to learn that there are differing scientific views on issues such as biological evolution."

Ohio had magnified the intelligent design debate to a national level. But in October 2002, the five-member majority on the Standards Committee had its own local decision to make. With approval from the school board, the committee first rescinded a tenth-grade standard that defined science as "limited to natural explanations." The replacement said: "Science is a systematic method of continuing investigation ... which leads to more adequate explanations of natural phenomena." Then it added a new "indicator" guiding tenth-grade life science teachers to: "Describe how scientists continue to investigate critically and analyze aspects of evolutionary theory."

Both sides had battled right up to the last hearings. Now that it was over, both declared victory. In Washington, the American Association for the Advancement of Science was less sanguine about the Ohio saga. In a resolution, it urged "citizen across the nation" to oppose the intelligent design push because it threatened "the quality of science education." By December, the Ohio School Board was ready to adopt the science standards, but with one final amendment. The new indicator, it said, did "not mandate the teaching or testing of intelligent design." Lattimer was pleased. During the year spent writing the standards, he said, "the public input was ignored." But finally, there was no escape from public opinion: "A large majority of Ohioans favors the teach-the-controversy approach."

10

THE TREE OF LIFE

The competition between the publicly funded Human Genome Project and the private company Celera Genomics to decipher the three billion codes of the human genome was at a fever pitch in spring of 2000. To prepare for the inevitable public unveiling of a full human genome, the two sides, represented by the government's Francis Collins and Celera founder Craig Venter, had to get together. Collins proposed a meeting, and over beer and pizza Ari Patrinos, head of the project for the Department of Energy, helped the two gene hunters reach a friendly agreement. They would appear jointly at the White House to announce the completion of a draft of the human genome by their respective teams.

On that day, American civil religion met genetic science. President Clinton said science was "learning the language in which God created life," and Collins described the DNA code as "our own instruction book, previously known only to God." What was not fully described until early the next year was the human genome's unexpected complexity and how it complicated the human place on the tree of life—the overarching metaphor for the treelike relationship of all living things, past and present

According to the official findings published in February 2001—splashed across the pages of the journals *Nature* and *Science* and on front pages of newspapers everywhere—if God invented the code, he used far fewer genes than had previously been believed necessary to produce something so complex as a human being. The findings suggested, for example, that humans are produced by only twice the number of protein-encoding genes required to make a fruit fly, worm or plant. Humans, moreover, have a relatively small number of genes that mice do not have. This implies that more has to be done with less: an astonishing interactive complexity is necessary within the genome.

Beyond the science, for believers and atheists alike these discoveries must elicit humility and awe. For believers such as Collins, a top scientist, public servant and churchgoing evangelical Christian, the complexity in itself was marvelous enough to deepen his wonder at the created world. "As we uncover things about life, about our own lives, about our own biology, we are glimpsing what really was God's plan, even though the plan was implemented through this Darwinian scheme," Collins said in his office later in that momentous year. "If you don't accept God being outside of time, that might seem rather odd. Blind chance bothers people a lot. They think, 'Well, God wouldn't play dice that way.'" Collins resolves the paradox by accepting that God is both sovereign and beyond the time and space of physical nature. Given a transcendent God,

> There was a design involved for sure. But the mechanism by which that design played out to our minds, which are bounded in space and time, appears to be through the random acts of evolution. Yet if one is a believer in the fact that God intended to have creatures with whom he could have fellowship, he had that whole plan worked out. It was therefore not a chance event.

About a year after the human genome's unveiling, some of the nation's leading naturalists met at the American Museum of Natural History in New York City for "the first major scientific forum in decades to address the 'Tree of Life,' the pattern of relationships that links all Earth's species." Infused with a naturalistic outlook, the gathering conveyed both the humility and hubris of science, captured in a visionary speech by the Harvard insect expert Edward O. Wilson. Mapping the tree of life took field biologists "almost to the breaking point," he said, because it involved so many specimens and an "almost unimaginably complicated evolutionary history." Yet Wilson is an optimist. In the next fifty years, he predicted,

> [we will have] a complete account of Earth's biodiversty, pole to pole, bacteria to whale, at every level of organization from genome to ecosystem, yielding an as complete as possible cause-and-effect explanation of the

biosphere and a correct and verifiable family tree for all the millions of species. In short, a unified biology.

Such a unitary vision evokes a time when naturalists were believers in divine creation. William Whewell—a hero of Wilson's for his idea of the consilience, or unity, of knowledge—was among the natural theologians who saw God's work in a remarkable created order. In Whewell's era, the first half of the nineteenth century, the unity of Creation was conceived as a hierarchical Great Chain of Being, in which groups of living things were "embranchments" from basic forms created by God. Indeed, two generations before Darwin sketched his tree in *On the Origin of Species* in 1859, a God-given tree of life already adorned some frontispieces of science books.

As embodied in the believing or unbelieving stances of a Collins or a Wilson, the scientist may regard the tree of life—a tremendous entity extending into the deep past and into the far future—either as God's work or as self-generated. The believing tradition had begun the categorization of living things with the Swedish botanist Carl Linnaeus (d. 1778), who invented the convention of binomial nomenclature (as in *Homo sapiens,* the genus *Homo* and the species *sapiens*). Linnaeus theorized that God had created a single pair for each genus, which had then differentiated over time. To this, the great comparative anatomist Georges Cuvier added the concept of four kingdoms or "embranchments" of life: the radiates, mollusks, articulates and vertebrates. Cuvier saw species as basically fixed by a "correlation of parts" that constituted each one, never to be disassociated and changed into something else.

Darwinian evolution swept over these two systems, adopting a similar classification but leaving all creatures open to change; their commonality derived not from a Creator, but from "one or a few" common ancestors. From a few simple types, the tree of life branched out, with slight variations at first but then into entirely different kinds of organisms—a process scientists characterize as going from diversity (small variation) to disparity (great differences). With the revolution in genetics beginning in the 1950s, the visible tree of life was found to have an unseen internal blueprint. Rapidly, the science of life faced the promise and peril of two separate tracks of description. One was the inner "gene phylogeny" (ancestry of genes), and the other an outer "organismal phylogeny" (ancestry of organismic shapes).

With the inner and outer tracks having histories that must be correlated, the work of the naturalist becomes as intricate as the cosmologist's, who witnesses an expanding universe by light that carries ancient images. Because most organisms on the historical tree of life no longer exist—an estimated 99 percent have become extinct—and because the fossil remains are relatively few, the internal tracking by molecular biology hit science "like a tidal wave," in Edward O. Wilson's phrase. It overwhelmed the old-fashioned approach of building a tree based on diagnosing the shapes of organisms. In theory, the inner genes and outer morphology were supposed to match closely, but by the time of the human genome project, it was already clear that the tree was not always so simple.

Despite its name, the Human Genome Project also focused on the genetic totality of organisms such as the bacterium *e. coli,* yeast, the roundworm, the fruit fly and the mouse. In other molecular biology laboratories scientists did parallel work, adding to the total of sixty-one species that had been sequenced by early 2002. The independent labs had also probed twenty thousand species for the sequence of a particular molecule that all organisms have.

With the tendency for the new biology to do everything by gene comparisons, Wilson, who began as an insect collector, urged a revival of descriptive systematics. "The molecular geneticist has so much money, and there are so many of them," he said. "And they are so ambitious."

Whatever the funding, they all take one common concept to the bank: that the tree has absolute physical continuity. In accordance with Wilson's "cause-and-effect explanation of the biosphere," they should be able to trace every leaf and twig back along its branches to the trunk and then to a common root. Though the tree is massively extended, it is entirely self-contained, much like the cosmologist Stephen Hawking's no-boundary universe. And as Hawking might ask of a no-boundary tree of life, "What place then for God?"

The Human Genome Project's Francis Collins knows the debate, often called "the God of the gaps" issue, pretty well. The only gap that makes sense to him at this time is the ultimate origin of life.

There's this huge problem currently with scientific explanations of how we got from having nothing to a self-replicating system, and in a very inhospitable environment four billion years ago. If you wanted to be a God of the gaps person, that would be the gap I would pick.

Right after life's beginning, the sapling began to branch. Ever since the revolution in molecular biology, this stage has been the target. By the 1970s, scientists had expanded the idea of three organismal kingdoms at the root to five kingdoms, with the large animals and plants receiving the most attention. Accordingly, study of the tree of life was dominated by zoologists and botanists.

In the 1960s, however, American cell biologist Lynn Margulis had enough of this bias against tiny organisms. Drawing on the speculations of others, she wrote a heretical paper stating that microbes and cells invaded each other, which enabled the "evolution" of more complex organisms. Her book *The Origin of the Eukaryotic Cells* (1970) threw down the gauntlet. Reluctant biologists had to start testing her "symbiogenesis" theory, which held that symbiotic exchange of parts gave rise to early life (and maybe larger-scale life, too). By 1975, her theory proved valid at the cell level, making a small chink in the neo-Darwinian armor.

Two of the labs that tested Margulis's hypothesis were those of Carl R. Woese and W. Ford Doolittle. But they were neither zoologists like Haeckel nor microbiologists like Margulis. They worked at the level of biological molecules, where genes and DNA operated—down at the level that they believed would yield real understanding. Woese's laboratory at the University of Illinois was the first to spawn a small revolution as he looked at the molecular makeup of the very root of the tree. It was he who proposed that life arises not from five kingdoms but from three more fundamental superkingdoms, later called domains. This conceptual advance made the front page of the *New York Times* in the fall of 1977.

By studying a particular molecule that all life presumably has had—the ribosomal RNA molecule—Woese argued that even before bacteria arose 3.5 billion years ago, there were entities he called archaeabacteria. By 1990, he decided that archaea were so distinct that they constituted a separate domain of the tree of life. Today, Woese's three domains of archaea, bacteria and eucarya are the standard for the field. And he located a standard molecule that science could investigate in every organism. As his colleague Ford

Doolittle describes it, "Woese's major achievement was to get everybody on the RNA standard, and to construct a massive phylogenetic edifice. It's probably the best tree we have based on a single molecule."

A decade after Woese's declaration about the three domains, Doolittle threw his own hat into the ring. Based on work at his molecular biology laboratory in Nova Scotia, he declared in 1999 and 2000 that an "uprooting of the tree of life" may be necessary because there was so much "lateral transfer" at the very dawn of life, a process that undermined the very idea of a common ancestor. By the time of the Tree of Life conference, even an orthodox Darwinian like E. O. Wilson was speaking of the "still tangled and problematic trunk of bacteria and archaea."

In his presentation, Doolittle assured fellow experts that the uprooting affected nothing above the three-part basal stem of the tree of life. Still, Doolittle said, "My view does challenge Darwin in a couple of ways." It threw into doubt a first ancestor, on one hand, and undercut the idea that gene mutation is the only cause of new evolutionary forms, on the other. "The mechanism of adaptation may be borrowing genes rather than making your own genes better."

Doolittle, a native of Illinois, has been looking at the genetic tree of life since high school in the mid-1950s, when he washed dishes at one of the pioneering laboratories in the technology of DNA gene sequencing. He thus had a front-row seat when molecular biology began its dramatic expansion. And he believes it is the most powerful tool we can deploy in understanding evolution.

"Lateral gene transfer could be so massive that there is no gene that would track organismal history all the way back to the beginning," Doolittle said, chatting before his formal presentation at the conference. "It doesn't make a lot of sense to talk about the last common ancestor." He prefers concepts such as "a common ancestral population," which still means life was invented only once, but the universal genetic code came out of a promiscuous collection of early DNA precursors: "A community evolves, and eventually that community gets all the properties a modern cell has. But there was never a single cell to which we can trace it all."

Woese would make the same case in a 2002 paper, saying that "primitive cellular evolution is basically communal" and "it is the community as a whole, the ecosystem, which evolves." Only after that communal period, Woese argues, did novel cells emerge and begin to cross a point that he calls the "Darwinian threshold."

All these excavations at the root of the tree have interested creationists, yet the last thing Doolittle wants to do is give them aid and comfort. He knows that his work is also widely cited by the intelligent design movement, at least to question standard textbook claims about a Darwinian common ancestor. In this context he says:

> Of course there was a tree of life. Cells give rise to cells [by division] and all life is related. Imagine we had a movie camera running from the beginning of life. We record every single cell division that happened. That would have a roughly treelike structure.

But inevitably, the tree becomes far more complicated and "not treelike." Doolittle knows this is an opening for people looking for God's action in nature, so he's put a little thought into the God question, though he himself is led to disbelief:

> If for some personal reason you believed in God, a God who intervenes in the world, then I guess there is plenty of place for him to intervene because we simply have not proven very much about what happened in the totality of life's history. But I think it is unfair, as some creationists do, to take any apparent chink in the armor of the Darwinian synthesis as evidence that there is room for God. I've come up with another materialistic, naturalistic explanation for the data. It's not anti-Darwinian because Darwin didn't even know about genes or that much about bacteria.

He likes to think Darwin would agree with him today. "It's not fair to treat us [Darwinists] as a religion, of whom Darwin is our prophet, and then say, 'Oh, you're deviating from the true religion.' That's just not how science works." And tree-of-life science is not easy.

> There's uncertainty—and I'm not saying that makes room for God—but it's harder to figure out the tree of life than one would have thought. [For example], people would be willing to die for chimps being our sister taxon. But there are other things they wouldn't be willing to die for—yet. And

you would think, "My gosh, with all the fossil records worked out, and all the comparative anatomy, we should know this." So it's harder to do than you think.

Doolittle believes that the intelligent design theorists come to the axing of the trunk as honestly as any non-Darwinian can. But as a naturalist and a scientist, he is loath to see any meaning or purpose shoehorned into the data of nature, even where the data touch on the pregnant topic of origins:

> They say, "We look at the data, and we are not persuaded it can be explained this way." Well, at least that's an honest statement. But I'm persuaded that it can be explained in that way. To be a scientist is to say that I see nothing in biology that demands that I believe that there's a supernatural force at play. Or even a purpose.

FURTHER UP THE TREE, THE SO-CALLED CAMBRIAN "explosion" apparently gave rise to a riot of different basic life forms, and some scientists cannot get away from arguing over the "meaning" or "purpose" of such an unusual event.

Though the true nature of the Cambrian period, which began 530 million years ago, is debated, the image of an "explosion" won't go away. While a traditional tree moves from diversity to disparity, the Cambrian seems to begin with disparity and then diversifies further. In the most literal view of the fossil record, the earliest disparate body plans seem to have burst out of nothing. Palentologists and evolutionists find this hard to believe, but cannot find preceding organisms on the tree of life, presumably because they were too small and soft-bodied to have laid down traces in the strata.

The term Cambrian comes from the region in England where, in 1830, the British paleontologist William Buckland found the remarkable fossil layer. The era's most famous collections of fauna are from the Burgess Shale in Canada and the remote Ediacara Hills of South Australia. The ferment over such discoveries prompted a 1995 *Time* cover story on "Evolution's Big Bang." Little mentioned, however, was Darwin's own angst over the question more than a century earlier. "Darwin was fully aware that his theory might be difficult to reconcile with the seemingly abrupt appearance of the

Cambrian animals," says Simon Conway Morris of Cambridge University. And for creationists—which Conway Morris is not—the Cambrian explosion ranks as a discontinuity in the tree that certainly looks like God's creative activity.

Conway Morris, an expert on the Cambrian, resembles the late Stephen Jay Gould in his encyclopedic knowledge of fossils and organisms; but in their thinking on the significance of the Cambrian, the two scientists diverge dramatically. In his book *Wonderful Life,* Gould used the Burgess Shale data to argue that the Cambrian outburst produced Earth's optimum number of basic life forms, many of which then rapidly died off—an upside down "cone of life." Gould turned the tree into a bush with a profusion of broken and dead-end twigs. The message was clear: life is full of flukes and accidents, and the emergence of humans is just one of them. A magnificent wordsmith, Gould drew his title from the Frank Capra movie starring Jimmy Stewart: a suicidal man sees his life played back to him, and notices how one "contingent" boyhood event determined whether he lived or died. And so it is with biological life, morals and society. Gould made the term "contingency" chic.

To Conway Morris, the metaphor of a film rewinding is an unfortunate "intellectual game" that also gets the data from the Cambrian basically wrong. Using the more extensive and recent discoveries from deposits found in China, which preserved many pre-Cambrian soft-bodied organisms, Conway Morris argues that the Cambrian does appear to be a genuine explosion demanding an explanation. He rejects Gould's "enormous contingent muddle" and argues that it can be refuted on scientific grounds.

The refutation comes in the evidence of "convergence," or the tendency of life, at the level both of genes and of organisms, to take on similar shapes and functions everywhere. Darwin had noted convergence, too. But Conway Morris says that such "convergence and constraints of form" may be the dominant theme in the tree of life. "For all its exuberance, the forms of life are restricted and channeled." So the same kinds of eyes, brains, limbs and molecular machinery show up on distantly separated parts of the tree: "Again and again we arrive at the same solution." We find it in nature and also in the laboratory. He argues that of the immense random possibilities for a genetic code, "nature's choice might indeed be the best possible code." A laboratory experiment shows "startling evidence for optimization."

The same goes for the Cambrian, since the evidence to date rejects the "inverted cone of life" model proposed by Gould:

> In fact the constraints we see on evolution suggest that underlying the apparent riot of forms there is an interesting predictability. This suggests that the role of contingency in individual history has little bearing on the likelihood of the emergence of a particular biological property.

This apparently marvelous tendency of life "reinforces the reality of trends and direction in evolution," he says. "And this, to my mind, goes a long way to refute some of the main theses of Stephen Jay Gould," such as his notion that evolution's products are solely the result of blind, unlikely-to-be-repeated fortuity. Convergence points to a diametrically opposite conclusion, Conway Morris says, but raises the great circular question of origins:

> The ubiquity of convergence suggests there is some degree of biological reality and organization and coherence, rather than just a "great muddle." But are organisms similar because they have converged or because they are descendants of a common ancestor?

Conway Morris's approach does not so much point to discontinuity on the tree as hint at design. He knows this may be taken by creationists as another vulnerability of Darwinism. Though a Christian believer himself, he quickly notes that science forever prefers a natural explanation to a supernatural one. Still, with all the optimizing and convergence, "some people believe that they can read a message in there. I'm not sure one can." Yet every interpreter of nature may apply a worldview, as Conway Morris does on Sundays. "Design is imprinted in the universe," says the Cambrian fossil hunter. "That's the way it is because it was created by a God."

This returns him to his problem with Gould: he believes *Wonderful Life* was written "to buttress an ideological viewpoint" (for which the left-wing Gould was well known): that seeing God and purpose in nature leads to dictatorships, hierarchies and right-wing social policy. In rebuttal, Conway Morris argues that Gould unwittingly opens a road to contingent nihilism. "We might do better to accept our intelligence as a gift, and it may be a mistake to imagine that we shall not be called to account," he says.

THE TREE OF LIFE CONFERENCE WAS HELD in the Romanesque ballroom of the American Museum of Natural History, and presentations moved up the line of species from bacteria to reptiles and on to humans. At times, the auditorium seemed filled to capacity with students, teachers and the lecture-going public. The visual aids used by speakers showed a distinct trend, and that was the use of *cladistic* charts with which to organize taxonomic categories (e.g., classes, genera, species) of organisms. Three decades earlier, cladistics was unknown, but at this conference it was abundantly present.

Every presentation used the term *clade,* Latin for branch, even though the term was disdained by a previous generation of interpretive systematists. The clade and its map, the *cladogram,* has become the easiest possible way for naturalists to group organisms. The aim is to reveal shared characteristics of organisms as they actually are, without regard to theoretical claims of evolutionary descent. "Cladists" all believe in Darwin and an evolutionary tree, but concurring that the tree can never be mapped, they organize clades as if a historical evolutionary tree did not exist.

The paleontologist and cladist Henry Gee, a student of Colin Patterson, one of England's great Darwinian iconoclasts (who constantly questioned the scientific claims of Darwinism), has explained this new taxonomy as a necessary response to the insurmountable problem of Deep Time—that the distant past cannot be recounted. He wants to keep tree-of-life studies empirical, not wishful or speculative. "Once we realize that Deep Time can never support narratives of evolution, we are forced to accept that virtually everything we thought we knew about evolution is wrong," he writes. And that includes the very attempt to build a tree.

On a more modest scale, cladistics is a way to estimate the "relative degrees of cousinhood" of organisms. Because such comparisons are empirical, not speculative, "cladistics is the best philosophy for the scientific understanding of the history of life as we unearth it from Deep Time." He thinks of it as more than a technique, but less than a science; it is a way of seeing the "products of evolution as they are, not how we would like them to be."

It is clear why Henry Gee was not a plenary speaker in New York, where the museum had in fact adopted cladistics years earlier. "No science can ever be historical," Gee has written. He praised his mentor Patterson, a fish expert at the British Museum of Natural History, because he "wished to replace the elitist, authoritarian presentation of old-fashioned museum displays" with a more limited, empirical approach:

> The cladogram makes no presumptions about who is ancestral to whom, for such things cannot be known for certain. There are no "missing links," no chain of ancestry and descent, no sign of progressive advancement towards the acme that is humanity.

In this sense, Gee has taken a stance contrary to that of Conway Morris, sympathetic rather to Gould's insistence that humans not be elevated to the top of the heap, the apex of Creation or a Great Chain of Being. When Gee's iconoclasm on the tree of life was portrayed by creationists as a major blow for Darwinian evolution, Gee parried by saying it was not, and lest his science be taken as motivated by disbelief, he said that he too believed in God.

Understandably, the creationists have watched the cladistic revolution and the new genome frontier with interest and frequently amusement. First, the tree of life argues for absolute continuity, but its followers have gone over to cladistics, which seems to be saying that continuity, or ancestry, is no longer in the realm of science. Thus, continuity looks philosophical, not empirical. Second, the molecular work in a cladistic context seems to point to the existence of genetic types—shades of the "kinds" spoken of in Genesis. Suddenly, in the space age, the old-fashioned systems of Linnaeus and Cuvier, with their divine underpinnings and all, are beginning to look pretty good.

That, at least, is the remarkable public claim of one of the world's leading experts on butterflies. At the same London museum where Patterson had held forth, Bernard d'Abrera rose to prominence for his mastery of the butterfly, which he had studied from age three. In 2001, he came out with the beautifully illustrated *The Concise Atlas of Butterflies of the World,* running to 353 pages in coffee table size. A summa of his career, thirty years of work, it contains illustrations of nearly every genus of butterfly ever described. Here are all the ingredients for a possible butterfly tree of life. But then, a considerable section of the book is devoted to lambasting science's failure to fund preservation of butterflies and the environment; all the money, complains d'Abrera, is squandered looking for an elusive Darwinian tree.

"They fill the universities and the scientific institutions after their own kind, and relentlessly pursue useless theories about the past origins of species, which have no bearing whatsoever on the systematic extinction of species in their present," he wrote. His book is an attack on the "arrogant attitude" of modern materialist science, which claims it is not philosophical, but indeed is profoundly so, not allowing experts like himself to categorize nature's wonders in ways that acknowledge them, with Linnaean-like clarity, as God's creations. The author, who describes himself as a "Natural Historian and Philosopher," says his work is an antidote to "the very real excesses of evolutionist literature and its relentless propaganda." Accordingly, his chapters on biology, classification, philosophical argument and mimicry spare the reader any hint of the "evolutionary bias."

D'Abrera labels the bias in question the "Theory of the Accidental Origin and Evolution of Species by Chance." Breaking from that assumption, he "simply wishes to free himself and his readers of all that viscid, asphyxiating baggage, so as to leave the study of the lepidoptera [insects with two pairs of broad wings] entirely in the peace and tranquility of an objective science, based on observation, experimental demonstration, and above all, common sense."

This *cri du coeur* by such a prominent museum scientist is uncommon, to say the least. His suggestion that "the tree of life" is really more like a mosaic of creations reinforces the views of creationists. From this perspective, the tree is best envisioned through the metaphors of a lawn, a forest or even an orchard. In other words, either by God's design or by processes as yet beyond science's ability to explain, organic life is viewed as having many separate basal shoots from which arise the various kinds of life forms. The naturalistic view can now envisage separate lines arising from the communal pool of the first cellular organisms, but the case may equally be made for the Cambrian explosion as the origin of the forest. Focusing on discontinuities in nature, this version is amenable to many theists, though it is entirely based on the findings of secular-minded scientists.

One of the most influential in the past few decades has been Michael Denton, a British biochemist who has worked and taught in Australia and New Zealand. His 1986 book, *Evolution: A Theory in Crisis,* asserts that

Darwin's most basic tree-of-life argument, namely homology, has gone unproven.* "Homology has remained the mainstay of the argument for evolution right down to the present," Denton says, but still faces a scientific "failure to find a genetic and embryological basis for homology." Some common structures have different genetic codes, and some similar codes produce different structures. Embryos that look different at conception may look similar at a middle stage, but then their mature features often end up being shaped by new sets of biological mechanisms. In short, homology's "value as evidence for evolution is greatly diminished" as science begins to understand the vast complexity of genetics and embryology.

Denton is no creationist, and he has distanced himself from "special creation" ideas. But he does not mind working with critics of Darwinism, and he became a science fellow at the Discovery Institute. Denton has since argued strongly for a single branching tree of life, but with a plan for life "written into the order of things" and carried out by the miracle of genetics. His 1998 book, *Nature's Destiny: How the Laws of Biology Reveal Purpose in the Universe,* makes the case with the author's customary persuasive power. Denton posits a "directed evolution" not dissimilar from the idea of "oriented evolution" proposed by the great French naturalist Pierre Grassé, and he is open to the idea of genetic "saltations," or leaps, in which life's programming reaches a critical stage and "explosive evolution" produces drastic novelty. There is no God in his biological schema, but it lends support to the anthropic principle and a fine-tuned universe, and indirectly to beliefs in theistic evolution. Something *has* to do the directing.

One of Denton's colleagues at the Discovery Institute was science fellow Paul Nelson, whose doctorate in the philosophy of biology at the University of Chicago gave him standing in the debate on the common ancestry of life. Emboldened by works such as Denton's *Evolution* (1986), Nelson and others would emphasize the discontinuity of life, especially after the Cambrian explosion, and the constraints that seem to produce only certain types of creatures. "The problem Cuvier grasped is very much alive today,"

---

*Homology "occurs where a fundamentally similar organ or structure is modified to serve quite dissimilar ends. A good example of homologous resemblance is the similarity in the basic design of the forelimbs of terrestrial vertebrates." Michael Denton, *Evolution: A Theory in Crisis* (Adler & Adler, 1985), p. 48.

Nelson writes. "Cuvier saw his embranchments as functionally constrained in the range of possible variation." In this, Nelson has common cause with Conway Morris's search for convergence, and Denton's openness to purpose and saltations in biological history.

But he is ultimately looking for the discontinuity—the gap, indeed—where the mind of God could create, and again it is the metaphors of lawns, forests and orchards that seem most promising. Nelson has cited the work of P. Wilmer at length on the origin of the subkingdom of metazoa, or animals. Wilmer, in her highly regarded *Invertebrate Relationships,* asserts that the origin of animals does not resemble "a vine, or a neatly dichotomous tree." Instead, "the comparative evidence indicates that the history of animals must branch like a field of grass low down. . . . The overall effect is therefore not that of a neat lawn of grass, but rather an old-fashioned meadow, where a few hardy perennial designs flourish and branch among the grasses." Wilmer questions the perfect tree of Darwin, because similar life forms seem to appear again and again without ancestral ties. "Many kinds of invertebrates do appear to have been 'invented' several times over, with particular designs reappearing repeatedly," Wilmer writes. Perhaps "metazoan status itself was achieved more than once, so the 'animals' as a whole are polyphyletic." Though Wilmer's work is empirical and secular, its suggestion of discontinuity in animal history may be taken as not incompatible with creationist ideas, some of which attribute different "kinds," or archetypes of animals to divine creativity.

Another area of science where more information is making the tree harder to understand is genetic ancestry. The confidence of popular science in these "phylogenetic trees" is illustrated by a section in the National Academy of Science's book *Teaching about Evolution and the Nature of Science.* It uses a favorite example: a common molecule found in all organisms is called cytochrome C. This molecule transports energy in every living thing. When its DNA is examined, its degree of evolutionary change over time matches those on the presumed tree of life.

"The molecular divergence allows research to track evolutionary events by sequencing the DNA of different organisms," the book explains; this method determines that the lineage of humans and chimpanzees diverged about five million years ago, whereas the mouse and human lineage split eighty million years in the past. "Scientists today routinely use the differences they can measure between DNA sequences of organisms as 'molecular clocks' to decipher the relationship between living things." The book holds out hope that "as the chromosomes of more and more organisms are sequenced over the next few decades, these data will be used to reconstruct much of the missing history of life on earth—thereby compensating for many of the gaps that still remain in the fossil record."

Not too long after the book's publication, the geneticist Francisco Ayala, who was peerless in the 1980s in his fight against creationists, published his latest findings on how poorly the so-called "molecular clocks" work. If in 2001 Ayala questioned "whether there is a molecular clock at all," given that molecules he studied "evolve erratically," the next year he pointed out "a conflict between fossil- and molecular-based evolutionary time scales." It was a methodological problem, he said, but the upshot was this:

> Molecular approaches for dating the branches of the tree of life frequently lead to substantially deeper [further in the past] times of divergence than those inferred by paleontologists. The discrepancy between molecular and fossil estimates persists despite the booming growth of [molecular] sequence data sets.

For Ayala, this apparent clash between his findings and the claims of the National Academy book is part of the normal pugilism of rigorous science, not a proof of gaps for the interventions of God. But for Paul Nelson, who is a design theorist, this phylogenetic tree problem is yet another scientific confirmation that common ancestry is a philosophical assumption, not an empirically established fact. Indeed, Nelson says, common ancestry can at times look like a no less theological idea than Cuvier's belief that God created distinct kinds of life forms—a forest of life, not a tree of life.

DESPITE THE MOUNTING EVIDENCE AGAINST IT, the Darwinian tree model still prevails. And when the human genome had been unlocked and offered to the world on February 15, 2001, it was presented among images of the human species as a magnificent branch amid the upper foliage of the tree of life. The main surprise was that fewer genes seem needed to produce humans than once believed, though that low number was quickly disputed and the debate goes on.

Still, it appears that a few genes do a lot more, or many things at once, said genome expert Mark Bloom of the Biological Sciences Curriculum Study. Rather than assume that one gene does one job, science now has to look for "alternate expression from the same gene, gene regulation, gene interactions, and protein modifications." The genes in question are called "protein coding" because they give instructions for a particular protein, or building block, of the human being.

If the molecular tree of life is conceded to be more complex than previously surmised, the leaders of the genome revolution still see the future in a hopeful light. David Baltimore of the California Institute of Technology heralds the new knowledge, but adds that connecting the chimpanzee to humans with precise treelike clarity might get harder. "I wonder if we will learn much about the origin of speech, the elaboration of the frontal lobes and the opposable thumb, the advent of upright posture, or the sources of abstract reasoning ability, from a simple genomic comparison of human and chimp," Baltimore says. Everyone agrees that now the game is about finding clusters of genes, or key sets of regulatory genes that seem to tell the others what to do. For the tree of life, the question has become: how does science trace the common ancestry and branching of groups of genes? "Another half-century of work by armies of biologists may be needed before this key step of evolution is fully elucidated," Baltimore says of just the chimp-human branch.

At the National Institutes of Health, Francis Collins does not see the idea of evolution by natural selection being undercut by a more complex tree of life. What boggles the mind—and may add to religious awe—is our improved information concerning the "incredible elegance" of the gene system:

> How you could, on a digital platform, build a human being out of just thirty to thirty-five thousand instructions? On top of that, once we are developed, we still are capable of an amazing range of activities that all have to be specified in that information molecule. The idea that we can simply catalog these genes and their sequences and get a rough idea of what each might do based on its homology to other genes is probably way, way, way naïve.

Though he thinks that the new complexity of the genetic tree of life "does not upset too many apple carts" in Darwinian theory, Collins feels that it does make the branches more intriguing:

> The tree of life carried with it the expectation that branches don't reconnect with each other once you get out onto them. And we're really learning in virtually all species where you can look hard enough, including, it seems, ourselves, that there are such interconnections. DNA can be exchanged across barriers that we thought were pretty hard to breach.

Just as intriguing is the new prominence of regulatory genes, which had been known since the 1960s. Not only could one gene make three different proteins, but it seems that 20 percent of human genes also regulate other genes. "It does cause one, whether you are a believer or not, to stand back and marvel at how it can work, with such a limited set of basic instructions," Collins says. He said the regulators are taking a new prominence in all genetics. "But does that scream for design?" he asks. "I don't know that it does. A strict evolutionist will say that natural selection will get you there, and I don't think that can really be disputed." Again, he is wary of a God of the gaps proposal:

> The intelligent designers might be right, but I wouldn't want to hang my faith on it. If your faith is dependent on there being no new thing we'll discover that might explain a particular gap, then your belief is in a vulnerable position. I don't think that's something that God would expect.

The only gap that speaks deeply to Collins is the human tendency to seek a moral sense, or a transcendence. That is very much the kind of argument made by C. S. Lewis, and indeed after work in his genetic field, Collins often repairs to a seminar on Lewis's writings. Lewis did not comment on human susceptibility to disease—a major frontier for gene research—but he wrote widely on human meaning and behavior. What the gene revolution means for that, Collins said, has galvanized his religious instincts.

> The big danger of the current revolution in genomics, I think, is the genetic determinist view. It's an easy one for people to latch on to when you have a little bit of data for a genetic contribution. Over and over we

see people saying, "Well that means DNA is all there is." And we know that can't be right.

He frowns on geneticists' revival of the argument that free will is a fiction or that religious belief is just a biologically induced response to the world. "The people who wish to propagate a particular point of view will be able to figure out ways to use the new genetic data to support their perspective," he says. "Unless the hearers of those arguments are themselves pretty sophisticated about what the data is, they may be taken in."

For Francis Collins, the pervasiveness of the human moral sense makes belief in God more plausible and logical than disbelief. "A lot of the argument rests on the moral law and the existence of that within each of us. Where does that come from?" The evolutionist answer—that it came from brute survival—does not work for him; moral sense defies biological Darwinism and can even be in conflict with it. He asks: "What better place to look for evidence of a personal God than right there?"

11

MIND AND BRAIN

The Decade of the Brain, which spanned the 1990s, engendered a mood of optimism among neuroscientists. They heartened each other with the idea that because the mind must have material causes, consciousness itself must be explainable and they could find with the tools of science what religion had for centuries identified as the soul.

In "The Brain," a special 1998 issue of *Daedalus,* Vernon B. Mountcastle pointed out: "Few neuroscientists now take a non-naturalistic position." In case there were some cold feet about materialism and the mind, neurophilosopher Patricia Churchland cheered materialism as a "highly probable hypothesis." Its "rejection of Cartesian souls or spirits or 'spooky stuff' existing separately from the brain is no whimsy," she said. And with obvious irony, Nobelist Francis Crick wrote that the idea that the soul, or mind, has material causes is "an astonishing hypothesis." But it was the orthodox assumption of his peers in the Decade of the Brain.

Even in an age of materialist science, the brain—the most complex entity in the known universe—was approached with a certain amount of ambivalence, for professional science had to be careful about its public profile. Should it come off as bold and triumphant, or with a calculated modesty? Even within the field there were doubters and pessimists, whom the materialist philosopher Owen Flanagan called the "new mysterians"—those who felt less certain that science could conquer the mind.

The "old mysterians" were people who believed in the soul, the classic dualism of eternal mind and perishable body. Science had few worries about this group; they were dismissed as religious, not scientific. But the new mysterians were modern-day materialists who doubted the reach of science.

Flanagan accused them of postmodernism, of taking a position "designed to drive a railroad spike through the heart of scientism, the view that science will eventually explain whatever is natural."

Yet the mysterian tendency is contagious, even in the highest echelons. Surprisingly, physicist Steven Weinberg, a naturalist to the hilt, has said that a final theory of physics is an example of what may lie beyond human ability: "I think we may also have to bypass the problem of human consciousness. It doesn't mean there's anything supernatural about it. It may just be too hard for us."

Materialist thinking about the problem is usually traced to a passionate defender of soul/brain dualism, the seventeenth-century French mathematician and philosopher René Descartes. Wandering through the Royal Gardens, he was impressed by some water-driven robots and theorized that human and animal action was likewise a machine-like "reflex." For Descartes, only God and the soul—which he viewed as making contact in the pineal gland at the brain's core—were beyond mechanization. Modern science happily took Descartes's machine, but jettisoned the soul.

How this brain-machine worked was a question for the next two centuries. The choice was between the brain as a holistic process or as a collection of discrete local operations. Evidence mounted for the second explanation. The famous 1835 case of Phineas Gage, a New England railroad worker, was indicative: after an iron rod flew through his head, tearing the frontal cortex, his physical health and cognition, remarkably, remained intact. However, his moral judgment and behavior deteriorated, thus establishing a link with the damaged areas of his brain. In France a few years later, Dr. Paul Broca challenged the holistic view of speech: he was able to predict that a man's speech impairment originated from damage to a certain area of the brain, the frontal lobe. When the man died, Broca opened his head and found a lesion, or scar, at that location.

When psychology was born as the "science of consciousness" in the late 1800s, it looked for overall principles uniting the mind. The work of American psychologist William James defined many concepts in the field, such as "conscious mental life." But it was the "science" of the Viennese neuroanatomist Sigmund Freud that stole the show by explaining the psyche as a bundle of conflicting moods, wishes and fears stemming from the primitive needs for food and sex in the context of constraining family relations. Though Freud had (in theory) tied every human belief and desire to reflexes and nerves, his "science" of the subconsious was so conjectural that a materialist revolt came in the form of a highly mechanistic "behaviorism." Originating in 1913, it played out in the popular writings of B. F. Skinner. Behaviorists took a strong cue from Descartes's robots, strictly tying mental phenomena to stimulus-response conditioning of the nervous system. First-person accounts (which Freud had relied upon) were downgraded to "folk psychology," and the symbol of the era became I. P. Pavlov's salivating dog, whose conditioned response was supposed to explain everything.

With the end of the Second World War, advances in electronics and computers initiated a "cognitive revolution." As psychologist Steven Pinker of the Massachusetts Institute of Technology explained: "Once you have intelligent machines like computers and cybernetic systems, it becomes hard to maintain [behaviorist] notions that memory, plans, and goals are inherently mystical and unscientific." A new "computational theory of mind" showed how intangible thoughts worked on corporeal muscles—just as software works on hardware.

Excitement about the brain as a computer culminated with the hubris surrounding visions of Artificial Intelligence. There were entrepreneurs who predicted they would download their personalities onto hard drives, conferring immortality on their essential egos. Organicists, cool to this software-hardware reductionism, reacted with theories of biological complexity and hoped to detour science from such a robotic view of human consciousness.

Malcolm Jeeves, a neuropsychologist and a president of the Royal Society of Edinburgh, is a Christian who concedes that neuroresearch has "more tightly linked" mind and brain events, suggesting that one day there will be a single materialist explanation of the soul. Nevertheless, a crass reductionism can be avoided by taking a holistic view of the brain. "Psychological processes are not necessarily localized to one part of the brain," says Jeeves; they "often depend on the intact working of networks of systems of cells located in widely separated parts of the brain."

Soon enough, this complex interaction was said to create mind as an "emergent property" of the brain. The concept's prophet was American neuroscientist Roger Sperry, who in 1981 won the Nobel Prize in physiology for working out the dynamics of the brain's right and left hemispheres. Sperry gave authority to emergence by distancing it from dualism. "Mentalism, yes; dualism, no," he said in 1980. Consciousness was "a dynamic emergent property of brain activity, neither identical with, nor reducible to, the neural events of which it is mainly composed." Emergence became a synonym for the soul and a godsend for modernist theologians caught between old-fashioned dualism and rank materialist atheism.

The brain is a three-pound object described as having the consistency of gray porridge. Organized in two hemispheres, the brain keeps its form by virtue of an inner structure of "white matter," or glial cells. But only the "gray matter" neurons, nerve cells that come in a great variety of specializations in the brain, produce its powers. They form the brain's thin outside coating, the convoluted cerebral cortex. Neurons also congregate in several small, specialized organs and nerve strands at the brain core. While the core is home to the more primal forces of emotion and appetite, the cortex, especially at the front of the skull, is the seat of decision-making.

The functions controlled by the brain—breathing, heartbeat, smell, hearing, touch, sight, speech, feelings and logic—vary from being involuntary to requiring a "willfulness," and range from having a precise point of origin to being a mysterious echo across the cortex and core. Technology has vastly increased the precision with which local brain activity is measured. Scanners can photograph electrical currents and watch blood flow using radioactive molecules, while neuronal chemistry can be studied at the molecular level.

The fundamental revolution in understanding the brain came on two fronts: discovering the right-left dynamic of the brain, and cracking secrets of its basic workhorse, the neuron. Under the "double consciousness" regime of the brain, the right and left hemispheres specialize, transmitting signals to each other and making up for each other's deficits when damage occurs. Neurons, which are immensely larger than average cells, generate internal electrical signals. These run down a branch, or axon, and reach other cells across a gap called a synapse, making the leap via a puff of chemical transmitters. All told, the number of synapse firings in the brain each second could be as high as ten million billion.

When Congress and the White House declared the 1990s "The Decade of the Brain," all this physical knowledge was heralded as the key to medical breakthroughs. Lawmakers promised more money to research how "thought and emotion" might affect "development, health and behavior."

Here there is a major fork in the road for modern brain research. Should it focus on healing illnesses or on attempting to capture the soul? Brain researchers must make a choice, and here an emphasis on medicine may reflect what the philosopher Owen Flanagan calls "consciousness shyness." Although science is rarely characterized as "shy" about conquering the unknown, something of the sort may well be a factor in the search for consciousness: of the fifty members of the National Academy of Sciences listed under "systems neuroscience," just one, Lawrence Weiskrantz of Oxford University, states his research program as the "neural basis of consciousness."

Whether in medical research or in study of brain functions, the preferred approach has been to nibble at the edges of the mind or soul. This is an incremental strategy called the study of the "neurological corollary of consciousness," or NCC, which is constituted by the local phenomena of the brain, the "islands of tissue" in the gray matter where perception takes place. This has been called the "building block" approach, which assumes that by pinning down each piece, the entire brain—as a computer matrix, organic mosaic or biological machine—may finally be understood.

Yet for visionary materialists like Francis Crick, these local areas and their medical applications are not the Holy Grail:

> The main object of scientific research on the brain is not merely to understand and cure various medical conditions, important though this task may be, but to grasp the true nature of the human soul. Whether this term is metaphysical or literal is exactly what we are trying to discover.

Crick, of course, views a literal soul as a preposterous myth and metaphysics as a soft materialism.

With this and other prodding, the consciousness shyness began to fall away by the 1990s, and Crick's agenda-setting call for a "neurobiological theory of consciousness" began to propel a somewhat more independent movement to parallel the government's Decade of the Brain. There was no concerted stampede to understand consciousness, but rather a number of foot races—and disagreements.

An important benchmark, academically at least, was the first refereed journal on the subject, *Consciousness and Cognition,* which started in 1991. By 1993 there were rumblings about an international conference, which gelled the next year in Tucson, Arizona, as "Toward a Scientific Basis for Consciousness," opening up the once-taboo topic. Its most resonant aftermath may have been a distinction made by a key organizer, psychologist David Chalmers, between the "easy problems" of the neurological corollary of consciousness (NCC) and truly "hard problems" of consciousness. "It is with the hard problem that the central mystery lies," the very question of "how physical processes in the brain give rise to subjective experience," Chalmers wrote later.

The Tucson event, attended by several hundred of the most accomplished people in the field, was the wellspring of another division: a split over hard science and "softer" sciences. The question was whether to unfurl a wide or narrow tent over who was allowed to speak on the topic of consciousness. In 1997, the wide-tent *Journal of Consciousness Studies* reported that Crick "expressed his frustration at the broad public interest in the field."

The new world of "consciousness studies" was clearly not of one mind. And as with all big problems, such as those of cosmology, each subdiscipline tended to argue for a better way to go. In the journal *Psyche,* brain researcher Joshua Stern humorously delineated brain science's "parochialism":

> Physicists advocate qm [quantum mechanics], biologists neurons, and good computationalists like myself, computers, each looking with bemused condescension upon their eccentric neighbors. Can we get some bakers to participate in this forum, who will advocate that the roots of consciousness reside in the éclair?

The bifurcation into wide- and narrow-tent philosophies was amicable enough. The Tucson Conference, which became a regular forum, welcomed all comers, and the *Journal of Consciousness Studies* (1993) gave voice to this interdisciplinary attitude. Soon after Tucson I, those who preferred a narrow tent in the robust new field formed the Association for the Scientific Study of Consciousness, which now has roughly three hundred members.

Consciousness and Cognition (1991) and *Psyche* (1997) became the narrow-tent journals and defined the field as a "natural science" focused on three things: consciousness, voluntary control and self.

To the wide-tenters, that seemed like an undue narrowing, since it ejected healing, folk psychology, psychotherapy, ethics and religion from the science of mind. When the *Journal of Consciousness Studies* made its three-point case for a wide tent, the summary presented a snapshot of the debate for years to come:

1. No one has yet come up with any evidence for a theory of consciousness that will satisfy the demands of various skeptics, so the decision to focus the investigation at, say, the level of the neuronal network, has to be for pre-theoretical reasons.
2. We only know consciousness through our own experience, so arguments against including a first-person phenomenonlogical approach are a contradiction in terms.
3. The only form of consciousness that we know is human, and this is characteristically shaped by social, cultural and environmental factors.

In the thick of this debate, Crick and others knew well that the wider public and even Western social institutions are dualist to the core. More than 90 percent of Americans, for example, believe in God or a universal spirit. Belief in God does not always entail belief in a soul or an afterlife—fewer than eight in ten believe that the soul lives on, with Jews believing it less and evangelical Protestants more. But for believers, God and soul are typically, almost inevitably, two sides of the same coin. Society, too, presumes dualism when it holds individuals responsible for what they do. The law holds them accountable, even if their neurons "made them do it."

Here of course was a fertile debate for the philosophers, and two of the most interesting of them, Owen Flanagan and Howard Ducharme, took up the naturalism-versus-dualism debate against the backdrop of the ebullient 1960s and 1970s. Both Flanagan, a New York native, and Ducharme, who hails from rural Michigan, were once self-described hippies; Flanagan's semi-autobiographical *The Problem of the Soul* updates that identification to "aging hippie," noting his beard and long hair as a fifty-something university professor. With academic training the two men became sharp antagonists in the battle over the soul. Flanagan, a leading advocate of materialism, ended up adopting the humanist and atheist Buddhist notions of transient human identity; Ducharme became a classic Christian, and with the help of science argued for dualism and a lasting human soul.

For years a teacher at Wellesley College, Flanagan first came on the scene in 1981 with his influential summary text *The Science of the Mind*. He argued that modern thinking and science had dispensed with prescientific notions of mind, soul and free will, and he located the beginning of the debunking with Descartes, father of modern dualism. Like Descartes, Flanagan was reared a Catholic, but as a teenager he discovered the joys of skepticism. Though he learned from Thomas Aquinas's mental rigor, he rejected the God of his faith. Today, Flanagan relates that he still shudders when he sees a priest.

Descartes had three arguments for a mind as separate from the body, two purely logical and the third physical. The physical argument asserts that even if an arm were amputated, the unity of the soul would stay intact. Flanagan recognizes this argument's merits, but proceeds to have fun with it, asking, "What about both legs and both arms? Notice any difference in your mind? Still unpersuaded? Let's get rid of your head and all the neural machinery: any difference?"

But changes in the physical body do create a problem for the argument that a person's identity is based in matter alone. With normal cells dying and being replaced all the time, everyone gets a new body every six or seven years, and yet the individual's identity continues. "It is this sort of thinking that Descartes's third argument gives rise to and that gives dualism some of its considerable plausibility, some of its great intuitive appeal," says Flanagan. But for him, the rebuttal is clear: the physical basis of identity is not the body, but an unaltered DNA code and brain cells, or neurons, that don't change. "They can last a full lifetime, and those that die are not replaced."

Later in Flanagan's career, the Buddhist idea of physical particles congealing into identity, and then dissipating at death, appealed to him. In scientific terms, "The real self is not an extra ingredient in you or a further fact about you, as the soul is. The self is an abstract theoretical entity in the same way that force, mass, and energy are abstract theoretical entities"—but real nonetheless.

When Howard Ducharme began his premed studies at Hope College in Michigan, he was "somewhere between an agnostic and an atheist." Then one summer a friend was killed by electrocution; he happened to have been working on a summer job Ducharme had sought. For the first time he grappled with "the reality of life and death," and in time decided that God was as concrete as the biology he was studying. "A religious experience is a real phenomenon," he says.

Armed with his science diploma and eager to understand religious experience, he passed through Trinity Evangelical Divinity School in Chicago for a graduate degree in the philosophy of religion. Having written on the German phenomenologist Martin Heidegger, he was accepted at Oxford. But trained in biology, Ducharme was no dualist. "I thought like everyone else. 'An immaterial substance?' Give me a break!"

His Oxford studies, however, persuaded him that dualism was both challenging and interesting—especially when he uncovered work by Samuel Clarke, a little-known British dualist of the seventeenth century. Clarke's arguments for a soul, in fact, were used later by two of England's most famous natural theologians, Joseph Butler and Thomas Reid—thinkers, incidentally, that Owen Flanagan includes in his stable of "soulphiles," or those who want a soul to exist as desperately as Flanagan wants no God.

When Ducharme went to Oxford, dualism was not entirely anathema. In the early 1980s, the dualist and evolutionist Richard Swinburne had taken the Oxford chair in the philosophy of the Christian religion. Nevertheless, a panel of Oxford dons flunked a doctoral candidate ahead of Ducharme for arguing dualism. Ducharme took heed, and in his own dissertation, "The Moral Self, Moral Knowledge and God," he played the role of aloof historian of philosophy rather than questioning believer. "My thesis was all couched in, 'These are Samuel Clarke's arguments . . . .' and 'These would be Samuel Clarke–type replies to contemporary criticism. . . .'" He passed, and after teaching at the University of Tennessee became chairman of philosophy at the University of Akron in Ohio. Now, he says, "I plainly let people know I am a dualist, rather than just be accused of it."

Ducharme began writing and lecturing on biomedical ethics and enjoyed teaching introductory philosophy. Among the standard materials was a study of Thomas Hobbes's argument for egoism, which holds that people are solely motivated by physical preservation. To help students evaluate it critically, Ducharme hit on his "I went to kindergarten" argument. The logic is simple:

1. "I" am this body if materialism is true.
2. "I" went to kindergarten.
3. The kindergarten body is not the body of "I" today.
4. Therefore, materialism is false.

His conclusion? "Personal identity is different in kind than physical, bodily or biological substance."

Before long, Ducharme's talks on biomedical issues took philosophers, biologists and doctors (and even the occasional Nobel laureate) back to kindergarten to make his point. One day in New Zealand in 1998, he was challenged by a neurosurgeon. "He said, 'brain cells and the DNA don't change, and those are the physical things that make up the person.'"

It was Flanagan's argument writ large. Ducharme didn't have a strictly empirical comeback—at least not yet. That would change as the new field of "neurogenesis" bloomed. Ducharme was present at the 2000 meeting of the American Association for the Advancement of Science when research scientists announced "neurogenesis in the adult brain." The next year, the *New York Times* carried the front-page headline, "Brain May Grow New Cells Daily."

While medicine, which had found a weapon in its battle against degenerative brain diseases, cheered one kind of victory, Ducharme experienced another, metaphysical one: "The 100-year-old doctrine that 'the brain cells you are born with are the only cells you will ever have' was disproved." Science hinted that identity did not exist in perishable neurons—a support for dualism that "refutes the Flanagan claim," according to Ducharme.

Following up on his premed training, he monitored neurogenesis studies and the new findings of impermanence in human DNA, contrary to Flanagan's claim. In early 2001, Ducharme told a session at the National Institutes of Health Human Genome Conference that genetic identity is dynamic, not static—another plus for dualism. Scientists had discovered "jumping genes," for example, which could cause mutations when they leaped from one chromosome to another. Other scientists had found that tips of chromosomes fray with age and that "repair genes" fix genetic codes altered by environmental influences. "One's genetic identity in 2002 is not identical with one's genetic code in 1955," Ducharme said, adding another prop to his kindergarten argument.

This was brand-new science, but Ducharme still drew on the classic arguments of the natural theologians, for whom defining self-awareness was key. "Assume that I am my neurons, as the materialist asserts. Do I have any experience of bundles of electrical firings of neurons?" The answer is no, and the same goes for personal knowledge of one's genetic code. In short, "self-knowledge" is not knowledge of firing neurons or chemical codes on one's DNA. "We have direct experience and knowledge of our self and only book learning about neurons and genetic codes."

BACK IN THE EARLY 1950S, when Flanagan and Ducharme were literally going through kindergarten, the attack on dualism had been given a new impetus by the work of Oxford University's materialist philosopher Gilbert Ryle, editor of the venerable journal of philosophy *Mind.* Ryle was "professor of metaphysical philosophy." Yet his 1949 book, *The Concept of Mind,* rallied materialist forces to dominate mind studies.

A clever wordsmith, like Flanagan, Ryle contributed the metaphor of the "ghost in the machine" to the debate. And he told this story: Once upon a time a group of peasants came upon a modern locomotive. They peered between the pistons, wheels and boilers, but they saw no horses. So they exclaimed, "Certainly we cannot see, feel or hear a horse in there, so it must be a ghost-horse which, like the fairies, hides from mortal eyes." Ryle crowed, "Poor simple-minded peasants! Yet just such a story has been the official theory of the mind for the last three very scientific centuries."

Prodded by Ryle's book, the BBC organized a series of broadcasts on the physical basis of the mind. They chose as the foil to Ryle the country's most eminent neuroscientist, Sir Charles Scott Sherrington—a bench scientist who was open to the idea of God, the soul, and finally dualism. While Ryle spun out metaphysical tales, Sherrington found and named the *neuron* and *synapse* and in 1932 was awarded the Nobel Prize in physiology. A scrupulous empiricist during four decades at Oxford, Sherrington too became a philosopher. In his 1933 lecture "The Brain and Its Mechanism," he "denied our scientific right to join mental with physiological experience," the Nobel Foundation notes in his biography. Thus began Sherrington's public flirtation with dualism.

In his Gifford Lectures in 1938, he came out for a "limited dualism" that viewed the mind as "a mystery but not a miracle," in the words of his student John Eccles. Still, for the clerical audience the lecture was so far from advocating a soul that it had "little comfort to offer," Sherrington later admitted. "My 'self' is not an object which I can examine through sense," he said, acknowledging the subjectivity problem for science. Muscle and nerve action can be studied, but when it comes to personal experience "I am at the disadvantage that I cannot submit this to others besides myself to examine and report on." For such mild dualism, Pavlov, the arch-materialist, declared that Sherrington must have been "senile." But Sherrington had a disciple to develop his views for the next generation, while Pavlov did not.

That disciple was Wilfred Penfield of Spokane, Washington, a son and grandson of doctors. While an undergraduate philosophy student at Princeton, Penfield had read psychologist William James, who fired his curiosity about the brain and the mind. Choosing medicine as his field, beginning in 1913 he studied under Sherrington. From that master of physiology he learned, he said, that "the brain was an undiscovered country in which the mystery of the mind of man might some day be explained." He also heard Sherrington say that the proposition that "our being should consist of two fundamental elements offers, I suppose, no greater inherent improbability than that it should rest on only one." It was a classic conundrum: will the brain machine be deciphered, or will the investigator hit the wall of dualism, where a disquieting "spooky stuff" comes into play?

At the start of his illustrious career, Penfield decided that he wanted to explore this undiscovered country of the human machine. He studied in the shadow of the great Spanish neuroanatomists, learned about electrical probes and cerebral cortex surgery in Germany, and after being a lead surgeon in New York City, persuaded the Rockefeller Foundation to fund the cutting-edge Montreal Neurological Institute. After opening the institute in 1934, he elevated its international reputation by curing epilepsy with precise surgery on the temporal lobe, removing the damaged nerve tissue that triggered the wild electrochemical signals. *Time* magazine boosted his fame in 1948. The surgical probing of conscious states was so novel that one tabloid, confused about the science, trumpeted: "Science Finds the Human Soul."

While Penfield opposed psychosurgery on criminals, the Frankenstein Syndrome of his field, he completed surgeries on 1,132 epileptics. Not until 1961, however, did he report on a puzzling brain phenomenon: how the mind acted independently of the brain.

For surgery, he used a sixty-cycle, two-volt probe to work with the awake patient to find the locus of the epilepsy. With each touch, patients reported how they perceived voluntary and involuntary acts. They reported dreamy sensations and past memories played on inner mental screens. As the stimulation in the motor area of a brain hemisphere made one hand rise, the person made his other hand resist the movement. It suggested a split mechanism, Penfield reported. "Behind the 'brain action' of one hemisphere was the patient's mind," he said. "Behind the action of the other hemisphere was the electrode." He asked, "Is it another mechanism or is there in the mind something of different essence?" He was on the road to dualism.

When in retirement, he tried out the topic in a paper delivered at the American Philosophical Society, but it was diffuse and unfocused. Penfield had already theorized that the thalamus, a round organ atop the brain stem at its center (there are actually two thalami, one for each brain side) is the central switchboard of all mental activity. As he put it, "There is a switchboard operator as well as a switchboard."

Penfield didn't push forward on this sort of spiritual claim until an old schoolmate, Charles Hendel, who had headed the philosophy department at Yale University, urged him to expand his misfired paper; just tell the research story, Hendel said, and conclude with a philosophical note. "The testimony of your patients is convincing, and your development toward the mystery of the mind is convincing beyond any philosopher's argument," Hendel wrote. "Think it over."

The final product was *The Mystery of the Mind,* which left no doubts about Penfield's belief that "spirit" operated on brain matter: "The mind of the patient was as independent of the reflex action as was the mind of the surgeon who listened as he strove to understand. Thus, my argument favors independence of mind-action."

SIR JOHN ECCLES RODE INTO THE DUALISM DEBATE with his guns blazing. As their student, Eccles went beyond Sherrington's *recognizable mind* and *alleged unearthliness* and he exceeded the *spirit* of Penfield. Eccles spoke of the *soul* and the *supernatural*. With a Nobel for work on the electrical pathways in neurons and synapses, he ended up as the leading empirical theorist on how dualism worked. He called it *interactionism,* the process by which the mind made contact with the brain. He dismissed as a "nebular hypothesis" the idea that mind simply condensed out of matter, and proposed the "microsite hypothesis." It proposed that among the millions of micro-receptors on neurons, the quantum uncertainty of atoms allowed an opening for mind, a nonmaterial force, to act on brain matter without violating the laws of energy conservation.

In a strange twinning of intellects, the supernaturalist Eccles made common cause with science philosopher Karl Popper, a materialist. Their book-length conversation, *The Self and the Brain,* espoused dualism and a theory of mind that proposed its sudden *ex nihilo* appearance. Six years before his death in 1996, Eccles vividly professed his own truly astonishing hypothesis: that there was "a supernatural origin of my unique self-conscious mind." The failure of science to objectify the self, he said, "requires this hypothesis of an independent origin of the self or soul, which is then associated with a brain."

DURING THE 1959 DARWIN CENTENNIAL, the panel on "Evolution of the Mind" at one point grappled with the question of subjectivity—the internal part of mind experience that seems impenetrable to science. As the Oxford zoologist Niko Tinbergen expressed the problem, "It is very hard to imagine what a starfish feels when it is angry." That is, he added, "if it ever gets angry." Even Julian Huxley conceded that subjectivity might be an ultimate mystery.

The subjectivity problem continues to be acknowledged not just by religious believers, but by some materialists, those whom Flanagan flagged as "new mysterians." One of them is philosopher Thomas Nagel, who famously asked, "What Is It Like to Be a Bat?" The 1974 essay, which is yet another opening to postmodern thinking about science, said that while humans may imagine or describe bat life, they can never get inside of it. They can never be a bat. Hence the limits of science.

Religious believers who work in brain science have also developed ways to frame subjectivity, trying to go beyond the simple statement that it is something God puts in the brain. During the Science and the Spiritual Quest project, with its public forums in 1998 and 2001, two brain specialists—Ayub K. Ommaya, a Muslim Sufi, and Stanford University professor William Newsome, a Christian—proposed two kinds of solutions, neither of them dualistic. While Newsome, who appreciatively quotes Nagel's conundrum, locates human spiritual identity and freedom in the complexity of the nervous system—much as Nobel neuroscientist Roger Sperry might have—Ommaya identifies the black box of human subjectivity, and thus contact with God, with the emotional side of the brain.

Reared in Catholic schools in his native Pakistan, Ommaya was fifteen when he wrote to the famous American brain surgeon Penfield about his brain surgery. The letter that came in reply urged the young Pakistani to attend medical school. About a decade later, Ommaya was at Oxford on a Rhodes Scholarship, mastering neurosurgery and admiring Penfield's technique on intractable epilepsy. As if living a boyhood dream, Ommaya was present in Chicago when Penfield commented on his research during sessions of the American Association of Neurosurgery in 1971.

By 1960, the National Institutes of Health in the Maryland suburbs of Washington, D.C., had set up a surgery program that imitated Penfield's. The next year, Ommaya was invited to bring his experience to the team, of which he would soon become surgical chief. Before his forty years of surgery were up, Ommaya would complete some four thousand operations. Most repaired injuries or arterio-neuron malformations of the spine; others went after brain tumors. For a period, too, Ommaya became a latter-day Penfield. He operated on temporal-lobe epileptics and witnessed, like Penfield, double-mind effects of the right and left hemispheres.

Temporal-lobe epilepsy, a seizure-causing electrical neuronal storm in the temporal lobe, is rare but significant for one other feature: people who suffer from it sometimes show obsessive religious behavior. Doctors report that patients have fixations on cosmic meaning, write long undecipherable mystical tracts, convert to one religion after another or spend long periods praying in church. In 1997, one group of neuro-researchers found in an experiment that some temporal-lobe epilepsy patients showed a more elevated electroneurological response to religious words than to others. They declared, to much media excitement, to have possibly found the "God module"—in effect, the neurological corollary of consciousness (NCC) for the entire history of human religious experience.

Ommaya laughed when he saw the headlines. He had performed roughly 350 operations for temporal-lobe epilepsy, and only a quarter of the patients showed what he called "hyper-religiosity," which was not a large enough percentage to validate a God-module theory. What was more, the patients who did show the odd behavior were doing so under an "abnormal condition in the brain," which was emotionally entirely different from the normal religiosity attested by vastly larger numbers of people. "The God module is just a catchword," he says. Rather than arising from a spot in the brain, religious experience seems to emerge from the entire complex nervous system, "a function in the brain which is the capacity for religion, much like the capacity for speech and language."

When it comes to authentic religious experience, Ommaya looks to the seat of emotions, which is the limbic system. Rather than dualism, therefore, he has looked for a "unified" brain landscape, a material brain that produces language, memory and spirituality.

When he was twelve, Ommaya's Sufi father wanted to teach him not to fear death. He was to sleep for one night in a graveyard; it took three attempts until he succeeded. ("Sufi teaching is very practical," he says.) After some rough experience with disbelief at university, Ommaya found peace with his God.

During his student days at Oxford, the "cognitive revolution" had focused brain science on the logic-producing frontal lobes of the cerebral cortex. By the end of Ommaya's career, brain science had shifted its focus to the emotions. New research was showing that the limbic system, which had been identified only in 1937, was perhaps the most active, and even the dominant, network in the mental and sensory world. It made sense to Ommaya: all human motives usually begin with a feeling, followed by analysis. He came to believe that the emotions were the fulcrum of human balance, and even of religious transcendence.

Contemporary science doesn't feel comfortable with the quagmire of human emotions; but the cortex was tractable since it fit the computer paradigms of the new era. Ommaya explains:

> They don't want to consider emotions because you can't make subjectivity in a machine. And that's what emotion is, a subjective state. If we didn't have emotion, we would never have religion; it is the highest level of our mentality and feeling.

After the discovery of the limbic system, its extensions seemed to be found everywhere in the brain and the nervous system. A debate goes on: what else in the brain and spinal cord belongs to this core network? Ommaya does not underestimate the frontal lobe, which he likens to a hardworking bureaucrat in a large front office. But for now the limbic system, with greater input and output, is looking dominant. The cortex-limbic relationship explains what happened to Phineas Gage: the damage to his frontal lobe severed his judgments from his emotions. "The lack of empathy comes when you have damage mostly to the frontal lobes, while damage to the temporal lobes causes disturbances of memory and religiosity."

Ommaya cares not at all, even as a working scientist, if he is called a mystic or a mysterian. He has often given public talks on consciousness at the Smithsonian Institution. "People said I was a mystic. And I said, yes." For Ommaya, mystery is a perfectly good category for events in nature, from the transitions in evolution to the human mind, and particularly for God's action on the brain. But he believes that while "logical science" may not capture the self or subjective emotion, it may at least study the physical brain's capacity for spiritual experience.

That was the point of a well-known project at the University of Pennsylvania. Researchers there scanned the blood flow in the brain of a man practicing Tibetan Buddhist meditation and later the brain of a Franciscan nun after she had gone into deep prayer. At the point of transcendence—when the subjects reported a repose of the mind and an experience of something greater—the flow was monitored, and it showed a distinct pattern. The researchers found that not only did the blood concentrate in the front of the brain, which seemed logical at a time of concentration, but blood left an area of the brain that provides spatial coordination. They speculated that loss of that coordination led to the feeling of merging or elevation of one's identity into a larger reality. That works for Ommaya, who knows that all such research is preliminary. "This is a sign that the brain has this capacity. If there is one God, when you are transcendent, you are coming closer to understanding what the godhead is."

Though Ommaya has served on several committees for the National Academy of Sciences, he has never tried to get elected to that body. If he had been, he would describe his work as: "The understanding of the mind and spirituality on the basis of our brain." That will be his legacy in a final book: he will lay out his limbic-system theory of consciousness. "And the last chapter will be just like what a number of physicists have done, who usually end up with God," he says wryly. His conclusion will have the typical flavor of a mystic. "You can't define God," he summarizes. "We have to get as much as we can, but we still can't say it. Because we don't know what it is."

ONE OCTOBER DAY IN 2001, brain researcher William Newsome stood before a Science and the Spiritual Quest forum at Harvard and explained his search for the "fundamental principles" of the brain. A friendly group of Rhesus monkeys were his partners, he explained. Newsome's work on brain perception of motion won him election to the National Academy of Sciences a year earlier. As a member of the top echelons of science, he gets an occasional ribbing for being a churchgoing believer (his wife is an ordained minister), which he takes cheerfully enough.

The foundation of Newsome's work is discovery of specialized neurons in "cortical columns" in the gray matter, and when it comes to motion perception, they are specialized indeed. "You have up columns, you have down columns, you have right columns, and you have left columns," Newsome explains. By inserting harmless and painless micro-electrodes into columns in a monkey's brain, Newsome and his Stanford University team study how the mind works. The monkeys are trained to hit bars according to how visual objects move on a screen, and the related neuron firings disclose the activity of their minds.

It is a modest start, given the "avowed goal of neuroscience," which he describes as the understanding of all human thoughts and feelings "in terms of the electrochemical events that occur within that central nervous system." Whether that reductionist goal can be achieved is anyone's guess: "It's going to take some centuries for us to even start to get a glimmer." If forced to bet, "my suspicion is that we can do a lot, but I don't think we can do everything."

He might think otherwise if he hadn't confronted subjectivity in his experiments, the proverbial problem of "what it's like to be a bat." Likewise in his laboratory, he says, his work with the monkeys has "bumped up against this irreducibility of subjective experience." He explains: under normal conditions, when the monkey sees up or down motion, the proper neuron column fires. But if the researcher intervenes, stimulating the down-motion cell, the monkey reports down motion—no matter what the real motion on the screen.

How would the monkey explain this experience? "Would he say, 'Hey guys, I saw upward motion and reported upward motion'? Or would the monkey say, 'I saw downward motion on that trial, but I reported upward. I don't know why the hell I did that'?" What the electrode is actually doing to the monkey's experience is not entirely clear, and therein lies the problem of subjectivity. Newsome asks:

> Are we intervening at the level of perception, and really changing what is seen, or are we intervening somehow at the level of decisions? What is the subjective experience that accompanies electrical activity at this point in the cortex? [We] racked our brains for the last eight years trying to figure out how we would answer that question.

Indeed, Newsome has even contemplated being the first human subject of such experiments so he might see what it feels like, and writing up a scientific report afterward. "Even if I were to do that, would anyone else believe my first-person subjective experience?" he asks. "So I think the problem of subjectivity is a fundamental one."

From Crick to Newsome, and across most brain research and philosophizing in between, the seekers of the mind don't have to ask how the brain got here. For the most part, the brain and its remarkable ability can be taken as a "brute fact." It can be analyzed in the laboratory and through daily experience.

Yet for philosopher Alvin Plantinga, whom *Time* magazine called one of the world's "leading philosophers of God," the origin of human intelligence in natural history is the paramount puzzle. It might also be a profound proof of God. A dualist and evolutionist, Plantinga has argued that only if there is a God can the mind be trustworthy under Darwinian tenets. Purely naturalistic evolution (not backed up by God) would produce an unreliable brain in terms of intellectual beliefs, because survival value is the Darwinian explanation for everything, and brains ignorant of mathematics or philosophy could just as well have permitted human survival. If natural selection cared less about beliefs, and only about physical survival, "it would be unlikely that most of our beliefs are true, and unlikely that our cognitive faculties are for the most part reliable." Since we find them mostly true and reliable, it is more logical to think that God designed them to be so than to believe that natural selection produced that reliability. Flurry over Plantinga's argument is not likely to end soon: an entire volume of philosophers' reactions to his argument appeared in 2002.

The idea that the physical three-pound brain emerged by evolution is not being contested by Plantinga, and both naturalists and believers presume this to be the case. Evolution of the physical brain, as Plantinga puts it, is "the only game in town" for science. Belief in the brain's evolution took wing during the time of Darwin. His contemporary, the "social Darwinist" Herbert Spencer, argued that the mind evolved from matter as "differentiation," or complexity, of matter increased over time. William James considered that the concept of a soul still made sense, but he was purely Darwinian when he said that the physical mind "has in all probability been evolved, like other functions, for a use."

How it did so, and from what it derives its powers, is the mind-boggling question that divides brain theorists and philosophers alike. How can the quality of "mind" exist at all in matter? Some repeat the word "emergence" like a mantra. Others go so far as to say that consciousness resides in every particle, an idea called *panspychism*. Human consciousness is perhaps a confluence of these mind-particles.

Plantinga, the philosopher of God, is not the first to ask the embarrassing question he has brought to the forefront. In a letter written soon before he died, Darwin himself expressed angst over how a mind produced by natural selection could be trusted:

> With me the horrid doubt always arises whether the convictions of man's mind, which has been developed from the mind of the lower animals, are of any value or at all trustworthy. Would any one trust in the convictions of a monkey's mind, if there are any convictions in such a mind?

Similarly, the British evolutionist J. B. S. Haldane phrased the conundrum in terms of physics:

> If my mental processes are determined wholly by the motions of the atoms in my brain, I have no reason to suppose that my beliefs are true ... and hence I have no reason for supposing my brain to be composed of atoms.

Strict naturalists have proposed a solution, and the answer proposed by neurophilosopher Patricia Churchland—who rejects "spooky stuff"—is illustrative. Abstract knowledge of the universe was not required for Darwinian survival, but luckily it evolved nevertheless. "The brain did not evolve to know the nature of the sun as it is known by a physicist, nor to know itself as it is known by a neurophysiologist," Churchland explains. "But, in the right circumstances, it can come to know them anyhow." She says that science, though generated by this kind of trial and error, has become the highest form of reliable knowledge.

For Plantinga this is materialism's vicious circle, an explanation no better than a "God of the gaps" explanation. With philosophy's favorite method of thought experiments, he has attempted to show that all manner of false beliefs and outlandish fantasies could help in biological survival: "Natural selection doesn't care what you believe. ... Darwinian evolution doesn't select for belief except when belief is appropriately related to behavior." Therefore the human ability to discover reliable knowledge can be reconciled more logically with belief in a Creator who gave human minds the ability to apprehend it.

Evolution *and* God can explain the reliable human mind, Plantinga argues, "but the conjunction of naturalism with evolution is self-defeating. Things don't look hopeful for Darwinian naturalists."

12

LEAPS OF FAITH

A century ago, the American psychologist William James asked of natural science: does it leave room for God? Although he was a materialist and a Darwinian, James chose a leap of faith, or what he called the "will to believe." He took materialism right to the edge—but then stopped. The human will, he declared, was ultimately spiritual and free. The person, he said, was an "arch-ego" somehow beholden to God and to a metaphysical reality beyond the reach of science.

While such themes permeate James's writings, his 1902 Gifford Lectures, *The Varieties of Religious Experience,* convey a few other thoughts that remain compelling and relevant to the God-and-science discussion. Emphasizing personal experience, James was not an enthusiast for ritual, theological systems or organized religion. Accordingly, with regard to issues of science and personal faith he laid stress on three things: the concreteness of experience, the usefulness of belief, and the different temperaments of people.

James was the father of American pragmatism, and his definition of truth would cause shudders in both religionists and materialists: "Truth is the name of whatever proves itself to be good in the way of belief." He was not interested in first things or origins, but in "last things, fruits, consequences, facts."

Unlike today, when the God-and-science wars play out on school boards, in the media and even in national politics, in James's time these intellectual domains did not do battle. Yet he did have an adversary, which he named the "reigning intellectual tastes." This was the skeptical materialism of his time that demanded evidence before anything was conceded. It was the sort of materialism—objective, rationalistic and humorless—that was and is exceedingly abstract and quite unappealing to ordinary people. "Materialism will always fail of universal adoption," James said. Religious experience is universally more concrete to individuals.

As a pragmatic materialist and psychologist, James thought that atheistic belief had to be just as rooted in biological realities as religious belief. So the deeper question was: Which view was most helpful to a human being? He believed that hope and risk—the proverbial leap of faith—were the best choices, when compared with the psychological security provided by an overwrought skepticism. Materialists and rationalists lived on what James called the "agnostic veto" of every religious intuition. Confronted by the possibility of belief, he chided, these skeptics would say that "to yield to our fear of its being error is wiser and better than to yield to our hope that it may be true."

Those choices of belief or skepticism, James said, were rooted in a dichotomy of temperaments—one tough-minded and the other tender-minded. The first belonged to materialists, who forswore untested hopes, while the latter could lead to the experience of being "twice born," or transformed by contact with what is good, transcendent or divine. Biographers of William James point out that it was tender-mindedness that ultimately spoke to him, even though he was a tough-minded materialist in his science, frequently reproving specific religious beliefs as "absurd."

In several ways, James's ideas are relevant to the contemporary God-and-science debate. He lived in a time of materialist assumptions and unbridled optimism about the triumph of scientific naturalism; yet for educated Americans, it was an age of doubt. Because James spoke to that uncertainty, he has been called the "philosopher of the cusp." For the average man, he gave compelling reasons for freedom of the will and the aspiration of belief.

James's position came in reaction to the excessive abstraction of German thought and the naive materialism of British naturalism. Scientific abstraction had its role, James said, but could not compare to the concreteness of religion in its impact on human life. As his biographers document, he moved from theoretical and experimental science to metaphysics, which he saw as a more comprehensive way of considering reality.

Since the Darwin Centennial, perhaps a similar shift has taken place in the world of rational and scientific discussion. Many scientists acknowledge the limits of science, while continuing to draw a line between science and metaphysics. Still and all, they concur that both may be mentioned in the same breath. Let's not forget that ours is an age when the beginning of an "end of ideology" is cheered, and here many would include the scientific variety of ideology, or "scientism."

The sea change has been a recognition of the subjective element in science. Even the average research scientist must be motivated by some personal passion that inspires him to get up in the morning, often to face tedious laboratory work, orthodox programs and tight funding bureaucracies. And at the end of the day, most professional scientists would love to confess that their deeper ambition is to satisfy a thirst for truth, much as Einstein had declared at the outset of the twentieth century. Indeed, Einstein traced his motivation not to some external imperative of science, but to a "cosmic religious feeling," and said that his most powerful investigative tool was intuition.

Michael Polanyi called this motive "personal knowledge," while a contemporary thinker like John Polkinghorne, a physicist and Anglican priest, has labeled it "well-motivated belief." Polkinghorne has said that while science seeks to accumulate truths about natural processes, faith looks for an eternal definition of reality. Accordingly, he said, "I do not need to read the *Principia,*" Newton's seventeenth-century masterpiece, which is considered one of the very greatest works of science, but has now been left behind by later achievements. But, Polkinghorne continues, far older though the Bible is, "I certainly need to read the Bible." What he brings to life here is that classic motto of Christian thought: Belief is the first step toward understanding.

As always, furious debate rages over credos, and atheists and theists of combative temperament seem to like nothing better than to stoke the fires. These engagements notwithstanding, the vast majority of reasonable people agree that subjective orientation is the crucial human beginning point. One must believe something in order to proceed to the next thing. Indeed, when asked the profoundest and most puzzling of all questions, why is there something rather than nothing, many scientists and rationalists opt for God.

Over and above turf-war issues of careers and cultural prestige, why is the debate about choosing God in an age of science so fierce? The answer is actually quite simple: the war mostly takes place in the corridors of the ivory tower. The questions about God and science do not arise on Main

Street, but typically in academic and scientific circles and among the intellectually curious. As William James might say, there is a certain temperament behind the debate. In these circles, prestige clearly goes to the
tough-minded objectivist, not to the "tender-minded," with the aura of
childlike susceptibility the words evoke.

The tough-minded, such as physicist Lawrence Krauss, will say it is a
"bitter pill" indeed for people to be told by science that it can neither find
meaning in the universe nor even address the God question: "Science has
discovered absolutely nothing in the past century of remarkable activity that
has any spiritual implications." What science does teach, in the world according to Krauss, is that people should not try to impose their spiritual meanings on the universe: "One of the most significant legacies of science in the
twentieth century has been the recognition that the universe is the way it
is, whether we like it or not."

Polkinghorne, a colleague of nonbelieving scientists such as Fred Hoyle
and Martin Rees, acutely describes them as classically tough-minded individuals who are "wistful and wary about religion." He amplifies: "They are
wistful in the sense that science doesn't tell you everything you want to know.
They are wary, I think, because they think religion is subservient to authority, that the Bible or the Pope or somebody tells you, 'You've got to believe
this.' And they don't want to commit intellectual suicide, nor do I. They
just don't want to be credulous. But again, nor do I."

In summary then, the debate over scientific evidence of a God, and
even a benign personal God, is vitally important to believers for one pre-
vailing reason: in the age of science, belief must claim to be tough-minded
as well.

THIS BOOK BEGAN BY MAKING A DISTINCTION between the Spinozans, or pan-
theists, in today's science/religion dialogue, and the theists who hold to a
personal God. What has either group found in science that confirms their
suspicions of purpose, design or a Creator?

The physicist Paul Davies is a Spinozan, and his words well summarize
the sentiments of the pantheist wing of the search. "For what it's worth, looking at the universe through the eyes of the scientist, I get the overwhelming

impression of purpose and design," he said one day, sitting on the stone steps of Harvard Memorial Church. "The more we discover through science about nature, the more beautiful and harmonious and inspiring and ingenious it seems to be." For Davies, it is not necessary for there to be an agent who is behind the universe, giving it meaning; the meaning can be imposed by us. "I don't see any fundamental reason why we can't take meaning and purpose, or design, which are very human categories, and find ways of applying them to nature."

Establishment science calls this wishful thinking, or a version of James's tender-mindedness. But Davies replies that the purely materialist mode, which sets itself up as quintessentially tough-minded, actually entails absurdity.

> Most scientists would say that that deepest level is simply the laws of physics, and we just accept those laws as they are, and they exist as they are for no reason. They have to argue that the universe is strictly logical and rational all the way down to this bottom level, the laws of physics. But at that point, they have to perform a back flip and say, "Oh, but those laws of physics are just reasonless. There's no reason why they are." So the universe is ultimately absurd.

To argue for the rationality of science but the absurdity of the world it seeks to explain strikes Davies as inconsistent.

The Spinozans can leave matters there, but believers in a personal God usually want to do more with the evidence of design. Some of their general themes are clear, going all the way from a noninterventionist Creator on the one hand to a God who splices into the natural world with creative actions on the other. While the more evangelistic God-and-science advocates speak of proof or testimony to the God of the Bible—indeed, the Bible argues for such evidence in a few famous passages—most theists are happy simply to say that the evidence adds up to making a God-created universe "coherent," and thus reasonable.

They point to four kinds of evidence for divine design: the simplicity of nature's laws, the beauty of mathematics and the physical order, the intelligibility of the underlying order of things, and the fact that humans are able to apprehend all these things. To be sure, materialists and Spinozans have also made much of the beauty inherent in reality, either calling it a brute fact requiring no explanation or the human projection of an evolutionarily produced, incidental sentiment that, while not perhaps having survival value, cropped up nevertheless.

From the point of view of coherence, however, theists say God is a "better explanation" of the four factors combined. "The laws of nature seem to be carefully arranged so that they are discoverable by beings of our level of intelligence," says Robin Collins, a physicist and a Christian. "I believe this feature of the laws not only suggests design, but that it fits in a larger pattern that suggests a particular providential purpose for human beings." He argues that beauty, which seems to transcend natural selection, ends up as a strong point for the God camp. "Theism naturally explains these characteristics," he says.

George Coyne, a Jesuit priest and director of the Vatican Observatory, has watched the science/religion engagement for several decades. "I'm not very happy with the rationalization of religious belief," he says, pointing to some attempts to produce a scientific kind of theology. "Religious belief is an imponderable thing; it's an experience." An example he adduces is how Scripture does not teach about science, but informs the faith of the reader. "Scripture was written sometime between 500 years before Christ and 200 years after Christ," he said. "Modern science began in the seventeenth century. Now just compare that. There is no scientific teaching in Scripture. None."

What Coyne seeks is a balance of faith and reason, which has much to do with a proper ordering of the two.

> There are rational grounds for my belief, but reason is not its ultimate support. Belief is a leap in the dark. Belief is receiving a gift from God. Once I believe in God, then whatever I know of the universe can help explain that. It is not finding rational proof, but understanding it in more rational terms.

Such appeals to a leap of faith do not take "proof" of God off the table for many rationalists or scientists. Some logically conclude that if God exists, there must be a reflection of that reality in nature. This is a stance that someone like Robert Newman, a seminary professor of the Bible who has also earned a doctorate in astrophysics from Cornell University, comfortably takes.

"Obviously, if you're a theist, you believe God can decide what he's going to put in nature that might point beyond nature to himself," Newman says. "The findings about fine-tuning suggest he's put a great deal in nature that points beyond a haphazard universe to something that looks very carefully designed."

Newman describes the role of a traditional God in terms of providence, or the laws that bring about an orderly universe, and intervention, in which the Creator infuses new and special levels of order, whether in the creation of life or in the individual human being and human consciousness. He agrees that the notion of an intervening God raises again the "God of the gaps" problem, but insists there are gaps nevertheless.

> You've either got a God of the gaps or a natural law of the gaps. So you look at what kind of gaps they are. Some gaps are pretty large. In those cases, when you have to theorize billions or trillions of universes for natural law to fill those gaps, then I begin to suspect that we're really looking at evidence of some kind of intervention.

After a century of scientific growth and expansion, Newman believes its limits suggest that science may be ready for an expanded redefinition. This does not mean the inclusion of theology, but it may allow the rational discussion of logical indicators for a Creator.

> For more than a century, science has ruled out agency and intelligent causation, and it's proving an insufficient tool box to explain the universe. It is too poverty-stricken a model to explain it. They say, "We'll eventually find a naturalistic explanation for these things." Atheists have regularly scorned believers for saying, "Eventually God will explain it, or we'll explain a problem of Scripture." Well, the naturalists are now getting the same medicine.

Newman suspects, as do others, that the discovery of design has such consequences that it will be opposed whatever the evidence may be. "Once you come to believe there is a God, unless you're an idiot, you're going to want to find out more about it. You're going to ask, 'Has he intervened in our history? Has he communicated?'" He likens the situation to that of the dedicated scientists who believe there is extraterrestrial intelligence, and who ponder whether its representatives have visited Earth or communicated with humanity. Similarly, the option for God is not confined to the ivory tower, Newman says.

> If there's a God, then he might have purposes for the universe. He may have purposes for us. Are we cooperating with them? So suddenly you see your choice on this is going to make a huge difference. It's going to have an impact on, "What's life about? What am I doing with it?" So if you back up and look, God and no God are enormously different.

The science of today is considerably more advanced than in 1902, when William James delivered his lectures on *The Varieties of Religious Experience*. In his day, there was an ebullient hope that science would dispel all the mysteries of the world. When it comes to religious belief and its attendant moods and behaviors in 2003, James would surely not deviate from his conclusions about its concreteness and the tender-minded quality of awe before something greater. We don't know what he would say about contemporary science. But he would probably concede that—on the cusp between meaning and doubt—finding design in the universe is not only a useful but a tough-minded act indeed.

ACKNOWLEDGMENTS

For the layman, even the slightest understanding of scientific frontiers can be a Herculean task. Yet science offers itself as something to be understood by everyone, and I took the offer in 1995. To complete a book on the evolution-vs.-creation debate in modern America, I read voraciously and interviewed more than one hundred protagonists of the debate, mostly in the natural sciences. With my colleague Edward J. Larson, I surveyed scientists and theologians on their beliefs. Then came the opportunity to attend an array of conferences: the Science and the Spiritual Quest conferences in 1998 and 2001; two major Intelligent Design conferences, Mere Creation (1996) and Life after Materialism (2000); and events put on by the science-and-religion dialogue unit of the American Association for the Advancement of Science. A word of thanks to all of those hosts.

Those experiences were a windfall for this book, which expands beyond evolutionary biology to astronomy, cosmology, genetics and brain science. Again, a group of scientists patiently walked me through these fields and their opinions, and to them my deep appreciation is due. Interview subjects and others looked over parts of various chapters, an invaluable backup for someone untrained in science. My starting points for this story were two: the Darwin Centennial in 1959 and the Copernican Celebration in 1973. While I read the three-volume Centennial proceedings, without the research and summary of historian Vassiliki Betty Smocovitis, my sense of Chicago circa 1959 would have surely been lacking in life. Similarly, Owen Gingerich edited the Washington, D.C., events of the Copernican year, and wrote widely on other international gatherings. These were a gold mine as well, and I read nearly every word. For the contemporary action, the organizers of two other conferences, Design and Its Critics and The Nature of Nature, both in 2000, were helpful in providing audio and video records of the entire proceedings. A final word of thanks to my publisher, Peter Collier, no mean scribe himself, whose enthusiasm for the book was immediate, and whose leash on the author very long. Peter and my editor, Diarmid Cammell, have turned a plausible book into one that I hope is a pleasure to read.

BIBLIOGRAPHICAL ESSAY

Preface

Much has been written about the new science-and-religion activity in the 1990s, and Edward J. Larson and I were happy to contribute. See our "Scientists and Religion in America," *Scientific American,* September 1999. Three other popular writers on the trend stand out. See Gregg Easterbrook, "Science and God: A Warming Trend?" *Science,* 15 August 1997, and "Science Sees the Light," *New Republic,* 12 October 1998. See also Robert Wright, "Science, God and Man," *Time,* 28 December 1992. For the skeptic's approach, see Michael Shermer, *How We Believe: The Search for God in an Age of Science* (New York: W. H. Freeman and Co., 1999). Shermer conducted the survey on how believers view design in nature.

Chapter 1

For understanding the Darwin Centennial, two works are indispensable: Sol Tax, ed., *Evolution after Darwin,* 3 vols. (Chicago: University of Chicago Press, 1960), and Vassiliki Betty Smocovitis, "The 1959 Darwin Centennial Celebration in America," *Osiris* 14 (1999). Julian Huxley's "Evolutionary Vision" is in vol. 3 of *Evolution after Darwin* and Louis Leakey's paper on Zinj, "The Origin of the Genus Homo," in vol. 2. The Leakey story is told best by Virginia Morell in *Ancestral Passions: The Leakey Family and the Quest for Humankind's Beginnings* (New York: Simon and Schuster, 1995). For a sense of the era, find L. S. B. Leakey's "Finding the World's Earliest Man," *National Geographic,* September 1960. See also Richard Leakey, *The Origin of Humankind* (New York: Basic Books, 1994). Hal Hellman treats "Johanson versus the Leakeys" in his *Great Feuds in Science* (New York: Wiley,

1998), and more recently, see Donald C. Johanson, "The Leakey Family," *Time,* 21 January 2002.

Owen Gingerich, a student of Harlow Shapley's, wrote his entry in Charles Coulston Gillispie, ed., *Dictionary of Scientific Biography,* vol. 12 (New York: Scribner's Sons, 1970), and also, "Through Rugged Ways to the Galaxies," *Journal for the History of Astronomy,* February 1990. For Shapley's own words, see his *Through Rugged Ways to the Stars* (New York: Scribner's Sons, 1969). Much has been written on Huxley by others and by himself, but I gained a focus from Michael Ruse's *Monad to Man: The Concept of Progress in Evolutionary Biology* (Cambridge, Mass.: Harvard University Press, 1996) and Edward J. Larson, *Evolution's Workshop: God and Science on the Galapagos Islands* (New York: Basic Books, 2001).

An overview of American society in the 1950s and the *Look* magazine survey can be found in Eric F. Goldmen, *The Crucial Decade—and After: America, 1945–1960* (New York: Knopf, 1966). For the story of Toumai see the three articles in *Nature,* 11 July 2002: Michel Brunet, et al., "A New Hominid from the Upper Miocene of Chad, Central Africa"; Bernard Wood, "Paleonanthropology: Hominid Revelations from Chad"; and John Whitfield, "Oldest Member of Human Family Found."

Chapter 2

For understanding the modern synthesis, Ruse's *Monad to Man* draws candid contrasts, as does William B. Provine's *Sewall Wright and Evolutionary Biology* (Chicago: University of Chicago Press, 1986). Proceedings of the Darwin Centennial's "The Evolution of Life" panel are in Sol Tax, *Evolution after Darwin,* vol. 3 (Chicago: University of Chicago Press, 1960). A sampling of Polanyi's works can be found in Michael Polanyi, *Knowing and Being,* ed. Marjorie Green (Chicago: University of Chicago Press, 1969). His views on religion are discussed in Karl E. Peters, ed., "Science and Religion in the Thought of Michael Polanyi," *Zygon* 17 (March 1982).

Other sources for this chapter include: Theodosius Dobzhansky, "Darwinian or 'Oriented' Evolution?" *Evolution,* 30 June 1975; The Editor, "Forward," *Evolution,* March–June 1974; Theodore Roszak, *Making of a Counter Culture: Reflections on the Technocratic Society and Its Youthful Opposition*

(New York: Doubleday, 1968); Arthur Koestler, *The Sleepwalkers: A History of Man's Changing Vision of the Universe* (London: Hutchinson, 1958); Dobzhansky, "Nothing in Biology Makes Sense Except in the Light of Evolution," *American Biology Teacher,* March 1973; Thomas Kuhn, *The Structure of Scientific Revolutions,* 3rd ed. (Chicago: University of Chicago Press, 1970); Stephen Jay Gould, "Is a New and General Theory of Evolution Emerging?" *Paleobiology* 6 (1980); Niles Eldredge, *Unfinished Synthesis: Biological Hierarchies and Modern Evolutionary Thought* (New York: Oxford University Press, 1985); Eldredge and Gould, "Punctuated Equilibrium: An Alternative to Phyletic Gradualism," in T. J. M. Schopf, ed., *Models of Paleobiology* (San Francisco: Freeman Cooper, 1972).

For proceedings in the Copernican year, see Owen Gingerich, ed., *The Nature of Scientific Discovery: A Symposium Commemorating the 500th Anniversary of the Birth of Nicholas Copernicus* (Washington, D.C.: Smithsonian Institution Press, 1975); and Gingerich, "International Copernican Celebration in Poland," *Sky and Telescope,* December 1973. See also, Kendrick Frazier, "The Nature of Scientific Discovery," *Science News,* 5 May 1973.

Chapter 3

In this chapter I relied on interviews with George Ellis, Charles Misner, Paul Davies and John Leslie. Fred Hoyle presents his unorthodox case in *Nicholas Copernicus* (New York: Harper and Row, 1973). The two best introductory collections are John Leslie, ed., *Modern Cosmology and Philosophy* (Amherst, N.Y.: Prometheus Books, 1998), and Dennis Richard Danielson, ed., *The Book of the Cosmos: Imagining the Universe from Heraclitus to Hawking* (Cambridge, Mass.: Perseus Publishing, 2000). More specifically see: John Leslie, *Universes* (London: Routledge, 1989); Alan Lightman and Roberta Brawer, *Origins: The Lives and Worlds of Modern Cosmologists* (Cambridge, Mass.: Harvard University Press, 1990); George Ellis et al., eds., *The Renaissance of General Relativity and Cosmology* (Cambridge: Cambridge University Press, 1993); Brandon Carter, "Large Number Coincidences and the Anthropic Principle in Cosmology," in M. S. Longair, ed. *Confrontation of Cosmological Theories with Observational Data* (Boston: D. Reidel, 1974), 291–97; H. Bondi, *Cosmology* (Cambridge: Cambridge University Press, 1952); John Leslie, "Cosmology and Theology," *Stanford Encyclopedia of Philosophy,* 1998;

John Barrow and Frank Tipler, *The Anthropic Cosmological Principle* (Oxford: Clarendon Press, 1986); F. Bertola and U. Curi, eds., *The Anthropic Principle* (Cambridge: Cambridge University Press, 1993); B. J. Carr and M. J. Rees, "The Anthropic Principle and the Structure of the Physical World," *Nature* 278 (1978): 605–12; Paul Davies, *The Accidental Universe* (Cambridge: Cambridge University Press, 1982); Gerald L. Schroeder, *The Science of God: The Convergence of Scientific and Biblical Wisdom* (New York: Free Press, 1997); Hugh Ross, *The Fingerprint of God: Recent Scientific Discoveries Reveal the Unmistakable Identity of the Creator* (New Kensington, Pa.: Whitaker House, 1989).

Two other helpful works include Martin Rees, *Our Cosmic Habitat* (Princeton: Princeton University Press, 2001), and Stephen G. Brush, "How Cosmology Became a Science," *Scientific American,* August 1992. George Ellis's paper, "The Theology of the Anthropic Principle," is in Robert Russell, William R. Stoeger and George V. Coyne, eds., *Quantum Cosmology and the Laws of Nature: Scientific Perspectives on Divine Action* (Notre Dame, Ind.: University of Notre Dame Press, 1993).

Chapter 4

Allan Sandage, Virginia Trimble, George Ellis and George Coyne were interviewed for this chapter. For a Hubble biography see, Charles Coulston Gillispie, ed., *Dictionary of Scientific Biography,* vol. 6 (New York: Scribner's Sons, 1970); and on Sandage and others, Alan Lightman and Roberta Brawer, *Origins: The Lives and Worlds of Modern Cosmologists* (Cambridge, Mass.: Harvard University Press, 1990). See also Kitty Ferguson, *Measuring the Universe: Our Historic Quest to Chart the Horizons of Space and Time* (New York: Walker and Co., 1999). For views on scientific and theological eschatology see John Barrow and Frank Tipler, *The Anthropic Cosmological Principle* (Oxford: Clarendon Press, 1986); J. C. Polkinghorne and M. Welder, eds., *The End of the World and the Ends of God* (Philadelphia: Trinity Press International, 2000); and Polkinghorne, *The God of Hope and the End of the World* (New Haven, Conn.: Yale University Press, 2002).

For the "Great Debate" in 1996, see the *Publications of the Astronomical Society of the Pacific,* December 1996: this volume includes the papers by Tamman and Van Den Bergh and two brief histories, one by Owen Gingerich and the other by Virginia Trimble. For the "Great Debate" in 1998 see the *Publications of the Astronomical Society of the Pacific,* March 1999: this volume includes papers by Peebles and Turner. For the two popular accounts of the accelerating universe see, James Glanz, "Cosmic Motion Revealed," *Science,* 18 December 1998, vol. 282; and Michael D. Lemonick, "How the Universe Will End," *Time,* 25 June 2001. Corey Powell offers the Church of Einstein in *God in the Equation: How Einstein Became the Prophet of the New Religious Era* (New York: Free Press, 2002). For the Pius XII speech, "Modern Science and the Existence of God," see appendix in Robert A. Morrissey, ed., "Science and Religion," *Catholic Mind* 50 (March 1952): 182–92. William Lane Craig's comments are from his presentation, "Cosmology," at the Nature of Nature conference, April 14, 2000, at Baylor University.

Chapter 5

For this chapter, Philip Clayton, George Coyne, William D. Phillips, Paul Davies and John Polkinghorne were interviewed. The fullest biography of Templeton is: Robert L. Herrmann, *Sir John Templeton: From Wall Street to Humility Theology* (Radnor, Pa.: Templeton Foundation Press, 1998). See also Lawrence Minard, "John Templeton: Why Common Stocks Are a Girl's Best Friend," and "Defining the Undefinable," both in *Forbes,* 27 November 1978: 45–52; and John Marks Templeton, *The Humble Approach: Scientists Discover God* (New York: Seabury, 1981).

For the official account of the Galileo rehabilitation see two accounts in *Origins,* 12 November 1992: John Paul II, "Lessons on the Galileo Case"; Cardinal Paul Poupard, "Galileo: Report on Papal Commission Findings." See Coyne's dissenting account in his "The Church in Dialogue with Science: The Wojtyla Years," in *The New Catholic Encyclopedia* (Washington D.C.: The Catholic University of America Press, 2002). Russell's remarks to SSQ came from his prepared text. For a brief history of the Vatican projects, see Russell, "Introduction," in Russell et al., *Quantum Cosmology and the Laws of Nature: Scientific Perspectives on Divine Action* (Notre Dame, Ind.: University of Notre Dame Press, 1993). See the letter by John Paul II and responses in: Robert Russell, William R. Stoeger and George V. Coyne, eds., *John Paul II on Science and Religion: Reflections on the New View from Rome* (Vatican City: Vatican Observatory Publications, 1990). See also: Alister

Hardy, *The Spiritual Nature of Man: A Study of Contemporary Religious Experience* (Oxford: Clarendon Press, 1979); Sharon Begley, "Science Finds God," *Newsweek,* 20 July 1998. For a sampling of twelve SSQ I interviews, see W. Mark Richardson and Gordy Slack, eds., *Faith in Science: Scientists Search for Truth* (New York: Routledge, 2001).

Chapter 6

Interviews were conducted with Edward Peltzer and Harold Morowitz. For Stanley Miller's story, see Stanley L. Miller, "A Production of Amino Acids under Possible Primitive Earth Conditions," *Science* 117 (1953): 528–29; Miller and Leslie Orgel, *The Origins of Life on Earth* (Englewood Cliffs, N.J.: Prentice-Hall, 1974); and "From Primordial Soup to the Prebiotic Beach," an October 1996 Internet interview with Miller by Sean Henahan for Access Excellence, University of California at San Diego. In support of abiogenesis see: George Wald, "The Origin of Life," *Scientific American,* August 1954; Leslie Orgel, "The Origin of Life on the Earth," *Scientific American,* October 1994; Sidney W. Fox and K. Dose, *Molecular Evolution and the Origin of Life* (San Francisco: W. H. Freeman, 1972); and Dean Kenyon and Gary Steinman, *Biochemical Predestination* (New York: McGraw-Hill, 1969). For criticism of abiogenesis, see Charles B. Thaxton, Walter L. Bradley and Roger L. Olsen, *The Mystery of Life's Origin: Reassessing Current Theories,* 2nd ed. (Dallas: Lewis and Stanley, 1992). For Edward T. Peltzer's work, see Peltzer and Jeffrey L. Bada, "Alpha-Hydroxycarboxylic Acids in the Murchison Meteorite," *Nature* 272 (March 30): 443–44.

The RNA world began with W. Gilbert, "The RNA World," *Nature* 319 (1986): 618. See also Christian de Duve, *Vital Dust: Life As a Cosmic Imperative* (New York: Basic Books, 1995), and de Duve, "The Beginnings of Life on Earth," *American Scientist,* September–October, 1995. Another good summary is: Paul Davies, *The Fifth Miracle: The Search for the Origin and Meaning of Life* (New York: Simon and Schuster, 1999). Kenyon's criticism of the RNA world is in Gordon Mills and Kenyon, "What Do Ribozyme Engineering Experiments Really Tell Us about the Origin of Life?" *Origins and Design* (Winter 1996).

On outer space, see Francis H. Crick and Leslie E. Orgel, "Directed Panspermia," *Icarus* 19 (1973): 341. The ideas of Harold Morowitz are found in: Morowitz, "The First Two Billion Years of Life," *Origins,* 12 February 1998; Morowitz, *Beginnings of Cellular Life: Metabolism Recapitulates Biogenesis* (New Haven: Yale University Press, 1992); Morowitz, *Energy Flow in Biology: Biological Organization As a Problem in Thermal Physics* (New York: Academic Press, 1968); Morowitz, *Cosmic Joy and Local Pain: Musings of a Mystic Scientist* (New York: Scribner, 1987). On the antiquity of life, see J. W. Schopf, "The Oldest Fossils and What They Mean," in *Major Events in the History of Life,* ed. J. W. Schopf (Boston: Jones and Bartlett, 1992).

Chapter 7

Based on interviews with Charles Thaxton, Dennis Wagner, Stephen Meyer, Michael Behe, William Dembski, Jon Buell, Phillip Johnson, Bruce Chapman and John West. Articles and books of interest include: James Glanz, "Darwin vs. Design: Evolutionists' New Battle," *New York Times,* 8 April 2001, A1; Michael Polanyi, "Life Transcending Physics and Chemistry," *Chemical and Engineering News* 75 (1967): 54–66; Stephen Meyer, "A Scopes Trial for the 90s," *Wall Street Journal,* 6 December 1993, A14; Thaxton, Bradley and Olsen, *The Mystery of Life's Origin;* Jon Buell and Virginia Hearn, eds., *Darwinism: Science or Philosophy? Proceedings* (Richardson, Texas: Foundation for Thought and Ethics, 1994); William A. Dembski, ed., *Mere Creation: Science, Faith and Intelligent Design* (Downers Grove, Ill.: InterVarsity Press, 1998); Phillip Johnson, *The Wedge of Truth: Splitting the Foundations of Naturalism* (Downers Grove, Ill.: InterVarsity Press, 2000); David K. DeWolf, Stephen C. Meyer, Mark E. DeForrest, *Intelligent Design in Public School Science Curricula: A Legal Guidebook* (Richardson, Texas: Foundation for Thought and Ethics, 1999); Associated Press, "Space Face," in *Fort Worth Star-Telegram,* 8 July 1988, sec. 1, p. 12.

Chapter 8

For this chapter I interviewed Michael Behe, Guillermo Gonzalez, Stephen Meyer and William Dembski. References of interest include: Bruce Alberts, "The Cell As a Collection of Protein Machines," *Cell,* 6 February 1998; Behe, "Reply to My Critics: A Response to Reviews of Darwin's Black Box," *Biology and Philosophy* 16 (2001): 685–709; National Academy of Sciences,

Science and Creationism: A View from the National Academy of Sciences, 2nd ed. (Washington, D.C.: National Academy Press, 1999); Guillermo Gonzalez, Peter D. Ward and Donald Brownlee, "Refuges for Life in a Hostile Universe," *Scientific American,* October 2001, 62–67; Ward and Brownlee, *Rare Earth: Why Complex Life Is Uncommon in the Universe* (New York: Copernicus, 2000); William A. Dembski, *Intelligent Design: The Bridge between Science and Theology* (Downers Grove, Ill.: InterVarsity Press, 1999); Dembski, *The Design Inference* (New York: Cambridge University Press, 1999). Comments by Stephen C. Meyer from: "The Origin of Biological Information," Nature of Nature conference presentation, 14 April, 2000; "Is Design Good for Science?" Design and Its Critics conference presentation, 22 June 2000, and Meyer, "DNA and Other Designs," *First Things,* April 2000. For criticism of intelligent design as science, see Del Ratzsch, *Design, Nature and Science: The Status of Design in Natural Science* (Albany, N.Y.: State University of New York Press, 2001); Kenneth R. Miller, *Finding Darwin's God: A Scientist's Search for Common Ground between God and Evolution* (New York: Cliff Street Books, 2000); Branden Fitelson, Christopher Stephens and Elliott Sober, "How Not to Detect Design," a review of Dembski's *The Design Inference,* May 1999.

Chapter 9

For this chapter, Philip Clayton, Robert Lattimer, Phillip Johnson and Stephen Jay Gould were interviewed. I also attended the Ohio State School Board "information session" on March 11, 2002. Other references include: comments by Steven Weinberg and William Dembski, The Nature of Nature conference, 12–13 April 2002; Jon Wiener, "Cash for Courses," *Lingua Franca,* November–December 1995, 68–73; the protest letter is from science history professor Edward B. Davis of Messiah College, dated 21 December 1995. See also David L. Wheeler, "Foundation Seeks to Create Field Melding Science and Theology," *Chronicle of Higher Education,* 11 April 1997; Lawrence M. Krauss, "Article of Faith: Science and Religion don't Mix," *Chronicle,* 26 November 1999; Victor J. Stenger, "Has Science Found God?" *Free Inquiry,* Winter 1998–99; Richard Dawkins, "When Religion Steps on Science's Turf," *Free Inquiry,* Spring 1998; Discovery Institute, *Getting the Facts Straight: A Viewer's Guide to PBS's 'Evolution,'* (Seattle: Discovery

Institute Press, 2001); National Center for Science Education, "Setting the Record Straight: A Response to Creationist Misinformation about the PBS Series 'Evolution,'" September 2001 (a 61-page website publication); "A Scientific Dissent from Darwinism," *Weekly Standard*, 1 October 2001, 20–21; Frederick C. Crews, "Saving Us from Darwin," *New York Review of Books,* two parts, 4 and 18 October 2001; comments by Johnson from his "Weekly Update" on the Access Research Network website, 25 September and 9 October 2001; Lawrence Krauss, "Life, the Universe, and Nothing: Life and Death in an Ever-Expanding Universe," *Astrophysical Journal* 531 (1 March 2000): 22–30; Jonathan Wells, *Icons of Evolution: Science of Myth? Why Much of What We Teach about Evolution Is Wrong* (Washington, D.C.: Regnery Publishing, 2000). For the full U.S. Senate debate on the evolution language, see *Congressional Record,* 13 June 2001, amendment 779, bill S.1. The revised language in the *No Child Left Behind Act of 2001* was moved to the "Joint Explanatory Statement of the Committee of Conference," part A, title 1, item 78.

Chapter 10

This chapter includes interviews with Francis Collins, W. Ford Doolittle and Paul Nelson. I attended the conference "Assembling the Tree of Life: Science, Relevance and Challenges" at the American Museum of Natural History on May 30, 2002, where I taped comments by E. O. Wilson. Other sources for this chapter are: Lynn Margulis, "Gaia Is a Tough Bitch," in John Brockman, ed., *The Third Culture* (New York: Touchstone, 1995); Margulis, *Symbiosis in Cell Evolution* (San Francisco: W. H. Freeman, 1981); Margulis, "Kingdom Animalia: The Zoological Malaise from a Microbial Perspective," *American Zoologist* 30 (1990): 867; W. Ford Doolittle, "Phylogenetic Classification and the Universal Tree," *Science* 284 (1999), 2124–28; Doolittle, "Uprooting the Tree of Life," *Scientific American,* February 2000.

The comments by Simon Conway Morris are from his presentation, "Biological Complexity," at The Nature of Nature conference, 14 April 2000, and Conway Morris, *The Crucible of Creation: The Burgess Shale and the Rise of Animals* (Oxford: Oxford University Press, 1998). For Stephen J. Gould, see *Wonderful Life: The Burgess Shale and the Nature of History* (New York: W. W. Norton, 1989). See Bernard d'Abrera's long anti-Darwinian introduction to *The Concise Atlas of Butterflies of the World* (London: Hill House, 2001). For Michael Denton's views in 1986 see "The Failure of Homology," chapter in *Evolution: A Theory in Crisis* (London: Adler and Adler, 1986), and his more current views in "The Tree of Life," chapter in *Nature's Destiny: How the Laws of Biology Reveal Purpose in the Universe* (New York: Free Press, 1998).

Paul Nelson shares his views in "Applying Design within Biology," in William Dembski, ed., *Mere Creation: Science Faith and Intelligent Design* (Downers Grove, Ill.: InterVarsity Press, 1998), and with co-author Jonathan Wells in "Some Things in Biology don't Make Sense in the Light of Evolution," *Rhetoric and Public Affairs* 1 (Winter 1998): 557–63. Henry Gee's iconoclastic cladistics are found in his *In Search of Deep Time: Beyond the Fossil Record to a New History of Life* (New York: Free Press, 1999). Francisco Ayala reported his views on the molecular clock in Francisco Rodriguez-Trelles, Rosa Tarrio and Ayala, "Erratic Overdispersion of Three Molecular Clocks," *Proceedings of the National Academy of Sciences* 98 (25 September 2001): 11405, and in Ayala et al., "A Methodological Bias toward Overestimation of Molecular Evolutionary Time Scales," *Proceedings of the National Academy of Sciences* 99 (11 June 2002): 8112. See also, David Baltimore, "Our Genome Unveiled," *Nature,* 15 February 2001: 816

Chapter 11

Interviews for this chapter include Ayub K. Ommaya and Howard M. Ducharme. See Stephen R. Graubard, ed., "The Brain," *Daedalus* 127 (Spring 1998); Patricia Churchland is quoted from her essay, "Can Neurobiology Teach Us Anything about Consciousness?" 25 September 1995. Francis H. Crick's comments are from his *The Astonishing Hypothesis* (New York: Scribner's Sons, 1994). A good summary of the brain is Richard Restak, *Brainscapes* (New York: Hyperion, 1995). Owen Flanagan articulates his challenges to dualism in three works: *The Science of the Mind,* 2nd ed. (Cambridge, Mass.: MIT Press, 1991); *Consciousness Reconsidered* (Cambridge, Mass.: MIT Press, 1992); and the semi-autobiographical *The Problem of the Soul* (New York: Basic Books, 2002). For a defense of dualism see Howard M. Ducharme, "The Image of God and the Moral Identity of Persons: An Evaluation of the Holistic Theology of Persons," in *Law and Religion: Current*

Legal Issues, vol. 4, ed. Richard O'Dair and Andrew Lewis (Oxford: Oxford University Press, 2001). Other references include: Warren S. Brown, Nancey Murphy and H. Newton Malony, eds., *Whatever Happened to the Soul? Scientific and Theological Portraits of Human Nature* (Minneapolis: Fortress Press, 1997); David J. Chalmers, "The Puzzle of Conscious Experience," *Scientific American,* December 1995: 62–68; Sol Tax, ed., "The Evolution of Mind," in *Evolution after Darwin,* vol. 3 (Chicago: University of Chicago Press, 1960).

I have drawn on Alvin Plantinga's 1994 monograph, "Naturalism Defeated," which is based on his *Warrant and Proper Function* (New York: Oxford, 1993); he is quoted from his presentation, "Metaphysics: Are Evolution and Naturalism Incompatible?" at the Nature of Nature conference, 13 April 2000. For the story of Sherrington, see John C. Eccles and William C. Gibson, *Sherrington: His Life and Thought* (New York: Springer International, 1979). Penfield's story is told by Howard J. Lewis, *Something Hidden: A Biography of Wilder Penfield* (Garden City, N.J.: Doubleday, 1981), and in his own words, *The Mystery of the Mind: A Critical Study of Consciousness and the Human Brain* (Princeton, N.J.: Princeton University Press, 1975).

Epilogue

Here I rely on interviews with Paul Davies, John Polkinghorne, George Coyne and Robert Newman. The quotes and background on James are from William James, *The Varieties of Religious Experience: A Study of Human Nature* (New York: The Modern Library, 1994); Will Durant, *The Story of Philosophy* (New York: Simon and Schuster, 1961); and Gerald E. Myers, *William James: His Life and Thought* (New Haven: Yale University Press, 1986). For his analysis of temperament, see James, *Pragmatism: A New Name for Some Old Ways of Thinking* (New York: Longman Green and Co., 1907). Lawrence Krauss is quoted from his "Article of Faith: Science and Religion don't Mix," *Chronicle of Higher Education,* 26 November 1999.

INDEX